What readers are ~

'Remember starting a jigsaw
all the pieces on the table a
jigsaw, but YOU create YOUR pic
on YOU, YOUR vision and why 's
have your picture of your life, R
will help you put together the p____s in a logical and sequential
order! So stop dreaming, read the book and take action.'

Chris Brindley MBE

'I couldn't wait to get my hands on *Rise* given that Royston's
previous book, *Built to Grow*, completely changed my business.
I had high expectations and it didn't disappoint. *Rise* is literally
your personal success coach in your pocket. I thought I was a
pretty focused person but after reading *Rise* it has unleashed
another gear inside me that I knew was there, it just needed
unlocking!'

**Perry Power – Entrepreneur and digital
marketing guru**

'*Rise* stops you in your mental tracks and makes you grab a
pen and paper from the first chapter! Although you're invited to
make notes in the margins, you'll feel compelled to pass it on to
a friend. You'll want to share the real-world stories and practical
activities which really will make you ask: "Are you living on the
balcony or the dance floor of your life?" Each chapter, packed
with thought-provoking content, will challenge you to question
your "why".'

**Jayne Owen – Head of Learning and Development,
Princes Food**

'Recently I cycled Europe coast to coast covering nearly 200 miles across ten countries. Prior to that I ran 1,100 miles along the Camino de Santiago in France and Spain. I have adventured in Vietnam, climbed Mount Kilimanjaro, completed multiple Ironmans and even run a 145-mile non-stop running race. While this could sound like me trying to impress you, it's not. I'm simply trying to impress upon you the power of the ideas Royston lays out in *Rise*. But beware, they have the ability to take you on a journey beyond your wildest dreams. They sure did for me.'

Graeme Harvey – Extreme Sportsman
and Adventurer

'I've experienced first-hand the passion Royston has for helping people, teams and businesses realize their potential and be successful. The impact he has had on the leaders in our business has been profound. In *Rise*, I can again feel his passion leaping from the pages together with a practical and down-to-earth tone that resonates regardless of your status, position or current situation – unerringly insightful, real and totally applicable to any one of us. If you engage in this book and join Royston on this journey to maximize your potential, then success and a brighter future can be yours to enjoy.'

Joe Dent – Group HR Director, Princes Food

'Royston has succeeded in packaging the ideas in *Rise* into an easy and accessible read. There are life skills and tools which are relevant to all, and I challenge anyone to not take away golden nuggets they can quickly apply to be a better mother, partner, friend and rounded person. The book does what it says on the cover and gives you the motivation to start living the life you were meant to lead.'

Jenna Cottam – Director of Parenting for two
wonderful children

'I first had the pleasure of working with Royston in 2008, and since then we have shared great success in enabling people to be the best version of themselves and to truly recognize the value of identifying their personal and professional excellence. Royston's authentic approach has personally inspired me in my own career. He has played the role of coach, mentor and professional advisor, which I have valued immeasurably. *Rise* is a fantastic culmination of everything Royston represents. Thank you, Royston, for sharing and enabling people to discover their own unique version of success.'

Nebel Crowhurst – Head of People Experience, River Island

'Every teacher needs a copy of *Rise*. With growth mindset playing such a big part in today's curriculum, it's a great starting point to sense-check our own thinking using simple techniques and a strong framework to achieve personal and professional success!'

Nicola Cumberpatch – Teacher

'Success in sales is 80 per cent psychology and 20 per cent skill, which is why *Rise* has been a critical enabler in setting our team up for success and for creating that all-important momentum. *Rise* is an essential read for any team wanting to deliver accelerated and sustained peak performance.'

Adam Botterill – Sales Director, Marley Eternit

'Retirement can feel like the end of the biggest chapter in your life, but after reading *Rise* it made me realize it is in fact the start of a bigger and better one! A must-read for anyone going through a period of significant change.'

Peter Bowers – Retiree exploring the next chapter of life

'Royston has a unique ability to educate, entertain and inspire action, all at the same time. With *Rise*, Royston has condensed decades of personal transformation experience into a simple, authentic blueprint for life – just what you need to unleash your true personal potential.'

Tom Hacqouil – Managing Director, Infuse Group

'*Rise* is your personal satnav to a successful, purposeful and happy life. This inspirational book focuses on the importance of transforming dreams into reality by adopting the right mindset, skillset and toolset for any personal or professional situation. The beauty of this read is that the practical tips and techniques can be adopted by anyone – irrespective of age, gender or role – who wants to develop their own personal success formula for designing and living the life they want ... something which most people only dream of!'

Jacqui Hughes – Leadership and Personal Growth Expert

'We are all in charge of our own success but, sometimes, we need help in unlocking our potential or help with staying on track. It's reality, not theories, that set you up for success and the tips and tools in *Rise* are from the real world; giving a positive nudge to help and restore your attitude of action!'

James Devine – Deputy Chief Executive, Medway NHS Foundation Trust

Rise

Louise
_____

Every Success on your
RISE journey

Royston

12 Mar 19

Rise

Start living the life you were meant to lead

ROYSTON GUEST

JOHN
MURRAY
LEARNING

First published in Great Britain in 2019 by John Murray Learning.
An Hachette UK company.
Copyright © Royston Guest 2019
The right of Royston Guest to be identified as the Author of the Work has been asserted by him in accordance with the Copyright, Designs and Patents Act 1988.
Database right Hodder & Stoughton (makers)
All rights reserved. No part of this publication may be reproduced, stored in a retrieval system or transmitted in any form or by any means, electronic, mechanical, photocopying, recording or otherwise, without the prior written permission of the publisher, or as expressly permitted by law, or under terms agreed with the appropriate reprographic rights organization. Enquiries concerning reproduction outside the scope of the above should be sent to the Rights Department, John Murray Learning, at the address below.
You must not circulate this book in any other binding or cover and you must impose this same condition on any acquirer.
British Library Cataloguing in Publication Data: a catalogue record for this title is available from the British Library.
Library of Congress Catalog Card Number: on file.
Trade paperback ISBN 978 1 473 69538 2
eISBN 978 1 473 69539 9
Audio ISBN 978 1 473 69540 5
1
The publisher has used its best endeavours to ensure that any website addresses referred to in this book are correct and active at the time of going to press. However, the publisher and the author have no responsibility for the websites and can make no guarantee that a site will remain live or that the content will remain relevant, decent or appropriate.
The publisher has made every effort to mark as such all words which it believes to be trademarks. The publisher should also like to make it clear that the presence of a word in the book, whether marked or unmarked, in no way affects its legal status as a trademark.
Every reasonable effort has been made by the publisher to trace the copyright holders of material in this book. Any errors or omissions should be notified in writing to the publisher, who will endeavour to rectify the situation for any reprints and future editions.
Typeset by Cenveo® Publisher Services.
Printed and bound in Great Britain by CPI Group (UK) Ltd, Croydon, CR0 4YY.
John Murray Learning policy is to use papers that are natural, renewable and recyclable products and made from wood grown in sustainable forests. The logging and manufacturing processes are expected to conform to the environmental regulations of the country of origin.

Carmelite House
50 Victoria Embankment
London EC4Y 0DZ
www.hodder.co.uk

For the courageous, bold individual who is prepared to look in the mirror, challenge yourself to be the best you can be and truly live the life you were meant to lead ... *Rise* is written for you. Enjoy the journey!

Contents

Acknowledgements

1. *You meet thousands of people and none of them really touches you. And then you meet one person and your life is changed for ever.*

   To my wife, Jane:

   I am truly blessed that I have the love of my life, best friend and soulmate all wrapped into one. Thank you from the bottom of my heart for everything you do and everything that you are. The journey through this adventure called life would not be the same without you sharing it with me.

2. *Each day of our lives we make deposits in the memory banks of our children.*

   To my daughter, Eloise, and son, Ethan:

   Having children was one of the most defining moments of my life, and my goal in life is to give you two things: one is roots; the other, wings. Eloise and Ethan, you are both the centre of my universe and I am so proud when you call me Daddy. I know you will both fly in life and I will always be there to support you, love you unconditionally and, as the proud father, watch you flourish and grow.

3. *Family is not an important thing. It's everything.*

   To my family:

   Mum, Dad and Jean: your unconditional love, sacrifices and life experiences have helped mould me into who I am today. I hope you are proud of the business professional, husband and father I have become.

Justine, my big sister: you have always had my back. To watch you grow into the successful businesswoman, mum and wife you are makes me feel proud.

My in-laws, Mary and Eric: you welcomed me into your family and inner circle with unconditional love. Thank you for everything you do for us – your grandchildren adore you both.

4. *Friendship isn't about who you've known the longest. It's about who walked into your life, said, 'I'm here for you', and proved it.*

To my friends:

You can count on one hand the friends who are truly there for you. The ones who you know when you make that call and need them will be there, rain or shine. Peter, I had to call you out, especially as I knew I would never hear the end of it if I didn't! On a serious note ... you are living proof of the quote about friendship.

5. *Individual effort is important, but it's teamwork that makes the dream work!*

To my team:

I feel blessed to be surrounded by passionate, loyal and committed people. It is truly amazing what a team with a shared vision and purpose can achieve.

Kate and Luke: you have both been alongside me for over a decade. You are both talented individuals, and the positive difference you make every day is profound.

Laura, my EA: keeping me in check is no mean feat and you do it with a remarkable calmness and discipline. You are truly valued.

For all my colleagues across all our businesses: I am so proud of the great work, commitment, focus and drive you demonstrate every day in helping our clients grow their businesses and unlock people's potential. You truly are the best of the best at what you do and how you do it.

And, finally, to all our strategic partnerships who are an extension of our family and culture.

Additional special thanks to Colin Brown: the hours we spent piecing *Rise* together, taking it apart and rewriting until it was perfect required focus, tenacity and a unique skill. You have all three in abundance.

To Iain and the team at John Murray Learning: This book would not be what it is without your expertise and passion for the content.

6. *We don't meet people by accident. They are meant to cross our paths for a reason.*

And finally, to YOU, the reader:

If you are reading this right now, it is not by accident. It's because our paths were meant to converge. Thank you for letting me into your world and for sharing the ideas in *Rise* with you. If, by synchronicity, I should happen to spot you sitting and reading my book, allow me to sit down beside you. I would love to hear your thoughts. My passionate goal is that you rise like never before and truly start living the life you were meant to lead.

The Rise *Mission*

EVERY PERSON is equal and has the opportunity to achieve GREATNESS.

But the biggest blocker in achieving greatness is YOU through your limiting beliefs and closed mindset.

The greatest opportunity to make it happen is YOU.

Playing small does not serve the world.

The world needs you to think BIG and play BIG.

How?

By stepping out the safe harbour of your comfort zone.

By looking in your own mirror and challenging yourself – how high is high?

By turning off your autopilot and living with deliberate conscious intent as the architect of your own destiny.

And by taking ownership for your life, your choices, your actions and your results.

You're only ever one pathway from living the life you were meant to lead!

Your future is NOW! … *Take action: achieve more.*

About the author

From an early age Royston nurtured his entrepreneurial spirit and passion to make a difference, spending weekends and summer holidays working in his father's construction business.

A relentless itch to join the working world saw Royston kick-start his career at the age of 16, enrolling on a construction apprenticeship programme. He worked from the ground up, literally.

His thirst for learning and making things happen saw his career fast-track at companies like Balfour Beatty managing high-profile projects like the Liverpool Institute for Performing Arts, founded by Paul McCartney. A working stint in the USA gave Royston valuable insight into operating across cultural boundaries.

On returning to the UK, Royston was involved in the privatization of the rail industry and major private finance initiatives (PFIs) with Jarvis before joining Hoogovens, a Dutch business where he was involved in mergers and acquisitions.

His breadth and depth of 'hands on' business and life experiences led to Royston establishing his own consultancy and people development business, of which he is CEO.

Driving sustainable business growth and unlocking the real potential of individuals are two professional missions of Royston and his team – missions spanning over two decades and 27 countries and engaging with tens of thousands of businesses and individuals across a multitude of sectors, enterprises and governments.

His work led Royston to publish his first book, the number-one bestseller *Built to Grow,* a proven time-tested model full of strategies, tools and ideas to unlock business growth.

His professional mission to help business owners and leaders deliver accelerated, sustained and profitable business growth led to the launch of The Business Growth Pathway™, a powerful and intuitive online experience designed to critically assess the growth stage of any business.

Royston is also founder of living**your**future™, one of the most innovative and leading-edge personal transformation programmes on the market today. Following the programme's international success, Royston has created a unique framework and set of insights helping individuals achieve greatness by becoming the architect of their own destiny and start living the life they were meant to lead.

Whether he is speaking, facilitating, consulting or coaching, Royston's passion to make a real tangible difference is at the forefront of his work, and is what sets him apart from his peers.

Royston is married with two children and splits his time between Jersey, the UK and countries around the world speaking at events and conferences.

Introduction

When I was writing *Rise*, my second book, family, friends and colleagues asked the usual pointed question: 'What's it about?'

You might have heard of an elevator pitch, a statement that explains your idea in a way that anyone can understand in around 30 seconds. I know I have only seconds to grab your attention and only a few more to convince you to invest your precious time and headspace in the *Rise* journey; so here goes.

You can achieve greatness

There is a vast reservoir of untapped potential inside every one of us. This book is about unlocking your potential, unleashing your success and creating the future you want.

Rise is about placing you firmly in the driver's seat of your life, guided by an internal satnav, so that you know precisely where you're going, how you're going to get there, and who and what you want to become on the journey.

I've worked with tens of thousands of people over the past two decades, from all walks of life, and I passionately believe in your potential and even more ... I know it can become your reality. Here's why.

The itch that won't go away

We are all born with the potential to achieve greatness, yet many of us wake in the morning with an itch. And I'm not talking about a tingling of the skin. I'm talking about the itch that just won't go away. No matter how many times you scratch the surface, it's still there. Why? Because it's deep in your very being.

You know how it is. The alarm clock goes off in the morning like a starting gun, propelling you into a frenzy of activity, as you run through the playbook in your mind of all the things you need to do that day. It's easy to get sucked into the pace of the day and all the superficial stuff you need to take care of, but deep down you have a feeling something isn't quite right (it's your itch again).

We're like Charles Dickens' Scrooge, who had to be reminded of the gifts he was missing:

- The Ghost of Christmas Past showed him how he was allowing the past to shape his present in negative ways.

- The Ghost of Christmas Present showed him how much opportunity he had around him if he paid attention.

- And the Ghost of Christmas Future showed him that the future is unwritten and entirely his to shape.

If there is one lesson I've discovered from working with high achievers, it's that they are constantly learning from the past but not living there; they are living in the present with deliberate, conscious intent and shaping their future as the architect of their own destiny.

As you take the *Rise* journey, you'll do the work necessary to unpack your relationship with your past, your present and your future (no ghosts required!) and to maximize your ability to make the best of what each has to offer.

What is holding you back?

What is holding you back from your past, creating your itch or clouding your future?

- You may be going through a significant period of change in your life and feeling reflective about where you're at, where you want to be and what the future holds.

- You may be approaching a milestone birthday or the beginning of a new life stage.

- You may know what you want from life but not be sure how to get there.

- You may simply want to 'sense check' whether what you're currently doing will result in you achieving your goals.

- You may be in pain – not the broken leg type, but the incessant ache that comes from not having meaningful purpose and focus in life.

- You may be feeling lost through redundancy, break-up or divorce. You've lost your rudder and keep going off in directions that turn out to be blind alleys.

- You may be stuck in a rut or you have fallen out of love with your life, unable to move forward or back, with a desire to improve but uncertain about where to start.

- You may want to develop essential life skills and knowledge. You want to reach goals you've set. You want to create the right attitude and philosophy for living your future.

If any of these strike a chord, then you're in the right place, right here, right now, to start unlocking your potential. I passionately believe we are all a work in progress and there is so much more that we can do and be. And there is so much more fun and enjoyment we can squeeze out of this adventure called life. Here's how we're going to do it.

The balcony of your life

Are you spending enough time on the balcony of your life or too much time on the dance floor?

Visit a nightclub and you've got a couple of choices about where to spend your time: on the dance floor amid the energy and the chaos, or upstairs on the balcony, out of the fray, where you have the opportunity to stand back for a moment, observe and study it all with a much broader perspective.

The dance floor of life with its fast-paced jobs, demanding home lives, and 'always on' digital culture, is like a packed, heaving nightclub. It's easy to get caught up in the music. But a large part of your success lies in your ability to step off the dance floor, walk to the balcony and reflect on the following questions:

- Am I on the right dance floor?
- Am I dancing to the right music?
- Am I creating my own music or constantly dancing to someone else's?
- Am I the DJ or just a listener?
- Am I in the place I want to be?
- Am I living the life that I was meant to lead?

Spending time on the balcony of your life gives you the self-awareness to make conscious choices about how you want to shape your life, the areas you want to focus on, the value you can add and what you are prepared to do and not do. You will discover the music you are prepared to dance to and the tunes you are not. The balcony is the place where you develop the invaluable knack of dispassionately monitoring your own mental, emotional and physical states as you interact with the world around you.

Throughout this book I'll share a plethora of ideas, strategies and tools to enable you to work on your life instead of just relentlessly dancing in it. You will learn how to:

- start to consistently make time to stop, reflect and think
- live your life with deliberate, conscious intent
- operate at your full potential
- set yourself up for success, so that you can be the best version of you, every day.

How you will gain maximum value from Rise

I have purposely designed *Rise* around usability and the attainment of real, tangible results.

I believe fundamentally in the power of coaching, and I spend much of my time coaching individuals and groups to achieve higher performance or to overcome life's obstacles. It's for this reason that I've written this book using a coaching framework to give you the feeling of 14 individual one-on-one coaching sessions with me.

It goes without saying that this isn't just a book for light bedtime reading. In fact, it has been crafted specifically as a blueprint for helping you live the life you were meant to lead. It is designed to be:

- **practical** – with real-life stories that bring all the strategies, tools and ideas within the book to life
- **accessible** – written in an easy coaching style
- **interactive** – with Accelerator exercises throughout plus a toolkit for you to download
- **reflective** – with each chapter summarizing the key exercises and actions

- **supportive** – with an action planner to help you become consistent and disciplined as you incorporate *Rise* into your life.

And, finally, it's yours to personalize. You can scribble your thoughts and comments in the page margins, underline passages that are most compelling – why not share them through Instagram? – and refer regularly to the content. This will make it simple for you to find the most relevant information while embedding the lessons as you read and reread. As the author, I am giving you permission right now to gather all your coloured pens and make this copy all your own!

My ask of you

All I ask of you is that you work with me and make the commitment to follow the ideas, strategies and tools outlined. Read, learn and absorb with a curious, excited mind, focusing on troubleshooting and problem solving your own specific life challenges and greatest opportunities.

Not everything is going to be easy. That's on purpose. There's no real growth to be found within your own comfort zone. So, on your *Rise* journey, every day from this day forth begins at the edge of your comfort zone.

It's time to fulfil your true potential and start living the life you were meant to lead.

Are you ready? Then let's begin!

Royston

Your future starts now

'You can't go back and change the beginning. But you can start where you are and change the ending.'

C. S. Lewis

You and I are busy people. Our lives have many facets, with work, home, family, friends, colleagues, partners and perhaps children as well. And over the years, no doubt, commitments have crept in, almost unnoticed, to the point where, whether you know it or not, there are probably already multiple versions of you.

Think for a moment about how many versions of you there are. There's the personal you with family and friends, the professional you with colleagues and bosses, the you in a relationship, the you as a parent, as well as just you being you. Each version of you has to meet differing demands and expectations, each version of you dialled up or down as you and your life evolve.

When I first started my business, I was young and single and habitually put in 14-hour days, going hell for leather as I set about building my company. On a weekend I would wake up, go for a long cycle ride, or read the newspapers until mid-morning, and then head into the office to work for the rest of the day. The 'me' that existed in that period of my life was almost entirely weighted towards the professional me.

When I met my wife, Jane, she didn't live in the same country, much less the same city, so I had to make changes to my routine and my schedule in order to get the most out of both my career and my relationship. I had to learn to manage the tension between the professional me and the relationship me. Since I wanted to win at both, I had to learn how to play well at both.

A few years later, along came our children and I had to reset again, so I was able to give energy to all the dynamics that defined me:

- **The personal me**: I still wanted time to focus on my fitness and meet up with family and friends, but usually this 'me' was the one pushed aside due to the demands of the other 'me's.

- **The professional me**: I was still ambitious to build a world-class business and I was the driving force to make it happen.

- **The relationship me**: Our relationship was evolving to handle our new dynamic – children – but we both recognized that we needed to create time for us to be a couple. Easier said than done!

- **The parent me**: This one I had to learn on the job, and if you're a parent you'll know what this journey is like – rewarding, exhilarating and terrifying, all at once.

Managing the tensions between these various versions of 'me' is something I've had to learn and, if I'm being totally honest, am still learning, as new demands and challenges arise. The answer isn't to become universally excellent at all of them, but to understand clearly which one requires the most attention at any given point. Remember, there are many versions of you but only one physical you.

Managing the tensions between the different versions of you

It's not easy, but here's an insight into how I learned to manage the tensions during a particularly busy time in my life.

As I was writing this book, we'd just experienced our best year in business in five years. To me that was no surprise. You see, five years ago our first child was born and we've added another member to our family since then. Being a parent demands an endless stream of energy, activity and presence, so the 'hell for leather' professional version of Royston, who put in 14-hour days and travelled regularly away on business, had to be dialled down as the demands of the parent me and the relationship me took priority.

As the children grew and my wife returned to work, I shifted my focus back into the business. The result was the best year we'd had for five years. And I believe that's how it's supposed to work.

Unfortunately, far too many people struggle to manage the tensions, giving all their energy to one version at the expense or loss of another. I wouldn't have been able to make the judgement call I needed to make in order to shift my energy and focus for a few years if I had been permanently on the dance floor, spending no time on the balcony of my life.

Think about your multiple versions of you. Are any in tension? Are you getting the most out of each one? Do any need to change because you've entered a new stage in your life and you haven't pressed the reset button yet?

In Chapter 4, I'll focus specifically on a group of versions of you that are already having a massive impact on your life, whether you know it or not. But first I'd like to introduce you to three guiding principles that are critical as you embark on your journey of living the life you were meant to lead.

Guiding principle 1: Your past does not equal your future

To put it another way, you can be the way you are because of your past, or ... you can be the way you are **because** of your past.

In the Introduction I spoke about the importance of learning lessons from the past but not living in the past. I had a fairly turbulent childhood: my parents were from 'middle-class' backgrounds, putting in the hours to provide for the family and to give my sister and me the best education and opportunities in life, but when I was 11 they divorced. For me, it was a terrible age to have your family breaking up (not that any age is good, I suppose). It hit me hard and for a time I went off the rails. Mum remarried, and her new husband turned out to be a heavy drinker with a violent temper. I literally counted down the days until I was 16 and could leave school, start earning my own money, make a life of my own and be in control of my own destiny.

Now, among those childhood experiences were many life lessons:

1 Relationships are fragile and require work.

2 Sometimes people come into your life and have an unpleasant and negative impact.

3 Earning money requires a strong work ethic and it gives you freedom and choices.

But the *meaning* we attach *to those lessons* is what really shapes us. On the one hand, you might decide:

1 Because relationships are fragile and require work, I should keep them superficial and avoid any real commitment like marriage and children.

2 Because people can have an unpleasant impact, I should become hard and aggressive to counteract it.

4

3 Because earning money requires effort and commitment, I shouldn't bother pushing myself all that hard.

In other words, you become who you are *because of your past.*

Or you could take a different view:

1 Because relationships are fragile and require work, I should really think about the ones I want in my life and work on them to ensure that they remain valuable and rewarding, and, when it comes to my children, protect and nurture them.

2 Because people can have a negative and unpleasant impact, I should set myself a strong set of personal values and understand what I want most out of life and surround myself with like-minded individuals.

3 Because earning money requires effort and commitment, I should focus on contributing, innovating, adding value and making a real tangible difference so that the rewards will follow.

In other words, you become who you are *BECAUSE of your past.*

I chose the second set of responses, choosing to allow those life lessons to positively shape me, my actions, my life and who I wanted to become.

> Life is constantly testing us, and the quality of our life is determined by the quality of the choices we choose to make.

Guiding principle 2: Understand the power of your choices

One of the most interesting things about life is that first you make your choices but, ultimately, your choices make you.

The difference between those who achieve and those who fail to realize their potential lies in the quality of the choices they make. Why do some people make better choices than others and realize their potential? It's because they make their choices with conscious, deliberate intent. They are not sleepwalking through life. They do not live on autopilot, just going through the daily, mundane routine. They know that how they show up at their choice points is critical to their success.

Think about it for a moment. Every decision you've made, whether at a conscious or unconscious level, has got you to this moment in time, sitting with this book in your hands, looking for answers, regardless of your life stage, your age, your state of happiness or anything else.

The reality is that the quality of your life is in direct proportion to the quality of the choices you make every day. And it's not just the big life decisions that truly shape your destiny. It's the small incremental choices that really make the difference. The compound effect of those small choices every day will have an exponential impact on the quality of your life:

- Do you hit the snooze button on the alarm clock or get up and create some quality time to think and plan the day ahead?
- Do you drink the smoothie or the can of cola?
- Do you eat the chocolate or the piece of fruit?
- Do you make the extra couple of sales calls or call it a day?
- Do you drive to the gym or stay at home to watch TV?
- Do you decelerate or accelerate as you approach the finish line?

How good are the choices you've made in your life to date?

Keep this guiding principle at the forefront of your mind as you read and work through *Rise*, as there will be a host of choices for you to make and reflect on in order for you to live the life you were meant to lead.

> Remember: you make your choices and then your choices make you.

Guiding principle 3: Put some skin in the game!

You can't achieve success in life if you're on autopilot. Too many people live in 'the safe harbour of the known'. They do the same things over and over again, following the same routine and thought process thinking that, since it worked in the past, they can keep replicating it and it will work in the future. Some things will work, but a lot will not.

Albert Einstein defined insanity as doing the same things over and over and expecting different results. Real joy comes when you put 'skin in the game' and take some chances. Believe me, I've had some fantastic failures both personally and professionally but, boy, have I learned from them.

The most important thing is to put yourself in the arena of life, out there on the playing field, taking action and shaping your future. You can't win without leaving your safety zone and taking some calculated risks. No risk = no reward. The reality is that the more risks you take in pursuit of your goals, the greater your risk of failure, but also the greater your chances of brilliant success.

The real risk in life lies in living risk-free. Mark Twain made the point perfectly when he said: 'Twenty years from now you will be more disappointed by the things you didn't do than by the ones you did do. So throw off the bowlines. Sail away from the safe harbour, and catch the trade winds in your sails.'

That says it all, doesn't it? So go ahead, stretch today, step out of your comfort zone and remember that you can't win a game if you aren't even truly playing. How serious are you about living the life you were meant to lead? Are you truly committed?

Let me share part of a speech by Theodore Roosevelt, given more than 100 years ago, in 1910. While the language may seem a little archaic, the message is one that resonates with me every day. I hope it does for you.

It is not the critic who counts; not the man who points out how the strong man stumbles, or where the doer of deeds could have done them better. The credit belongs to the man who is actually in the arena, whose face is marred by dust and sweat and blood; who strives valiantly; who errs and comes short again and again; because there is no effort without error and shortcoming; but who does actually strive to do the deeds; who knows great enthusiasms, the great devotions; who spends himself in a worthy cause; who at the best knows in the end the triumph of high achievement, and who at the worst, if he fails, at least fails while daring greatly, so that his place shall never be with those cold and timid souls who neither knows victory nor defeat.

Take action: achieve more

Today is the day you ...?

This chapter considered the multiple versions of you – the personal you, the professional you, the relationship you and the parent you. Managing the tensions between each one is not achieved by becoming universally excellent at each one at the same time. It's about understanding clearly which one requires your attention at any given point. Remember that there are many versions of you but only one physical you.

Take this opportunity to reflect on the three guiding principles that will form a thread through this book:

1 Your past does not equal your future.
2 Understand the power of your choices.
3 Put some skin in the game!

Today is the day you embark on your journey of living the life you were meant to lead. Your future starts now!

2

Setting your standards of personal excellence

'Perfection is not attainable, but if we chase perfection we can catch excellence.'

Vince Lombardi

What if I told you that one of the biggest inhibitors to your own success is an often random, often baseless, but usually very powerful set of internalized, limiting beliefs that prevent you from setting your bar as high as you can actually go? And what if I told you that challenging your limiting beliefs will very often cause them to simply crumble and throw your potential, and your opportunities, wide open?

Let me share with you an amusing but insightful story about how a lone cow in West Texas overcame her own limiting beliefs one day, and broke through a barrier that had held back millions of other cows for over a century.

I haven't been to West Texas but I'm told the sweeping landscapes are so vast that it's simply not economical to hang a gate everywhere a road crosses a fence. In order to prevent cattle from roaming out of their pastures, cattle ranchers used what they call the cattle guard – a ditch in the road, covered by metal bars spaced closely enough together for vehicles to drive over but far enough apart that cattle cannot walk over them. It's a good solution, except for one thing: being jolted about as you drive over one is incredibly uncomfortable.

So some enterprising cowboys came up with an alternative solution: rather than a ditch covered in bars, why not just paint stripes on the road? It would be far easier to drive over, and since cattle aren't all that clever, the stripes would probably do the same job as a cattle guard.

They were right. The new solution looked to the cattle like the old solution, so they stayed in their pastures and grazed away. But then, one day, all that changed. As a pair of cowboys approached a herd way out on the range, they discovered that many of the cattle had crossed the cattle guard and were grazing across the road. It's impossible to know exactly how it changed, but the general idea was clear: one cow had tested the cattle guard, discovered it was just paint and had simply walked across.

The limiting belief was smashed for ever.

As soon as one cow had walked across, another followed, and another ... and another. That turn of events brought with it a number of questions. Had cattle typically been inclined to test the cattle guards, waiting for one they could cross? Or was it just one particularly clever cow who'd figured it out? Whichever it was, one of the herd had had the courage and curiosity to test the wisdom of the whole herd. In so doing, it found a flaw and simply tried a different way. The herd would never be the same again.

One of the many choices we have in life is to remain fenced in by herd wisdom, reducing us to mediocrity in the process. Or we can choose to examine the cattle guards, focus on the rewards and break through those barriers and, in doing so, set our own standards of personal excellence.

Which choice are you making? Where are you setting your standards of excellence?

Mediocrity is everywhere

Excellence is the driving force behind progress. Mediocrity stands in stark contrast to this.

The pursuit of perfection and excellence involves risk and the possibility of loss, but it has the potential for phenomenal gain. Mediocrity offers assurance and the comfort of knowing, but at the loss of opportunity. Mediocrity can seduce those with bold aspirations to let go of their dreams, or not to dream at all. Are you consciously or unconsciously falling into this trap?

Mediocrity operates like a virus. Its effects are debilitating and damaging, but if it is identified and countered its symptoms can be reduced or suppressed, even if it can never be eliminated. If ignored, its spread can be extensive and the result acute. Worse still, its influence can be all-encompassing. Mediocrity's power has primarily two aspects: it self-replicates, generating and reinforcing the very environment in which it thrives; and, the more it comes to dominate your thinking, the harder it is to recognize.

You don't have to travel very far these days to find mediocrity in abundance. It is the foundation on which society for many is built and viewed. In a mass-manufacturing age – where price is a major factor for most customers – products, services, attitudes, ideas and results risk not being as good as they could be. Think about the last time you had an exceptional customer experience or the last time you bought something that really lived up to your expectations. Did you have to think long and hard to find an example? Was it an exception rather than the norm?

The truth is that consumers, businesses and organizations value things differently today. Whole industries have become cursed with the herd mentality that thinks excellence is less important than value. Unfortunately, that herd mentality is driven by us, the ordinary consumer.

As airline passengers, we complain about the lack of legroom and the poor quality of the meal, but when we book our next flight, we'll specifically pick the cheapest one. When we buy gym memberships, we decline the additional cost of a personal trainer twice per week despite the fact that he or she may vastly reduce the time it will take us to achieve our goals.

We have education systems that promote the idea that we are all winners because we can't have any losers. Really? This is mediocrity at its most fatal. Surely, used in the right way, having winners and losers can help fast-track and unlock real potential, create aspiration for those not there yet, and foster growth among the many. Life is competitive and the faster we develop the skills in young people to be able to thrive, not just survive, the better equipped they'll be to deal with whatever life throws at them.

Pursuing excellence is a choice. It means you have to aim high, often without certainty, while you test where your personal limits and the boundaries of possibility lie. When we're comfortable with the knowledge that we may fail and we do it anyway, that's when real growth happens. It's the place where we might just discover excellence.

In the USA this is an accepted mindset, which explains why so many people in business, entertainment, politics and society in general are willing to reach out and try. And it's why so many of them make it. The entrepreneurial and business culture in the USA is huge. In other countries, however, if you fail, it can be viewed as a huge embarrassment, and therefore, for many it's better not to try in the first place. So you end up playing within the confines of your comfort zone.

You unconsciously subscribe to mediocrity and the herd mentality, even though deep inside you know there is a better way; even though all you really want to do is break free, play, push and practise on the edge of your comfort zone to test how high is high.

As the saying goes, you can't become excellent at anything without practice. And you can't practice until you decide to get started.

Are you ready to start accelerating through the gears?

What does excellence look and feel like?

I'd like you to go on a journey with me and experience this idea of excellence in everything you do. Not enough people spend time focused on being excellent. Excellence is an unwavering standard that good enough is not good enough.

How does excellence play out in everyday life? What does it look like, feel like and act like?

- It's the person training in the gym who sets out to do ten repetitions but chooses to do an 11th, a 12th and a 13th because they know that's where the real growth comes from.

- It's the sales professional who sets themselves a target unrelated to a clock or a spreadsheet, knowing it may take longer, but that winning takes extra effort.

- It's the employee who turns up for work 15 minutes early to get ready for the day so they can hit the ground running rather than strolling in five minutes late and starting the day in a state of chaos.

- It's the parent who makes sure their child cleans their teeth properly every morning and every night because they know that the discipline they set today will be with them for the rest of their life.

- It's the athlete who trains for hours and hours, seven days a week, relentlessly working at shaving half a second off their lap time, making the difference between a gold medal or no medal at all.

If you are going to achieve excellence in big things, you must develop good habits in little things. Excellence is not an exception; it's a prevailing attitude. It's a way of being.

Excellence is about stretching your comfort zone, challenging yourself to show up being the best you can be every day, in every moment, in every interaction. It's a restless, uncompromising, laser-beam focus to do the best and be the best in everything you do.

Ultimately, excellence becomes a self-fulfilling idea because a mind once stretched never returns to its original dimension.

And mediocrity ... well, that is locked away for ever.

Where are you currently on your journey to excellence?

Understanding the phrase 'a standard of excellence'

To truly understand the phrase 'a standard of excellence', let's explore the words 'standard' and 'excellence'.

A standard can be defined in multiple ways. At one point, it was a banner carried during times of war; it served as a rallying point to gather the troops. It was also a personal flag: one of a royal family or an organization. For example, the flag of the UK's royal family is called the Royal Standard.

Another definition of 'standard' is that it is something set up and established by authority as a rule of measure. For example, a standard ruler is 12 inches long; a standard workday is eight hours long; and a standard first date is dinner and a movie (or that's what my wife told me!). These standards were all set by someone else, and most of us simply follow them without question because they make eminent sense.

But you don't have to follow *all* the standards set by others. In life, you make your choices and your choices make you.

Raising the standards of your own life

What standards do you measure yourself against and hold yourself to account against?

I'm not talking here about the standards you display when people are watching. I'm talking about the standards you hold yourself accountable to *all* the time – because there's always one person watching and that person is your future self. Your future self is begging you to show some guts, to show some heart. To do that little extra *now*, to raise your game, so you can live with pride and all the physical and emotional trappings of success later.

Don't let your future self down.

If your standard is excellence, then the next step is to unpack what it means to be excellent in all aspects of your life. 'Excel', the root word of excellent, means 'to rise or project'. It's no surprise, then, that I called this book *Rise*.

To excel is to surpass others in accomplishments or achievement, to be distinguishable by superiority. This is not arrogant, egotistical superiority, but one that is confident, has integrity and authenticity, and moves with purpose. Excelling is going beyond the conventional limit, aiming to do better, transcending conventional wisdom, moving past the norm to reach another level, outdoing your own previous best, and challenging the competition.

It's about looking at things that are already great, and asking if they could be made even greater. It's asking how high is high?

Is 92 per cent good enough?

Recently I was having a lively debate with a good friend about key performance measures and metrics in our respective businesses, and he mentioned that his organization had recently hit a very healthy 92 per cent satisfaction rate on their latest customer experience survey, and he was struggling to convince his people of the need to improve on the score.

'But it's 92 per cent,' they said. 'It's significantly higher than our competitors', than the industry average and even the market in general.'

'Yes,' he said, 'but those aren't the standards we hold ourselves to.'

And together we began to explore this notion. On the one hand, his people have a right to be proud. The 92 per cent figure is excellent, but for whom – the customer or them? Where would it be terrible? Could 92 per cent ever be terrible?

And this is how he framed it with his team.

He announced at a team meeting that their business was going to participate in a sponsored parachute jump for their chosen charity and he was looking for 100 volunteers. It did not take long to fill the 100 spaces; in fact, they had a waiting list of people wanting to do it.

What came next is the critical part of the story. He announced that a parachute manufacturer had agreed to donate the parachutes and, when researching the company, he discovered that the manufacturer had a performance metric of 92 per cent for parachutes that opened. He asked the 100 volunteers if they thought a 92 per cent success rate was acceptable.

You can just imagine the silence that descended as people imagined themselves jumping out of a plane one Saturday morning, with the parachute strapped to their back having a 92 per cent chance of opening.

What would you say?

In 2017 in the UK 260,096 jumps were completed, according to the British Parachute Association. If an 'excellent' 92 per cent of those parachutes opened, that would mean 239,288 jumpers would land safely. But it would also mean that 20,807 wouldn't.

Not so excellent now, is it?

Accelerator exercise 2.1: Raise the bar

Let's do an exercise together.

Imagine two 6-foot people holding an imaginary high-jump bar at head height. I want you now to come up with three easy ways to get over the bar.

Now imagine that the bar has been raised from 6 feet to 100 feet in the air. Your next challenge is to think of five plus ways to get over the 100-foot bar.

Take a moment or two to do this. Suspend your disbelief, never mind about logic or any of the other potential constraints. Really stretch your mind to come up with solutions. You might want to draw two columns on a page and in the left-hand column, headed 6-foot bar, capture your three ideas, and in the right-hand column, headed 100-foot bar, capture your five-plus ideas.

Why do you think I've done this exercise with you?

What can you learn from the two different scenarios?

How did you answer those two questions?

Would the ideas that get you over the 6-foot bar get you over the 100-foot bar? In 99.9 per cent of cases the answer is no.

Would the ideas that get you over the 100-foot bar also get you over the 6-foot bar? The answer is yes, every single time. Now, here comes the entire purpose of the exercise, wrapped up in one question:

Where are you setting your bar?

Are you setting your bar at 6 feet and therefore having 6-foot thoughts on a daily basis, or are you setting your bar at 100 feet and therefore thinking openly and creatively about how you can achieve your goals?

Where are you setting your bar?

Stop, pause and reflect on the question for a moment. Really explore it, letting it penetrate deep into your psyche and the very essence of your being.

Where are you setting your bar?

'The greater danger for most of us lies not in setting our aim too high and falling short, but in setting our aim too low, and achieving our mark.'

Michelangelo

If you've set your bar at 6 feet it's almost as if you're thinking from a tunnel perspective, seeing only what is right in front of you. But at 100 feet, you're thinking not from a tunnel but a funnel perspective, which opens out to a wide-open space, truly seeing all that is around you. You're thinking outside the constraints and seeing far greater possibilities.

And isn't it interesting that the higher you set the bar, the more creative you become in thinking of ways to get over it? Did your ideas get more creative? I am certain they did! I would bet that when you worked through the exercise, you found it much easier to come up with a long list of ideas for getting over the 100-foot bar than you did to get over the 6-foot bar. Why? Creativity. Imagination. The removal of constraints. Working without boundaries or limitations.

Now you could argue that I asked for three ideas for the 6-foot bar and five plus ideas on the 100-foot bar, and therefore I actively asked for more 100-foot solutions. But there's an important reason for this.

What difference does it make when you add the word 'plus' to the end of the number?

It removes the limiting beliefs.

Think about it for a moment. If you think of me as your success coach on your *Rise* journey and I ask you to come up with three ideas as part of an exercise, what are you going to do? Exactly that. Come up with three ideas and then stop.

However, if I ask you to come up with five-PLUS ideas, what are you going to do? Come up with five-PLUS ideas, which is why your right-hand column will usually have at least double the amount of ideas compared to the left-hand column.

So many people are moving through life creating 'false' limiting beliefs and false ceilings about what they can and can't achieve. What limiting beliefs have you created for yourself either consciously or unconsciously?

Just imagine if from now on you improved your quality of thinking by 100 per cent PLUS, what difference it would make to your life. Do you think it might make a difference to the results you achieve?

You bet it would.

Change your thinking to change the game

Sometimes, as I share this exercise, a sceptic in the room might say, 'Ah but, you're missing a key point here; the ideas which get you over the 100-foot bar are more expensive and some of them are not practical.'

As you can imagine, I have a response and it is simply this: the purpose of the exercise has absolutely nothing to do with the complexity or cost of the ideas and strategies put forward. It has everything to do with the level of thinking that goes into the input bowl. Change your thinking and you change the game!

I'll talk more about this subject later when I delve deeper into how to program your winning mentality. For now, the key principle is that the great advantage we have as human beings over any other animal species is that we have 100 per cent control over how we choose to think. It's a choice.

So many people are searching for the magic key to unlock the door to the source of power, and yet we all have the key already in our hands. And we can use it the moment we learn to control our thinking.

Where are you aiming to go in your life?

Where are you setting your bar?

Think of it this way: if you aim for 6 feet in life, where are you likely to get to? 5 feet? 7 feet? ... Somewhere around 6 feet, that's for sure ...

But if you aim for 100 feet, where are you likely to get to? 20 feet? 52 feet? 78 feet? One thing's for sure: you'll be above 6 feet.

Shining examples of 100-foot thinking

If there is only one thing you take away from this chapter, it is that high achievers, whatever their chosen field of endeavour, think BIG. They have proactively programmed their mentality to daily/weekly/monthly/yearly 100-foot thinking. The great news is that they are no different from you. You have exactly the same potential and the same opportunity.

Dick Fosbury

You may not be familiar with the term 'Fosbury Flop', but if you've ever seen someone do the high jump, it's the backward body arc that athletes lean into as they leap over the bar. It is the standard technique for today's high jumpers. But it wasn't always this way.

The technique was named after Dick Fosbury, an American athlete who won the gold medal in the 1968 Summer Olympics using his own invented technique. In the years that followed, it became the standard. Prior to 1968, every jumper was using a technique that turned out to be very inefficient. And yet they all did it, year in and year out, clearing the bar by jumping forward.

Dick Fosbury was the only athlete to go over the bar backwards in the 1968 Games, and he caused a significant stir when he did. Athletes began to pay attention and, by 1972, 28 out of 40 high jumpers were doing the Fosbury Flop. In 1980 that number rose to 23 out of 28.

The biggest reason for the change, which caused athletes to be able to jump higher than ever before, was one person's willingness to ask probing questions, try out a new idea, and work hard to perfect it. Someone dared to change the rules.

Dick Fosbury is the epitome of the 100-foot thinker, and the kind of person who can (and did) change the world of high jumping.

The New Zealand All Blacks

The New Zealand All Blacks rugby team has had similar success, rewriting the rules of what is possible and setting 100-foot standards for themselves – individually and as a team.

Evidence of the All Blacks' excellence is the fact that they have won 84 per cent of their games since 2004 and 75 per cent of their games since 1901. That's a remarkable record, unrivalled by any other rugby team. It's no wonder that they are revered as one of the greatest sporting teams of all time.

Their secret is a little different, however. While they believe in great rugby and look for great rugby players to join their team, the barrier for entry – the 100-foot bar – is about something else entirely. The All Blacks believe in *whanau*, a sense of extended family, as their team's core value. They know that you win games by playing great rugby, but they believe you can only play great rugby by being a part of a meaningful team.

Whanau is a deep-rooted core value that demands a way of thinking, acting and being from each player who dons the black jersey and it is demonstrated through rituals such as 'sweeping the sheds'. At the end of each match, win or lose, the All Blacks players clean the changing room themselves, being sure to leave it better than they found it. Sweeping the sheds is a demonstration of *whanau*. If you don't have it, you are deemed to lack the humility required to be a member of the team.

Their purpose, their mantra, their reason for being is 'inspiring and unifying New Zealanders'. This is played out in their personal standards of excellence – their 100-foot bar – where all players put the shirt first and commit to always leaving it in a better place.

Some might say it's a coincidence that they win as many games as they do, but their success is no accident. It's a conscious, deliberate choice built on a solid foundation and core of unwavering standards of personal excellence and 100-foot thinking.

100-foot thinking in business

Steve Jobs of Apple was an absolute believer in setting 100-foot bars and, under his leadership, Apple successfully disrupted one industry after another, from publishing in the 1980s to music, telephony and mobile computing in the early 2000s.

The challenge, as Jobs frequently saw it, was that customers were awash with solutions, products, ideas and services that were created by people thinking 6-foot thoughts, and as a consequence were just enough to be helpful but never enough to be inspiring or revolutionary. By applying 100-foot thinking, he catapulted Apple so high that competitors were never able to match it. From the day Apple entered the music industry, it dominated it. From the day it entered the mobile phone industry, it set the rules based on 100-foot thinking.

Another example of 100-foot thinking is Sara Blakely, the billionaire entrepreneur, who initially planned a career as an attorney but reconsidered after scoring too low on the Law School Admission Test. After a short stint working at Disney, Blakely accepted a job with office supply company Danka, where she sold fax machines door to door. With 5,000 dollars of savings she then started Spanx, an American intimate apparel company. Forbes now lists her as the 93rd most powerful woman in the world.

Richard Branson is another great example of a 100-foot thinker. With his Virgin Group of companies he has moved from one industry to the next, disrupting entire industries, improving products and services, transforming the customer experience in every bold move.

There is a long list of more great 100-foot thinkers whose names you know because of their exceptional achievements, which shine through their own personal standards of excellence. Mark Zuckerberg of Facebook set himself the goal of creating a community where people could share information to the entire world and so far has a user base of more than 2 billion in less than a decade and a half. Bill Gates set out to put a computer in every home.

The list could go on … Henry Ford, Dale Carnegie, Oprah Winfrey, Enzo Ferrari, Diane Hendricks, one of the USA's wealthiest female entrepreneurs, Arianna Huffington and Sir James Dyson come easily to mind, for example.

100-foot thinking in politics

The greatest names in politics – Nelson Mandela, Winston Churchill, Barack Obama, Martin Luther King Jr, Margaret Thatcher, Mahatma Gandhi – are all household names because they set their standards of excellence in leadership at 100 feet. They all have their legacies, and their achievements will be studied and recognized for years to come.

> To achieve excellence in big things, you must develop the habits in little things.

Accelerator exercise 2.2: Develop your own 100-foot thinking

So you've decided 100-foot thinking is where you want to be. This is great news and, while you may not get to 100 feet first time out, one thing is certain: if you've been setting your bar up to now at 6 feet you are going to gain quick wins and forward momentum in a heartbeat.

Here's an exercise focused on how you can develop your 100-foot thinking. Take a piece of paper and a pen or an electronic gadget, whichever you prefer, and capture the following for both your personal and professional goals:

1 Think of one or two areas of your life – personally and professionally – where you'd like to kick on to the next level and raise your standards and your game. Call this your 6-foot performance.
2 What would 25-foot, 50-foot and 100-foot performance look like, feel like and act like for each?
3 What actions could you take immediately to create forward momentum and traction in reaching those goals?

Some examples to stimulate your thinking

At school age I was a keen tennis player, became captain of my local club, and played at a senior level. I didn't reach this level of success through talent, however; I did it by setting my own standards at 100 feet. Two school friends and I all joined the tennis club at the same time. While they spent most of their time playing against each other, I chose to always play against people who were better than me, and, whenever I could, against the best players at the club. I didn't mind losing so long as I gained valuable lessons and played the best game I could. It's no surprise that I kicked on to a level of performance which left my two school friends firmly behind.

A delegate on one of my programmes was a triathlon runner who typically completed his races in the middle of the pack, but wanted to break into the top 250. That was his 6-foot bar. He then set himself stretch goals: break into the top 200 his 50-foot target, break into the top 150, his 75-foot target, break into the top 100, his 100-foot goal. He called this his 100/100 BHAG goal (Big Hairy Audacious Goal). That change of mindset focused him, and the next time out he finished 122nd.

If you work in sales or anything target-oriented, think how this could apply in terms of setting your targets. If your target for this year is x, make x your 6-foot performance – the minimum you have to achieve. Then set yourself 25-foot, 50-foot and 100-foot targets and really think about how you would need to be thinking, feeling and acting in order to deliver against them.

With some creative thinking, it's almost a certainty that you can find ideas right now that easily lift you higher than 6 feet.

What if, for every single target you have to hit from this day on, you add the word PLUS to it? Improve by 20 per cent? Make it 20 per cent PLUS. Achieve profits of 30 per cent? How about 30 per cent PLUS? As you add the word PLUS, you remove the limiting belief you have set for yourself.

Remember the quote: a mind once stretched never returns to its original dimension!

What examples can you think of in your own life where you know you can improve? Set yourself some 100-foot targets and watch what happens. You may not hit them first time, but you'll massively improve on what you're achieving right now. The moment you start to action them, you'll be surprised how quickly you'll see improvements.

Excellence is waiting for you!

An internal standard with external benchmarks

There's one final point I want to make. Thinking big for you and me might mean something quite different from what thinking big meant for Steve Jobs or means for Richard Branson. It doesn't mean that you should aim to emulate them. Your race is not with them. You are running your own race, living your own life, setting your own standards of excellence aligned to what you want to achieve. It's about living life according to your definition of success, not anyone else's.

It's therefore critical that you take care in where you set your frame of reference and what you judge your own success against. This means answering the following questions:

Are you internally or externally referenced?

How do *you* know when you've done a good job?

Don't overthink your answers. The first thing that pops into your conscious mind is the one I want. If I were to ask a room full of people the same question, I would expect to hear a range of answers: 'My boss told me.' 'My colleague said "Well done."' 'My customer said I gave them great service.' But I would also hear: 'I don't need to be told; I know when I've done a good job and when I haven't.'

The difference between the two is that the first group is externally referenced, meaning that they take their validation from other people, while the second group is internally referenced, meaning that they create their own internal validation. I am sure you can think of people in both your personal and professional life who fall into one or the other of the two groups.

One of the businesses I run has a team of 30 consultant trainers and I estimate that 60 per cent of them are internally referenced and 40 per cent externally referenced. And within these two groups are variations on the scale. Some of the team have absolutely no need or desire for praise or recognition from me or their leader, while, at the other end of the scale, others like to call frequently to share feedback, testimonials and insights. Neither approach is right or wrong; it simply reflects their particular view of their world.

One of the goals of this book is for you to develop a greater understanding of yourself and others in terms of motivation, drivers and how we're all wired. Through this greater understanding, you'll be able to manage your own mindset and state better and also become a far greater influencer, communicator, leader and friend to others.

Are you more internally or externally referenced, or perhaps a bit of both?

If you're externally referenced, make sure you're getting your external validation from authentic sources. If you've set your personal standards of excellence high, seek feedback and advice from people whose standards are also high – people you respect and trust. Once you have your external validation benchmarked, start to trust yourself. Build your confidence with your own internal references and validation about whether you are meeting and delivering against your own personal standards of excellence.

If you're internally referenced, you may not need any external validation, as you know when you've done a great job or whether there is opportunity to raise your standards and your game further. You become your own personal success coach. But even for the internally referenced person, every now and then external validation, to ensure you're on the right track, is a positive thing. There's nothing like receiving positive feedback from a colleague, a superior peer or a loved one, to give your confidence a boost.

Excellence as your standard

It's good to be competitive – important, even. But the most meaningful competition you will ever have is with yourself. If you can challenge yourself to always be excellent, stop yourself from accepting second best in the work you do, in the way you present yourself to the world, in the way you manage your relationships and order and manage your life, you can achieve excellence.

Most of us fail in this critical test. Most people demand excellence from time to time, but allow their standards to slip when it suits them. And as life rolls on, they often have cause to wonder why some people seem to be doing so much better. The difference between regular achievement, which compounds over time to exceptional success, and sporadic achievement, which ultimately ascends to nothing, is a consistently high standard of excellence.

But remember, just because someone is winning while you're not, it doesn't mean that you're losing. It just means that winning is possible. Life is not a zero-sum game where one person has to lose if someone else wins. The truth is that there's plenty of winning to go around, and it's rarely a surprise to find that those who win most regularly are those who aim to do so.

An inspirational poem

Perhaps the American poet Jessie B. Rittenhouse (1869–1948) captured it best when she wrote:

> I bargained with Life for a penny,
> And Life would pay no more,
> However I begged at evening
> When I counted my scanty store;
>
> For Life is a just employer,
> He gives you what you ask,
> But once you have set the wages,
> Why, you must bear the task.
>
> I worked for a menial's hire
> Only to learn, dismayed,
> That any wage I had asked of Life,
> Life would have willingly paid.

What wage are you asking of life?
What's the wage you're asking from all areas of your life? Is it high enough?
Have you set your bar at 6 feet or 100 feet?
Where are you setting your personal standards of excellence?

Take action: achieve more

Ready to set your personal standards of excellence?

This chapter examined excellence and how you can strive for it in everything you do by simply setting your bar high and letting go of your limiting beliefs. Here are two action-able, momentum-building Accelerator exercises to help you change your thinking, so that you can change your game ...

Accelerator exercise 2.1: Raise the bar

Reset your expectations for yourself about where you are setting your bar in the pursuit of excellence ...

If you think 6-foot thoughts, you'll limit your performance and your chances of achieving excellence.

If you think 100-foot thoughts, you'll not only be able to achieve all your 6-foot goals, but also 20-foot goals ... and 47-foot goals ... and 71-foot goals.

Consider where you are currently setting your bar person-ally and professionally.

Accelerator exercise 2.2: Develop your 100-foot thinking

Think of one or two areas of your life where you'd like to kick on to the next level and raise your standard and game. This is your 6-foot performance.

Consider what 25-foot, 50-foot and 100-foot performance would look like, feel like and act like, for each.

What actions could you take immediately to create for-ward momentum and traction in reaching those goals?

If you challenge yourself always to be excellent, in your thoughts, actions and words, you will achieve excellence.

Why success is not an accident

'We are going to be the future, let us make today's dreams tomorrow's realities.'

Malala Yousafzai

Success is not a place but a way of thinking, feeling and subsequently acting as you embark on this exciting journey with the deliberate, conscious intent of turning a successful future into your reality.

If you ask any high achiever, whatever field they're in, to describe their success and how they're so good at what they do, you'll often hear an answer like, 'Well, it just happens.' For some, achieving success in their specialist field has been quite natural. Others have learned to accept that success demands hard work, sacrifice and courage. It might be that they are humble, internally referenced individuals who let their results do the talking. Or it might be that they've been doing what they do for so long that they've become unconscious in their actions, simply going through the motions on autopilot.

Let's be clear, nothing 'just' happens. Whether you're operating in a conscious state or not, achieving success in any facet of your life takes a pattern of thinking, feeling and acting that delivers a desired outcome. And the great news is that, once you become conscious and deliberate about developing, practising and applying your own individual formula for success, you can replicate it.

Replication minimizes the alternative option of trial and error, and means that you can create consistent, predictable, repeatable results every time. Think about it. Why would you do something that delivers the precise outcome you were looking for only to do something completely different next time? That has to be the definition of insanity! Yet people fall into this trap every day.

It doesn't have to be this way for you.

The five secrets of success

Over the past two decades, I have focused my time and energy on understanding what differentiates high achievers from the rest and, in doing so, I've identified five secrets of their success.

In applying these five secrets (Figure 3.1), both personally and with thousands of people through my living**your**future™ programme, I've been able to help individuals and organizations to increase not only the outcomes they achieve, but also the predictability of their results in the future.

Mastering these five secrets will accelerate your focus, your confidence and your self-belief, empowering and enabling you with the knowledge, skills and framework to start living the life you were meant to lead.

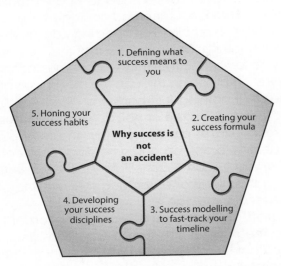

FIGURE 3.1 The five secrets of success and how they interlock

The interlocking nature of the secrets

The five secrets are not islands, but rather interlocking pieces of the same jigsaw. High achievers delivering consistent, sustainable, repeatable results do not just achieve mastery and excellence in one or two of these secrets, but in *all five*. They understand that the power is in all five secrets working in unison.

I'll deep dive into the first three secrets in this chapter. I'll cover the final two in Chapter 13: Being your own performance coach, where they'll mean more in that context.

Secret 1: Defining what success means to you

We all have junctures in our lives that shape our future selves and who we become. I can recall one such defining moment in my life, which really helped shape my thinking behind this first secret.

I was working in South Africa on a project with ABSA Bank and over a period of 12 months I was back and forth from the UK a dozen times. One random Friday I headed off with Elisha, the Managing Director from our joint venture partner, for some lunch.

It was a stunning day. The sun was shining as we sat outside a beautiful restaurant chatting and talking. There was a pause in the conversation and Elisha asked me a question that literally floored me. She said; 'Royston, we've been working together for nearly a year now and we've come to know each other pretty well. I have a good handle on Royston the businessperson and your professional goals, but I don't know much about you as a person. Royston, what does success mean to you personally?'

That single question left me dumbstruck. I just sat back in my chair, paused for what probably felt like an eternity and, being the candid person I am, responded: 'Elisha, that is a great question and, if I'm honest, I don't have an answer.'

I wrestled with that question for a good few days and here's why. At that time in my life I had just turned 30. I was single, travelling the world, building my business and having the time of my life. I had no 'personal' responsibilities, no partner or wife, and certainly no children. My business was my life. It was my child, which I was bringing up in the world. My existence between my 'business life' and 'personal life' had become one with no demarcation between the two. While this suited me fine for that particular stage in my life, was it healthy? Was it sustainable? Was I who I wanted to become?

Since that moment, this whole question of success has fascinated me and it has become a central pillar to my work when I am helping people to unlock their real potential and live the life they are meant to lead.

What does success mean to you?

Have you ever considered this question or taken time out to answer it? And I mean properly answer it. Create some quiet time, take out your pad and pen or preferred gadget and actually commit it to black and white.

What does success mean to you?

Success is such an emotive word, which we each define differently. Success for one person could be at opposite ends of the scale for the next. However, if you examine the words and actions of some of the most successful people today and throughout history, those individuals who have truly made a dent on the world and created a lasting legacy, you'll find they each have something in common:

- A clear set of motivational drivers
- A reason for being
- A clear answer to the question 'Why?'
- A purposeful intent that drives what they do and how they do it.

Some examples to stimulate your thinking

Mother Teresa looked after the downtrodden and the lepers in India's inner cities, not just because she was kind and generous, but because she believed she was doing the work chosen for her by God.

Winston Churchill is best remembered for successfully leading Britain through the Second World War, famous for his inspiring speeches and his refusal to give in even when things were going badly. His personal mission was protecting the nation, a legacy that will live on for eternity.

Success for Larry Page and Sergey Brin, co-founders of Google, was defined as changing the way the world communicates one click at a time. This was a lofty goal back in 1998, but defining their purpose and what success meant to them was what drove them to turn their vision into reality.

Roger Federer, revered as one of the greatest tennis players of all time, was driven by a desire to 'excite and delight crowds and positively position the game of tennis as an aspirational sport for future generations'.

Earl Nightingale, the father of personal development in the early twentieth century, summed success up as 'the progressive realization of a worthy goal or ideal'.

All the examples described above offer great insights to help you get to the core of what success means to you. Think about why you get out of bed in the morning. What makes you excited about the day ahead? Why do you care? What difference do you make? Who cares about you? Think about these things and you begin to raise your conscious awareness of your own motivational drivers, which in turn will help unlock your 'Why?' and ultimately your definition of success.

Why is this so important? It's because every person experiences important moments in their lives, but there is one that stands out above all others: it's the moment you change from someone drifting through life to someone with real purpose.

Having a compelling 'Why?', a clear definition of success and reason for being, infuses your life with purpose and meaning. The 'Why?' is your North Star, your anchor point, and, if it is compelling and strong enough, you'll figure out the what and the how.

Success by your own standards

Before I share some pointers to help answer the 'What does success mean to you?' question, I want to draw out a couple of key distinctions.

The critical part of the question is the word 'you'. You must measure success by your own standards, not anyone else's. This is so important. There will be a number of people who will try to weigh in and influence your definition according to their own preferences, biases and beliefs – if you allow them to. These people – perhaps parents, grandparents, siblings, friends or even random strangers – will often happily offer their advice, if you let them. It can sometimes feel like a tug of war as you're pulled from pillar to post, everyone else having a view and opinion on what you should do and who you should be.

But remember, they are not living your life – you are!

It's good to take advice and seek counsel from those whose opinions you value. But when it comes down to it, you and only you can make the decisions and choices about how you live your life and how you define what success means. Are you living by your own definition of success or are you living by the standards and definitions of others?

An example that is imprinted firmly on my mind is a friend who was married for 22 years and then got divorced. She remarried later in life. I remember having a conversation about her first marriage and she said: 'Royston, I knew when I was walking down the aisle that I was making a mistake and I should never have got married.' Yet she stayed with that person for 22 years.

The pressure external forces can have on how you define and live your life, and the compromises you make in order to please others, can lead to a fundamental lack of fulfilment or purpose, which in turn leads to unhappiness and resentment. You end up living with a feeling that you are not living the life you were meant to lead.

My friend above is not unique. I am sure you know people close to you who have fallen into a similar trap. You may even be one of them.

These influences do not just come from those closest to you. How influenced are you by societal conventions, for example? In the UK it is common for individuals to aspire to be homeowners, and embedded in our thinking from a young age is the idea that owning property is a sign of success. In other parts of Europe the thinking is quite different, with property rental being the norm.

Your work, your success

A few years back, I ran a workshop for the heads of Finance and their deputies at a leading logistics company. One of the sessions was about this very subject: what does success mean to you? During the break, a woman came up to me – she was number two at her distribution site – and said: 'Royston, if I'm hearing correctly, what you're saying is that if I don't want to run my own distribution site and just want to be a great number two then that's OK? Is that what you're saying?'

My response reiterated the point that it doesn't matter what I think; it was her definition of success that mattered. What did she think? Seeing her physical demeanour almost shedding the weighted blocks she had been carrying around was awe-inspiring. She had been putting herself under huge amounts of pressure to be someone she didn't want to be, simply because her manager had suggested she should strive to be number one.

We concluded our chat when I said to her, 'Here's the deal: if I were a finance director running a distribution site and you came to me and said, "I have no aspirations to be number one, but I do want to be a world-class number two," I would have you work with me every day of the week.'

It's so important to define success by your own standards. If you are an exceptional technician, plumber, mechanic, accountant, salesperson, pilot or anything else for that matter, and you're content with what you do and are excellent at it, why would you choose instead to be a manager or business owner? Ah! Because society says you should. Because the narrative we tell ourselves is that we should.

If being the next Richard Branson is your measure of success, then by all means aim for it and do the things required to build a brilliant business empire. But know this: if your measure of success is to be truly excellent at the job you're doing now, that's absolutely OK too.

Be aware of the old adage: never compare your insides to someone else's outsides. If you spend time on social media sites you can easily program your mind into believing that everyone is living a perfect life. They're on holiday, they're out to dinner, they're among friends, smiling and happy. In the meantime, you're at home or at work, feeling that you might be losing out on all the fun and excitement life seems to offer everyone else but you.

That's a dangerous misconception. If you choose to post photographs, insights and updates about your life on social media, it's almost a guarantee that you share positive updates when you're on holiday, out to dinner, among friends, smiling and happy. You may be surprised how many people think you're the one having all the fun and excitement.

These types of posts are usually a rose-tinted picture of a snapshot in time. What people choose to show you about their lives can, if you're not careful, skew your perceptions about how easy things are for them and how difficult and challenging they are for you. This is not only a false perception but also an irrelevant one. Don't waste your time or brainpower measuring your happiness or success against someone else's social posts.

This reinforces the point I made in the previous chapter about the externally versus internally referenced person. If you want to look externally in shaping your definition of success, great, but when you've carved out your final definition it has to be driven from within.

> Living your authentic and fulfilled definition of success is an inside–out job, not an outside–in one!

A word of caution for parents

Success is only real if it is individual. As parents or grandparents, it is crucial that we let our children or grandchildren develop into who they are instead of who we want them to be.

Many parents get to an age and look at what they haven't achieved in their own lives and try to live out success through their children, quite often pushing them down a path where the child doesn't want to go. That's rarely a recipe for a fulfilled human being, however young or old they may be. You have to let them find their own identity. A client and close friend of mine dropped her son off at boarding school recently and sat in on an induction presentation during which the head teacher said: 'Well done, parents; you have done your part. Now it's time for us to do our part, the chance for us to let your children flourish and develop into the people we know they have the potential to become, not mini-versions of yourselves.'

Breaking down your definition of success

In our naivety and desire to deliver and make stuff happen, we've all attempted to tackle goals or projects on a monstrous skyscraper scale. It can be overwhelming even knowing where to begin. But once you have a starting point and break it down into bite-size chunks, it becomes easier. And of course momentum breeds momentum.

The question 'What does success mean to you?' is like the monstrous skyscraper, just too big to answer as one question. So I break it down into two important parts:

- Part 1: What does success mean to you personally?
- Part 2: What does success mean to you professionally?

And there's a third part, to ensure that you've thought through the other two properly:

- Part 3: Are your two definitions aligned or are they in tension?

Let's look at Part 3 first, as this will give context and structure when answering the other two parts. From the tens of thousands of people with whom I have shared this exercise, I have met very few people who can:

1 articulate their personal and professional definitions of success
2 acknowledge the tensions and trade-offs they make in order to manage the two divergent paths.

In my mind this is because they do not spend anywhere near enough time consciously thinking about the definitions, tensions and trade-offs.

The yin and yang symbol from Chinese dualistic philosophy (Figure 3.2) represents a key guiding principle of the select few who truly manage to create alignment between personal and professional success. They do not constrain themselves with what author Jim Collins describes as the 'tyranny of the "or"'.

FIGURE 3.2

The 'tyranny of the "or"' pushes people to believe that things must be either A *or* B, but *not both*. It makes such proclamations as:

- 'You can have change *or* stability.'
- 'You can be conservative *or* bold.'
- 'You can have low cost *or* high quality.'
- 'You can invest for the future *or* do well in the short term.'
- 'You can play to win *or* play not to lose.'
- 'You can have a successful career *or* be a great parent.'

Instead of being constrained by the 'tyranny of the "or"', you can liberate yourself both personally and professionally with the 'genius of the "and"'. Instead of choosing between A *or* B, you can figure out a way to have A *and* B. In the case of success, you can have both personal *and* professional success.

It takes focus and yes, there may be short-term trade-offs, but one does not have to be at the expense of the other.

Be clear about your trade-offs

When you are really clear about what success means to you, both personally and professionally, you can design your life, fully aware of the tensions and trade-offs you're making.

Different stages of your life are like different chapters in which your definition of success may change, as will the importance you place on the different elements.

When you were a child, without responsibilities, you may have placed enormous value on your ability to run fast, jump high or get a record score on a video game. As you got older, your view of success may have skewed towards being great at sports, or getting high marks at school and university or securing your first job. After that, you might measure success by the job you get, the car you drive and the money you make. As life progresses, you might get married and your view of success will begin to be influenced by your relationship. Then, children may come along and a whole new ball game starts. Success is about how happy they are and how well you're able to nurture, protect and educate them, and your whole measure of success shifts again. Later in life, as your parents, your superheroes, start to get older, you add the new role of trying to be a great provider or carer to them, too.

That's life. It swings like a pendulum from side to side, and that's how your definition of success shifts. Being mindful of this will ensure that you're never chasing things you don't actually want.

So many successful people achieve high levels of professional success only to find, when they get there, that their personal relationships have fallen apart. They've missed birthdays, anniversaries, weekends and holidays; they're estranged from their children and their partner. Often it's because they've stuck to a single version of success, even as life evolved around them. Because they didn't evolve their definition of success as their life evolved, they have ended up in a place that is now completely wrong for them.

Being conscious of your changing scenario means that you can make and accept the trade-offs. This isn't an exercise you do once in your life and stick to it, but quite the opposite: it's an organic, fluid, agile process that needs revisiting frequently. This will ensure that:

- the definitions are still relevant
- the tensions are manageable
- the trade-offs you're making are working for you, not against you.

Be a pragmatic optimist

This book is not about setting yourself up with false expectations. You need to be the pragmatic optimist – pragmatic because it has to work in the real world and optimist because you should strive for improvement and a better way of doing things. Tensions are a given, but isn't it better to proactively manage them instead of retrospectively figuring out how to fix them?

A number of years ago, Bryan Dyson, then the President and CEO of Coca-Cola Enterprises, delivered a commencement speech at Georgia Tech, USA. In it he referenced James Patterson's metaphor explaining the difference between glass and rubber balls. The insight is as valuable today as it was then, particularly in defining success personally and professionally:

Imagine life as a game in which you are juggling some five balls in the air. You name them – work, family, health, friends and spirit – and you're keeping all of these in the air. You will soon understand that work is a rubber ball. If you drop it, it will bounce back. But the other four balls – family, health, friends and spirit – are made of glass. If you drop one of these, they will be irrevocably scuffed, marked, nicked, damaged or even shattered. They will never be the same. You must understand that and strive for balance in your life.

I have worked with so many individuals who would be perceived as successful from the outside, but who have broken down before my eyes in the closed confines of a private conversation. They will talk about how they have focused entirely on their careers at the expense of everything else. How they have been divorced three times or that their biggest regret is they missed their children growing up, or they don't have a close relationship with them now in later years. In developing your definition of success, identify your rubber balls and your glass balls. Handle the glass ones with care, because you never get them back!

Accelerator exercise 3.1: Personalize your definition of success

I'm going to share an exercise that will help you personalize your definition of success and provide guidance for making choices around possible tensions and alignment. This exercise is not an attempt to immediately craft a well-groomed, pithy sentence to define success. That will come with time; what is more important now is to capture phrases or words that have meaning for you.

Step 1: Get creative

Brainstorm. Be creative. Get your thoughts down first. You can always finesse and polish them into sentences, a storyboard or a couple of paragraphs at a later date.

If you like mind maps or are visual and prefer pictures, great. Use the approach that works best for you.

If you're struggling to make a start, here are some questions to help:

1 What's important to you personally?
2 What's important to you professionally?
3 What does success look like, feel like and act like for you?

I have found over the years that some people find it easier to articulate what they definitely don't want it to be about:

1 What doesn't success look like to you personally?
2 What doesn't it look like to you professionally?
3 What doesn't it look like, feel like and act like for you?

In answering the second set of questions, flipping your answers over from the negative to the positive will give you an idea of what success does look like.

Blending emotion and logic

In 1961, when President John F. Kennedy committed to sending US astronauts to the moon by the end of the decade, he wasn't speaking from the point of view of logic. The first men had only just gone into space and the technology to get to the moon didn't exist. What he did, however, was create an aspirational image of success and commit the USA to developing the technology, the machines and the training and to finding the men and women to make it happen.

Take the same approach. Dig deep into your feelings, needs, wants, desires, aspirations and dreams yet to be fulfilled; the things you ache for when you think about them long and hard. Answering the questions above, particularly the 'think, feel, act' questions, will ignite your sensory experience making the hairs on the back of your neck stand up with a feeling of nervous excitement as you carve out your definition of success.

Be detailed, be specific, keep drilling down your thoughts and ideas. I often hear people respond to the success question with: 'Royston, I just want to be happy!' While this is a great overarching goal, what do you think my question back to them is?

'OK, great, but what does happiness mean to you?'

'Well, it means being in a meaningful relationship; it means spending time with friends, laughing often, going out for long walks, spending quality time with the kids, being valued and appreciated at work, doing purposeful work' ... The list could go on.

Now spend some time completing Step 1 of the exercise and committing to black and white your key words, phrases and sentences.

Step 2: Piece success together

You now have two options. Your first alternative is to leave your words, phrases or sentences as a list of goals, as in the example below:

Personal goals	Professional goals
Run a marathon	Build high-performing businesses, leaders, teams and individuals
Plan our wedding	Be a 'go to' coach and mentor (internally/ externally)
Achieve financial freedom by 60 years of age	Make a big positive impact on how we give back to our communities
Spend quality one-on-one time with the children	Work for and learn from the very best leaders
Establish a social network beyond my work colleagues	Develop my career by passing the required exams and qualifications
Get involved in my community (sports club / giving back to the community)	Provide for my family
Have freedom to travel / seek out new experiences (time/health/wealth)	Work for a business where I feel valued
Buy a property abroad	Pass my probation
Have fun and maintain a good work/life balance	Find my dream job
Maintain my health and wellbeing	

Your second alternative is to piece them together into one overarching storyboard which flows seamlessly. This could be a series of compelling statements that will stir your emotions and ignite your motivation, creating clarity and focus to be the most successful version of you.

I've included my own definition of both personal and professional success below. I hope it will give you a feel for what yours could look like when it is finished. Believe me, it took me many takes to get to these definitions and they constantly evolve as my thinking and goals change.

They don't need to be long and you don't need to over-engineer and make them complicated. Simplicity is key! They just need to be a true reflection of the authentic you and your goals, aspirations and dreams.

Royston personal

Success to me personally means three things: HEALTH, WISDOM AND WEALTH.

HEALTH means having all my faculties about me and being conscious about the choices and things I do today and the impact on my long-term wellbeing.

WISDOM means living in the present, learning from the past and shaping the future – living life with deliberate intent.

WEALTH means appreciating all the simple pleasures that life has to offer and not being needy of the material things. It means having a wonderful family who are the focus and anchor of what I do and why I do it and giving them the most important gift of all: time and presence and maintaining my work/life focus. It means remaining true to my values and beliefs and remaining grounded and never losing sight of the priorities and what's truly important in life: family, friends and leaving a positive legacy.

Royston professional

My two professional missions in life are, first, delivering accelerated, sustained and profitable business growth through building high-performing, legacy organizations, and second, unlocking the real potential of individuals and helping them to be the best version of themselves every day. This means:

- having fun at work and working with people on projects where we can make a positive impact and difference
- working in partnership with clients and people who have shared values and a shared vision
- managing the positive tension between work and life and being clear about what I am doing, why I am doing it and the trade-offs I make.

Step 3: Validate your definition

The final step is to hold up your definition of success and ask yourself whether this is really what success means to you. Does it stir your emotions and make sense logically? Is it exciting? Does it move you to action? Can you picture and see yourself living out this definition of success? What does it feel like? What will it sound like as you share and hear people talking about your successes and whether you are authentically living to the definition?

If the answer is no to any of the above, go back and rework your definition. If you can honestly, hand on heart, answer yes, then fantastic, you have completed your working blueprint of your success definition.

The hidden gem from completing this exercise

Think about it for a moment. When two people first get together in an intimate relationship, which they both believe could be the one for life, there are hours of conversations about goals, aspirations and dreams on both sides. But what can happen over time is that these conversations subside and become less frequent. Where there was once aligned or convergent thinking around their definition of success, there are now individual definitions heading in different directions. The result is two people with little in common or – worst case – a failed relationship.

Armed with your definition of success, you'll be better equipped to communicate and share your wants and needs with your boss, peer colleagues, team, partner, children and so on. Plus, you'll be much better equipped to help others unlock their own definition, too.

As you read the next chapters, you'll find you want to add, tweak and change parts of your current definition of success. And it doesn't stop with this book. You'll find that defining success is a never-ending process as your thinking and experiences evolve, and your aspirations and expectations of what you want from life grow. That's what makes life so exciting and a dynamic, fluid journey of discovery.

To end this first secret, I'd like to share the following short story with you. It's one of my favourites and has certainly influenced my definition of success over the years.

'The Mexican Fisherman', inspired by Heinrich Böll

An American investment banker was standing on the pier of a little coastal village in Mexico, when a small boat docked with just one fisherman. Inside the small boat were several large yellow-fin tuna. The American complimented the Mexican on the quality of his fish and asked how long it took to catch them.

The Mexican replied, 'Only a little while.'

The American then asked why he didn't stay out longer to catch more fish?

The Mexican said he had enough to support his family's immediate needs.

The American then asked, 'But what do you do with the rest of your time?'

The Mexican fisherman said, 'I sleep late, fish a little, play with my children, take a siesta with my wife Maria and then stroll into the village each evening where I sip wine and play guitar with my amigos. I have a full and busy life.'

The American scoffed, 'I'm a Harvard MBA. I can help you. If you spend more time fishing, you can buy a bigger boat with the proceeds. With the proceeds from the bigger boat, you could buy several boats until eventually you have a fleet of fishing boats.'

The fisherman listened with polite interest. 'And then?' he asked.

'Then, instead of selling your catch to a middleman, you would sell directly to the processor, eventually opening your own cannery. You would control the product, processing and distribution.'

'And then?' the fisherman asked again.

'You would need to leave this small coastal fishing village and move to Mexico City, then Los Angeles and eventually New York City, from where you would run your expanding enterprise.'

'And how long would this all take?' asked the fisherman.

'Fifteen to twenty years,' said the banker.

'But what then?'

The banker laughed. 'That's the best part. When the time is right, you would announce an IPO (Initial Public Offering) and sell your company stock to the public. You'd become very rich. You would make millions.'

'Millions! And then what?' asked the fisherman.

The American said, 'Then you would retire, move to a small coastal fishing village where you would sleep late, fish a little, play with your kids, take a siesta with your wife Maria, stroll to the village in the evenings where you could sip wine and play your guitar with your amigos.'

The moral of the story is that it's so easy to get caught up in the pace of life, becoming so busy rushing around from one activity to the next, spinning multiple plates, that you don't make time to stop and think. Still today, when I catch myself rushing from one place to the next and feel I'm losing the balance in my life, I reread 'The Mexican Fisherman'. It helps me put everything into perspective and redress the scales.

Secret 2: Creating your success formula

Defining what success means to you is only the first piece of the jigsaw. Now comes the real work – turning your definition of success into reality. And to do that you need to create success formulas.

The great news is that we all have areas of our lives where we already apply success formulas. Perhaps you don't describe or think about them as formulas; you may call them plans, routines, systems, rituals, regimens or just 'the way you do it'. But if you're repeating something regularly in the same way because you know it gets you the result you want, that's a success formula.

Cleaning your teeth

Is there a success formula for maintaining healthy teeth? You bet there is! Any dentist could probably talk for hours about the intimate details of the formula and, most importantly, why it is so important.

Brushing and cleaning your teeth is a simple example, but it's also a serious subject. Having an easy success formula for something as basic as cleaning your teeth twice a day, or even after every meal, can prevent catastrophic consequences in years to come. That may seem like an exaggeration, but really it isn't. In Britain there is a tooth decay epidemic, which in recent years saw around 170 youngsters have teeth extracted in hospital every day, with sugar and poor dental hygiene blamed for creating an oral health crisis.

New data by Britain's National Health Service (NHS) reveals that in 2016–17 there were 42,911 hospital procedures to remove multiple teeth from patients aged 18 and under – at a cost of more than £36 million. Those are scary numbers.

If a simple three-minute clean twice a day can prevent real medical challenges later in life, you can see how a small commitment now can have a massive impact over time.

Your morning routine

With a success formula, your mornings can play out one way. Without one, they can be something very different. Picture a couple of different scenarios:

Scenario 1: You wake up and hit the snooze button for 30 minutes. When you do eventually climb out of bed, you're already on the back foot. You rush around getting ready, delayed because you haven't ironed a clean shirt or blouse, miss breakfast due to lack of time, rush out of the door with a quick goodbye, knowing you will now hit the rush-hour traffic, making you late for the first important meeting of the day. How are you feeling? Fraught, anxious, rushed, stressed, hungry?

Scenario 2: You wake up just before the alarm goes off. You climb out of bed and go into the bathroom to wash. You put on your crisply ironed shirt or blouse, which you prepared the evening before, you enjoy breakfast while catching up on the morning news or reading through the file you need for your first meeting or simply talking through the day ahead with your loved one. You are out of the door knowing you will arrive at work on time, prepared and ready for the day ahead. How are you feeling? Calm, in control, positive?

The above focuses only on you having to look after yourself. For parents, the morning routine takes on a whole new meaning! Trust me, with a five-year-old and a three-year-old, I know. If you're a parent, you will know what I mean. It's like a military operation remembering school uniform, PE kits, swimming kits, homework, lunchboxes and school forms, then doing a drop-off at nursery, then another drop-off at school before finally you get to catch your breath.

The difference a disciplined, well-executed success formula can have on your life is limitless. It can place you 100 per cent in the driver's seat!

Training for a marathon

If you've ever trained for or run a marathon, I'm sure you never just turned up on the day of the race and started running. Six months before the race, you may have started your research to find a training plan (a success formula) to follow, detailing precisely how to build up the intensity of your training, week by week, step by step, right up to the time of the race.

Sport is a great source of examples of success formulas in action. This is because the margins of error and the difference between winning and losing can be tenths of a second, one pass, or a single point. This is about elite performance, the best of the best in action.

Watch a Formula One racing team perform a pit stop in the middle of a Grand Prix, or a golfer following the same ritual every time they set up their next shot. You even hear of professionals who have their own particular foibles or nuances. Some might call them superstitious rituals but they would say it is part of their success formula.

Michael Jordan, one of the all-time great basketball players, never forgot his roots. Jordan wore his lucky shorts from his days at the University of North Carolina at Chapel Hill underneath his Chicago Bulls uniform in every NBA game.

Rafael Nadal is described in the tennis world as having neurotic on- and off-court habits. Nadal takes a cold shower 45 minutes before every match, he towels down after every point (even for aces and double faults), he points the labels of his drinking bottles towards the end of the court he's about to play from, and he never stands up from his chair before his opponent.

Tiger Woods wears a red shirt on the final day of golf tournaments, because his mother told him it is his power colour. He's done it consistently since 1996.

Success formulas in business

To find success formulas in action in business, you need to look no further than franchising. Franchises have a far higher success rate than comparable non-franchised start-up businesses. The franchisor has a proven system that works and, providing you follow that system, you will succeed. According to Bloomberg, 80 per cent of new businesses fail within five years and 80 per cent of new franchise businesses succeed in the same period.

McDonald's is probably the first franchise model that pops into your mind and it's no wonder. McDonald's has succeeded in driving the franchise concept to such a powerful level that it now has more than 37,000 restaurants in over 100 countries, with more than 69 million people eating at one of its franchises every single day. When you go into a McDonald's, it doesn't matter where you are in the world, they all serve the same core list of food items (with some regional differences added to the offering) and present them in the same way.

In business, think about monthly board meetings, performance metrics, key performance indicators and dashboards, project plans, monthly profit and loss statements ... These are all success formulas for running a business effectively.

When I'm delivering keynote addresses at conferences, I have a well-defined and deliberately structured success formula. Before I even start putting the talk together, I have a call with the client so that I can be clear about the audience, the purpose of the event, the overall goal and the outcomes they are looking for. Then, on the day, I always go early so that I can see the previous speakers, get a feel for the energy in the room, and develop a sense of how I can pick up the flow and build the energy levels when I hit the stage.

That morning, I will already have written out the three key things I want the audience to do differently at the end. Just before I go on stage, I reread the three key things and think about the audience. I do my breathing ritual to fill my body with oxygen and sharpen my senses, build my energy levels and make sure I am in the performance zone, so when I walk on to that stage I am fast out of the blocks and hit the ground running.

Success formulas in action

I've created a simple model (Figure 3.3) to help you in the creation and application of your own success formulas:

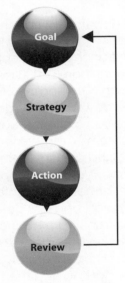

FIGURE 3.3 The four steps to success

1 Define success or the **goal** that you want to achieve.
2 Create a **strategy**, a success formula, a game plan for how you're going to turn your defined success or goal into reality.

3 Take massive **action**, aligned to your strategy, which gets you closer to your goal with every step.

4 **Review** it on a regular basis, as this is the only way you'll know whether it is working or not. This is the step that ultimately plagues most people, and the principal reason why a success formula will fail.

The power of simplicity

You might be thinking that this is an overly simplistic model and way of looking at things. However, its power is in its simplicity. As human beings, we have an innate ability to over-engineer and complicate life.

The grounded reality is that every decision you've ever made in your life to date has got you to the point where you are reading this book, this page, these precise words right now. Whether you are happy with where you are in your life right now is down to choices you have consciously or unconsciously made. And if you're not happy with where you are, it's down to one of three reasons:

- First, you haven't defined what you want your life to look like (Secret 1: Defining success).

- Second, you haven't created a strategy or game plan to turn success into reality (Secret 2: Creating your success formula).

- Third, you're not taking action in alignment with your plan.

The only way you'll know which one it is, is if you are reviewing your success formula on a regular basis.

In your review, focus on the positives as well as what you learn. That may sound obvious, but think about it for a moment. When we are doing a post-mortem, we're great at thinking of all the things that have gone wrong but not so great at thinking of the things that have gone well. For example, if you've just come out of a meeting that went really well, don't fall into the usual trap of giving yourself a two-second 'Well done, good meeting' and then rushing straight into the next thing. You could lose valuable parts of your future success formula. Make the time to stop and create some quiet reflective time for yourself and ask the following question: Why did that meeting go so well?

As you unpack the answer, the essence of your success formula will be revealed. For example:

> I'd done my preparation and planning before the meeting and circulated the agenda so everyone knew what they needed to do and bring. I was there ten minutes early, so I could do a final run-through in my mind and really tune into the meeting. We started and finished on time. I appointed a person to keep track of the time so we did not overrun on specific agenda items. I had another person in the meeting to capture all the actions and outputs, so I could focus on keeping the discussions on track.

Wherever you see high performance, whether it's from a team, an individual or an organization, in sports or in business, I guarantee one thing: their success is not an accident. They are following a success formula to deliver consistent, repeatable, predictable results every time.

This book is ultimately one big success formula. *Rise* is the recipe book that draws together all the key ingredients into one framework to help you start living the life you are meant to lead. Your life is one *big* success formula with many moving parts and individual success formulas contributing to the overall performance of the whole – you.

Accelerator exercise 3.2: Create your formulas for success

This exercise has two main steps:

Step 1: Discover your success formula

1 First, identify the success formulas you already have up and running in your life, or those scenarios where you've used success formulas to great effect for specific things you've done – for example running a marathon, moving house or running projects at work.

2 Now attach the new language of success formulas to the examples you have identified and then unpack the actions, the sequence of events and the key milestones that made it work and allowed you to deliver the specific desired outcome. Think of as many as you can and write them down.

3 Think about how you can replicate those formulas for achieving success in other areas of your life. Imagine how much certainty you could create if you started applying success formulas in those areas of your life where you're not achieving your desired outcomes.

Step 2: Reflect on the formulas described in this book

Now reflect on the success formulas you've discovered so far in this book and the chapters we've already covered. These are success formulas in their own right, which you can use and apply today.

Armed with your definition of success and your success formulas for how you're going to turn your goals into reality, you're now ready to fast-track your timeline through Secret 3: Success modelling. Remember, as Tony Robbins tells us, 'Most people overestimate what they can accomplish in a year – and under-estimate what they can achieve in a decade.'

Secret 3: Success modelling to fast-track your timeline

'Learn from the mistakes of others. You can't live long enough to make them all yourself.'

Eleanor Roosevelt

You don't need to be an expert in everything. You can fast-track your success by learning from the experts.

In my business growth book *Built to Grow* I talk about two choices you have when growing your business. The same principle applies equally to your personal growth, and I want to share it with you here.

When it comes to doing anything new, you have two choices: the first is to put in the hard yards, learning through trial and error as you reinvent the wheel; the second is to learn from those who have already navigated a pathway to success.

I consider myself to have been fortunate and learned early in my career that observing and emulating the habits, processes and attitudes of successful people was a reliable way to fast-track my own success. On reflection, this was one of my most important life lessons and it has stayed with me ever since.

Leaving school at 16, I was keen to get into the real world and start earning money, and my first opportunity was an apprenticeship at a construction company where I com-pleted a four-year rotation through each department of the business. That could have been a long process of trial and error for me but, instead, my very wise site manager advised me that, as I moved into the various departments, I should ask the three best people in each area what they thought I needed to know in order to be successful from day one.

I strongly believe that success modelling is the one idea that can fast-track your success. It doesn't mean there isn't some trial and error involved. When a child learns to walk, you can advise them a hundred times to be careful of a change in level because if they fall down it will hurt. However, sometimes you just have to let them experience the fall (in a controlled environment, of course), pick up a few bumps and grazes and cry a little to know it's not a good thing to do.

Why does a second sibling generally develop faster than the first? It's because they have a role model to emulate and copy; they are 'success modelling' from an early age. The optimum solution therefore is a blend of the two: modelling other people's success while testing out some of your own thinking and ideas, making some healthy mistakes and learning from them fast.

Your personalized success modelling strategy

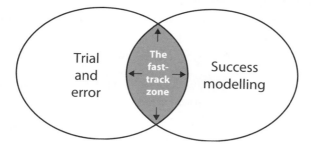

FIGURE 3.4 The fast-track zone in success modelling

The overlap where these two strategies meet is what I call the 'fast-track zone' (Figure 3.4). This is where you model successful behaviour, and then learn through trial and error as you perfect and apply it to your own life. The fast-track zone is where you can really build momentum. It's the place where people find they can shift up a gear and move their entire being and life to the next level in terms of confidence, self-belief, self-esteem and, yes, tangible results.

Here are five ways to create your personalized success modelling strategy:

1 INTERVIEW HIGH ACHIEVERS

We all know successful people who have achieved great things, but you may be surprised to discover how willing they often are to share their success, if only they were asked to do so. Bill Gates once said that he is amazed by how many people ask him for a million dollars and dismayed by how few people ask him for advice on how to make a million of their own.

So here's what I'd like you to do over the next couple of weeks: make a list of people in your immediate circle who you would define as 'successful'. Make it a mix of people from your both your personal and professional life. They should be individuals from whom you feel you are going to gain important insights in your journey of turning your definition of success into reality. Call or email them, tell them why you want to meet them and offer to buy lunch in exchange for asking some questions.

In the toolkit https://www.roystonguest.com/RISE-toolkit/ I've included 42 great questions you could ask. There are no doubt many more, but this list has served me well for many years. Here's a sample:

- What's your definition of success, personally and professionally?
- How do you manage the work/life quandary and balance?
- What's your view/take on goal setting? Have you written down your goals? Personal goals? Professional goals? Or both?

- What do you think are the secrets of your success?
- What would you say are the skills essential for success in business and in life?

2 Get a mentor or even a series of mentors

Ask the people you've just interviewed if they would be willing to give you an hour of their time every month on the condition that you ask them challenging questions so you can both learn and reflect deeply on success.

Mentoring is growing in popularity and, again, you'll be amazed how open people are to helping and supporting you on your growth journey.

3 Engage a formal coach

Whether that be in the area of fitness, nutrition, a business coach, a wealth coach, life coach or someone to help you manage your calendar and commitments better … The right coach can massively accelerate your journey.

4 Connect with as many learning opportunities as you can

On a daily basis, work on filling in the gaps in your knowledge. Think TED Talks, podcasts, books and audio books as great ways to learn new things.

Design a programme to align with your own preferred learning style. For example, if you don't like picking up a physical book to read, most good books are available in audio format. You can listen while driving, working out in the gym, walking or sitting on the train.

5 Create a virtual board

A personal favourite, which I'd encourage you to consider, is to set up your own virtual board. This is a group of people who you're never going to formally engage as coaches, but who you enjoy learning from, or believe can add a lot of value in developing your own performance. I have a virtual board of people, including Tony Robbins, Robin Sharma, Brendon Burchard and Russell Brunson, among others, whom I follow and actively learn from. I subscribe to all their newsletters, read their blogs, look at their seminars and purchase their programmes, and they give me a frame of reference that enables me to set an elite benchmark for my own performance.

So there you have it: the powerful concept of success modelling. This is definitely a quick win and a strategy you can implement immediately to start reaping the benefits quickly.

By now, I'm sure you're seeing the interlocking nature of the first three secrets:

Secret 1: Defining what success means to you

Secret 2: Creating your success formula

Secret 3: Success modelling to fast-track your timeline.

And as promised, here's the essence of the final two secrets, which are covered in detail in Chapter 13: Being your own performance coach.

Secret 4: Developing your success disciplines

'Once you have commitment, you need the discipline and hard work to get you there.'

Haile Gebrselassie

Warren Buffett, considered one of the most successful investors in the world, was speaking with Bill Gates, founder of Microsoft, at Harvard Business School. They were addressing students of the final graduating year, who were just about to start their careers. During the Q&A session at the end, a student asked: 'Mr Buffett, if there was one final thought you could share with us as we head into the world of work and start our careers, what would it be?' This was a great question and Buffett's response was, 'Get your habits right while you're young, because once embedded they will serve you in creating a compelling future.'

This was an insightful response, particularly the words 'because once embedded'. This is the difference that makes the difference for high achievers: consistency of action – consistency over time that in turn leads to habit.

You can invest quality time defining what success means to you personally and professionally. You can create your success formula and a personalized success modelling strategy and on paper you are set up for success, only to fall down on disciplined execution. I've seen so many people achieve some quick wins, but delivering accelerated, sustained and repeatable results requires a whole new set of skills and disciplines. It requires focus, it requires rigour, and it requires boundless levels of energy, commitment and resilience.

Secret 5: Honing your success habits

'We are what we repeatedly do. Excellence, then, is not an act but a habit.'

Will Durrant

There is a saying, 'There are no crowds lining the extra mile'. Masters of their craft, whatever their specialist field of endeavour, are part of a select group of people who really live by this saying. Why? Because the extra mile is where they spend most of their time. They don't subscribe to the tribe of life, the herd mentality. For them, a life of mediocrity is not an option.

Instead, they invest their time every day in being the best of the best, raising their personal standards and chasing perfection. Even though perfection isn't truly attainable, they know that by going the extra mile they may just catch excellence on the journey. Their journey is a never-ending pursuit of personal mastery. And their vehicle to get there is their discipline, which over time leads to habit.

Since the overarching theme of this book is that you strive for personal mastery in designing and shaping your life, it makes sense to cover this particular secret at the end of the book, because it details precisely the ideas over which each of us should strive to achieve mastery. These are the essential thinking and skills that will ensure you are on the road to building the life you have always dreamed of.

Take action: achieve more

Now's the time to define what success means to you.

This chapter introduced the five secrets of success: defining what success means to you, creating your success formula, success modelling, developing your success disciplines and honing your success habits.

Success never 'just happens' but is an act of conscious, deliberate intent on both a personal and professional level, managing tensions that exist between the two. Learn how to balance them and you'll remain focused on your definition of success.

I shared two powerful, thought-provoking Accelerator exercises to help define what success means to you:

Accelerator exercise 3.1: Personalize your definition of success

You must measure success by your own standards, not anyone else's. Success is only real if it is individual to you, so now's the time for you to own it:

- What does success mean to you personally?
- What does success mean to you professionally?
- Are your two definitions aligned, or are they in tension?

Accelerator exercise 3.2: Create your formulas for success

This is about identifying, replicating and applying your success formulas to all areas of your life.

- What was it that allowed you to deliver the specific desired outcome?

Unpack the actions, the sequence of events, the key milestones that made it a success formula for you. Your life is one big success formula made up of many moving parts, all contributing to the overall performance of the whole – you!

We all run a business called 'ME Unlimited'

'Your attitude will always dictate your altitude in life.'

Zig Ziglar

If your life were a business, would you invest in it?

It wouldn't take more than a few minutes of searching online to find a virtual library of videos featuring the most successful people on earth – Bill Gates, Oprah Winfrey, Richard Branson and others – describing their best tips for achieving business and financial success and their ideal work/life balance. This can be a great way to step inside the mind of some of your icons because the ideas they have to share can be invaluable.

But there's a problem: *they're* not living *your* life. *You* are. And living *your* life well is about accepting responsibility, taking control, making decisions and getting things done.

This is usually the subtext of all useful self-help advice. There are no get-rich-quick schemes, no wild pendulum swings and no magic elixirs when it comes to success. The greatest, most successful people in the world all got there by planning, creating life and work strategies, and then putting in long, hard hours to make it all happen.

We can all be guilty of passing the buck when it comes to our own struggles. Some people make it a mantra to complain about how things aren't going well and to pass the blame for their failure or hardship elsewhere. The government is always an easy scapegoat, no matter who is in charge. It's the economy, the 'system' or even the weather!

To achieve great success now or in the future, you simply can't think that way. No matter how you measure success, it is achieved by people who take total – note, TOTAL – responsibility for their lives, actions and results. The same rule applies to you and me.

The concept of responsibility

Let's stop for a moment to reflect on the word 'responsibility' and the related word 'responsible'. What do these words mean? Responsible can be defined simply as a combination of the words 'response' and 'able' – able to respond.

Often, however, the concept of 'responsibility' and 'being responsible' is mired in negative connotations. When we were youngsters it was often an accusation:

- Who is responsible for breaking that window?
- Who is responsible for this mess?
- Who is responsible for these muddy footprints?

You've probably attended a meeting where the question has been asked: 'Who's responsible for this action?' And everyone starts looking at their feet, twitching or playing with their pen, not wanting to make eye contact in case even a fleeting glance results in the action or task coming their way.

Being responsible sounds so final ... If it doesn't work, you're the one to blame. What it actually means, though, is quite different and it could be better articulated with the question: 'Who's going to own this one?' Doesn't that sound more positive, more enabling, and much less likely that you'll be in trouble for getting it wrong? And guess who owns and is in control of your life? Yes, it's you – even though, some days, it may feel that it's your boss, your partner, your children or your friends.

This may require a mind shift for you. There's nothing wrong with that. On the other hand, it might already be part of your mantra or your DNA, your personal philosophy or your belief system. It may be wired into the very essence of who you are. Either way, the most important part about getting on the path to success is about making the decision to start.

The million-dollar question

Here is the million-dollar question:

If your life were a business, would you invest in it?

What would your answer be?

The title of this chapter is 'We all run a business called "Me Unlimited"' and Me Unlimited, aka you, has unlimited potential to maximize the results of whatever you set your heart, mind and attention to. If you had to float Me Unlimited on the stock market, how confident would you be of its success?

As you write the prospectus for investors, how credible would the overall goals be? Would a potential investor pick up your prospectus and say 'Yes, 100 per cent I am going to invest' or would they say 'This just isn't viable'?

Your seven director roles

As with any business, there are multiple roles to ensure that the daily operations happen. This is no different for you, but there is one fundamental distinction: in your business you play all the roles. These are the seven director roles that make up your board: Chairperson, Sales and Marketing Director, Finance Director, Planning and Administration Director, Wellbeing Director, Learning Director and Communications Director. These roles collectively control your life, both personally and professionally.

Fulfilling the seven roles with focus and deliberate intent is one of the most powerful personal transformation exercises you'll ever complete. The whole mental process starts with knowing that you are in control of your own destiny and that you always have a choice. You can't always control what happens to you, but you can control how you react to it and what you do about it.

Taking total ownership of your choices is the most liberating thing in the world. You go from feeling like a passenger to being the driver. And being the driver is the first step to being out in front, winning a Formula One Grand Prix. Not all drivers will do that, admittedly. But I guarantee that no passenger ever will.

It doesn't mean you have to be selfish or focus on your own success at the expense of others. In fact, by taking ownership and being in control, you put yourself in a far better position to help those around you to accomplish their goals and maximize their potential.

Let's look in detail at the seven directors of your life and the roles they play.

Your first role: Chairperson

> 'If I have seen further than others, it is by standing upon the shoulders of giants.'
>
> *Isaac Newton*

As Chairperson, you are responsible for your vision and values and for setting the direction of travel, culture, environment, cadence and pace of your life. It is from this role that all other things flow, as it has overall responsibility for shaping the attitude and performance of the other six directors. Attitude cascades from the top, so having a great Chairperson is essential to success.

Unfortunately, we all know that bosses can be flawed. Steve Jobs was a visionary genius with exacting standards and an almost supernatural sense for trends, but he was a dire interpersonal communicator: Richard Branson is a pioneering dreamer with the power to execute ideas of any scale, but seems highly unlikely to be enthused by the idea of paperwork.

One of the tasks of the Chairperson is to keep all six of the other directors in check by playing to their strengths and compensating for their weaknesses while being aligned to a unified vision/purpose. Creating this overarching vision and purpose for your life is a central role of the Chairperson as it defines the attitude and mindset in which you will turn your goals into reality.

> All the rewards of life come from taking personal owner-ship and responsibility for our lives, actions and results.

Your second role: Sales and Marketing Director

'A spray-and-pray approach won't cut it, if you want real results.'

The sales side

On the sales side of the Sales and Marketing Director role, you must have a clear picture of how much money you are going to generate in your business over the next 12 months. Without this you don't have any real control over your financial situation.

In a random room of people, the vast majority would declare that they *don't* sell, *can't* sell or at least *don't like* selling. That's a real pity, because selling is critical to success.

You already spend much of your life selling. As a child you sold your parents again and again on the idea of buying you sweets or letting you stay up late. As an adult, you must at some point have sold your partner on the idea of going out with you or convinced your boss to let you have an extra day off or a pay rise. These are all examples of you doing a sales job. We sell all the time and we're usually a lot better at it than we give ourselves credit for.

If you're not earning the income for the life you want to live, then don't limit your sales strategy to just one revenue stream. What other revenue can you generate? It might be a second job, a part-time business selling unwanted items online, renting out a bedroom or even your house (think Airbnb), investing in stocks and shares or an investment portfolio, buying another property and renting it out. Revenue streams can and should come from multiple sources to maximize your earning potential and reduce over-dependency on one area.

> Irrespective of your source of income, every day should be about proving your value, your worth and your importance.

The marketing side

As Marketing Director, your focus should be on safeguarding and promoting your personal brand, making sure your messaging, image, achievements and activities are in alignment with the way you wish to be seen, thought of, and what you want people to believe about you. As Jeff Bezos, CEO and founder of Amazon, once said: 'Your brand is what people say about you when you're not in the room.'

So what do people say about you? And more importantly, what do you want them to say? Your personal brand is central to maximizing and unlocking your real potential, both personally and professionally.

You don't want to be a talented, high-performing individual who never realizes their real potential because you are the best-kept secret in the marketplace. You don't want to be playing small. You must communicate your brand to the outside world, making sure that there is only one authentic version of the truth – across social media, your CV and your biography.

Your third role: Finance Director

'Many people have too much month at the end of the
money ... instead of too much money at the end of
the month.'

Which way round is it for you?

One of British author W. Somerset Maugham's most col-
ourful characters was the tetchy art tutor Monsieur Foinet (in
Of Human Bondage, 1915), who delivered one of the greatest lines in English literature when he said: 'Money is like a
sixth sense without which you cannot make a complete use
of the other five. Without an adequate income half the possibilities of life are shut off.'

It's one of those statements that makes you sit up and
take notice, isn't it? But it's not just earning money that is
important, but what you do with it once you've earned it.
How you treat your money says a great deal about your reality. American billionaire Mark Cuban said a few years back
that 'If you use a credit card, you don't want to be rich. The
first step to getting rich requires discipline.'

As your own Finance Director, you are responsible for the
finances of your life, including budgeting, maintaining accurate records and making sure you look after your money
wisely. Having too much money at the end of each month is
your goal! You carry considerable responsibility for whether
or not you are 'investible'.

Imagine attending the Annual General Meeting (AGM)
of a big blue-chip company you were considering investing in. During the meeting a shareholder asks the Sales and
Marketing and Finance Directors the following questions:

- 'Do you have a sales forecast?'
- 'Do you have a budget?'
- 'Do you maintain accurate accounting records?'

- 'Do you have a detailed 12-month Profit & Loss Statement?'
- 'What's the monthly and yearly net profit forecast?'

Imagine if all those questions got a resounding 'no' in response. Would you still invest your hard-earned money? No way! It's no different with you: you, too, are investing, but the commodity you are using is your life.

There's no correlation between people who start out wealthy and people who end up that way. Your success is a result of things totally in your control: your attitude and mindset towards your wealth, your effective money management, planning, discipline and actions.

Money may not buy happiness, but it can certainly take the pressure off, and can give you more life, more freedom and more choices.

Your fourth role: Planning and Administration Director

'Our goals can only be reached through a vehicle of a plan, in which we must fervently believe, and upon which we must vigorously act. There is no other route to success.'

Pablo Picasso

This director operates at two levels: the creative one of setting goals, creating roadmaps and planning to achieve your dreams: and the more mundane one of keeping your admin in line so that you don't trip yourself up with unnecessary roadblocks or distractions.

They're quite different, but they're both equally important.

The planning side

This is where you get to have fun, setting yourself audacious goals personally and professionally. It's exciting and it's your invitation to dream as big as you dare. This director works closely with your Chairperson, translating the vision and purpose of your life into a set of deliverable goals, that are tangible and measurable.

If planning is on its game, you needn't worry about getting to the end of your life and looking back on unfilled potential and unmet goals. Your goals will have been translated into reality!

The admin side

Administration. I can sense your energy levels dropping even as you read the word! It's not lofty or exciting, but it's this role more than any other that prevents you hitting avoidable roadblocks. It's critical for maintaining control of your life, your business, your relationships and everything else. You may think this is the boring stuff, but the reality is that, if you don't keep on top of your admin, it will get on top of you.

You've probably heard the expression 'tidy desk, tidy mind', and this role takes care of all the 'stuff' that can clutter your mind and derail you from focusing on the important things that will truly help you reach your personal and professional goals. This role is also responsible for maximizing your time and resources. You have only finite supplies of those on any given day. So many people talk about how busy they are, as if being busy were a mark of success. It's far more important to be productive than busy, and those two things are definitely not the same.

Both components of this role – the sexy and the mundane – are critical to the success of your life. In sport, the striker or quarterback or championship driver is the leading face that gets fans' blood pumping, but behind the scenes, the faceless heroes – including the physiotherapists, coaches, handlers, advisers and managers – are just as criti-cal to their success.

You can be carried away by the other roles, but you'll put your success in peril if you don't embrace both parts of this role with equal vigour.

Your fifth role: Wellbeing Director

'Wellbeing is the complete integration of body, mind, and spirit – the realization that everything we do, think, feel and believe has an effect on our overall state of wellbeing.'

We operate in two zones. The first, the performance zone, is when you're 'on it', doing your thing, being the best version of you. The second, the recovery zone, is where you move into your personal life. This is where you come down from the highs or lows of the day, reflect on what's gone well or not gone well, and question what you have learned that will help you be better tomorrow.

The time you allocate and invest in the recovery zone is not just a 'nice do' – it's a 'must do' if you want to maximize your potential in the performance zone. Wellbeing is not a 'medical fix' but a way of living – a lifestyle sensitive and responsive to all the dimensions of body, mind, and spirit. It is a critical role in your business.

Your greatest wealth is your health and this is a central reason why this role is Wellbeing Director and not Fitness Director. Fitness is just one component of wellbeing but well-being also includes paying attention to things like exercise, diet, relaxation, sleep, avoiding burnout, mindfulness, dental check-ups, eye tests and more.

Can you put your hand on your heart and say you are currently doing everything within your control to look after your wellbeing?

Your sixth role: Learning Director

'The day you stop learning is the day you stop earning.'

Anon.

If there is one thing that differentiates all the high achievers I have had the privilege to work with, it is their insatiable thirst for learning, for knowledge and, most importantly, their bias for translating knowledge into action. High performers always have a book on the go, surround themselves with like-minded people, have a curiosity for life, and constantly ask questions. They are always listening, learning, feeding their minds and translating ideas into action. They stay on the lookout for the next strategy, idea or tool that is going to give them the edge, personally and professionally. They are thinkers and, perhaps more importantly, they are doers.

In life, you fall into one of two camps: you're either a rock or a sponge. Successful people are sponges. They spend their life being their own performance coach, taking 100 per cent ownership for their own development and learning, recognizing that life is a never-ending journey of discovery where there is always room for improvement.

There has never been an easier time to learn, with resources available at the touch of a button. There really is no excuse for not having an ongoing strategy for development and learning. The day you stop learning is the day you stop earning, and the day you stop learning is the day you lose your edge and stop being the best version of yourself you can be.

Your seventh role: Communications Director

'We are more connected than we have ever been, but the question is: are we really *connecting*?'

This role is responsible for how you interact with others and how conversations are managed internally, with yourself. That's so often overlooked. The saying goes that, if you spoke about other people the way you speak about yourself, you'd have a permanent black eye!

Knowing how to communicate effectively includes your ability to listen; your ability to interrogate people and ideas in an open and inquisitive way with the desire to understand; your ability to build rapport, to empathize; and to read both spoken and unspoken language. Your ability to communicate well with the outside world, including your family, your partner and your customers, is directly proportionate to your potential for success.

But there's a challenge. We are more connected than ever through technology and social media, but ask yourself this: are you truly connecting? If there has been one significant change in the way people interact over the past decade, it's through social media. But technology is not a replacement for developing rich, high-quality relationships. In fact, the reverse is true.

One knock-on effect of social media is that the ability to connect with people is becoming a scarce resource. If you are to be a truly effective communicator, you should consider adopting the following five principles to ensure that you're not just connected but truly connecting:

1 Be present

The best gift you can give someone is the gift of your presence. Not just physically, but your full self, tuned in. Think about it for a moment. How many times have you been mid-flow in conversation but your mind is already thinking about the next call or meeting? How many times have you been asked a question in a meeting when your attention has gone AWOL and you have no idea where the conversation was or how to answer?

In these moments, you are there in body but not in mind and, since I am sure that's never your deliberate intent, it's completely at odds with the underlying philosophy of Me Unlimited.

2 Ask yourself: are you listening?

What I mean is, are you *really* listening? It is so often true that listening is the most violated of communication skills. Many people hear the words but don't get the message, simply because they are just waiting for their turn to talk.

Listening is one of the single most important skills to master and the starting point is understanding the three different kinds of listening:

- Inattentive listening is where you're not really interested in what the other person is saying, or you do not have the time or inclination to listen.

- Competitive listening is where you're absorbed in your own thoughts and thinking, as opposed to tuning into what the speaker is saying. Your own internal voice is competing with the external voice of the speaker.

- Supportive listening is the key to success as a listener. This is when someone is truly listening to what you are saying, completely tuned into the moment and into you. Their eyes are with you, their body language is with you and they appear to be fully immersed and absorbed in what you are saying. They make you feel as if you're the only person in the room. Their listening is supportive and, as a result, you are confident that you will not be interrupted, you're confident in delivering your message and you're confident in getting your points across in a natural, persuasive style with maximum impact.

3 Pay attention to the detail

This is intrinsically linked to Principle 2 but it's much, much more than that. Great leaders, communicators and influencers all have the habit of paying attention to the details. They always remember the small things. And in a world where the big things make little difference, it's the LITTLE things that make a BIG difference.

It's about remembering the names of employees, their partners and their children, for example, and keeping tabs on people's birthdays, anniversaries, hobbies and favourite sports teams – details, details, details.

4 Have a real conversation

Or, more specifically, pick up the telephone! I wish I had a pound for every time I've said to a colleague 'Just pick up the phone and give them a call', only to check back later and they respond with 'I've sent them an email.'

Too many people hide behind technology and, specifically, email. But in a world that has become really impersonal, the personal touch is more important than ever. Picking up the telephone and actually having a conversation is such a simple but powerful way of ensuring that you are connecting. Walk over to a colleague's desk instead of sending an email. Sit around the dinner table as a family with no gadgets and just talk.

Some of these ideas sound so basic and simple, yet in the fast-paced, frenetic world we're living in, we forget the simple things, which really do make the difference. Be brilliant at the basics!

5 In your conversation, be empathetic, not sympathetic

Empathy is understanding how others feel, and it comes from understanding what the other person is thinking, feeling and experiencing. It's like an out-of-body experience, when you transport yourself into the other person's shoes and see the world through their eyes, not yours. It truly is a great skill to master.

Sympathy is feeling sorry for someone and can actually be very disempowering for them, as this perspective tends to place you above them. Put yourself in other people's shoes, but don't do their walking!

Putting yourself in the driver's seat

With seven roles with seven sets of responsibilities, sometimes it can feel like you're leading a pinball life, bouncing around at ridiculous speeds, feeling out of control, reactive to things you need to do both personally and professionally. When you do manage to get your head up for breath and turn autopilot mode off, a day, a week or even a month has passed and you wonder what has been happening and where the time has gone. Well, life is not for living in autopilot: it's time to put *you* firmly in the driver's seat of your life.

Me Unlimited is a great tool, a way of thinking and framework that can give you structure, focus and discipline. To help you get maximum value from it, I want to share a simple Accelerator exercise with you.

First, download the template from the toolkit https://www.roystonguest.com/RISE-toolkit/. Switch off your phone, switch off your email, put this book to one side and work through the following steps.

Note: You might want to review the descriptors for each role as you complete steps 1–3. I've also included below some additional questions to consider, to help stimulate your thinking as you complete the exercise.

Accelerator exercise 4.1: Review your performance

Step 1 Give yourself a mark out of 10 for how you think you are currently performing in each of the seven director roles. Then give yourself a mark out of 10 for where you want to be.

Now here is an important point. You might be thinking, 'Surely I want to be 10 in all these directorships?' Perhaps. But don't make the gap between where you are now and where you want to be too big. For example, you may score yourself a 2 in your role as Planning Director, because you don't currently set goals. Creating goals in your personal and business life and committing these to writing within 30 days might get you to 5, but in order to get to a 7, you should be reviewing your goals on a regular basis (weekly, with quarterly updates). Getting to a 10 takes time. That's OK. This is *your* life – and you've got some living to do yet.

Step 2 On the graph, plot your marks for each director, starting with the 'where you are now' scores first, and then connect the scores with a line. How balanced is your business? How well are the directors performing? Once you have done this, you may wish to use another colour to plot where you want to be. Would this make your business more balanced?

Step 3 In the last column, add a maximum of three actions you *must* take to achieve the desired mark against each of the seven director roles to make your business more balanced.

Questions to consider

CHAIRPERSON

1 How does your attitude and outlook on life affect those around you – personally and professionally?

2 How visionary are you in creating a compelling picture of your future?

3 What do you do to create a fun environment for those close to you?

4 What's the performance culture and the tone and pace you want to create for your life?

SALES AND MARKETING DIRECTOR

1 What are your financial ambitions?

2 How can/will you generate the income you desire/ need?

3 How is your personal brand and impact perceived and understood? Does this help or hinder you in realizing your full potential?

4 Where do you want to take your career in the next year, the next five years and the next ten years?

5 On a scale of 1 to 10 (1 = low, 10 = high), how confident are you in achieving your ambitions?

FINANCE DIRECTOR

1 Do you have too much money at the end of the month or too much month at the end of the money?

2 How do you stay in control of your personal finances?

3 Can you afford the life you'd like to lead?

4 Have you set aside three months of financial reserves to cover unforeseen circumstances (if you're unable to work or need to pay for exceptional costs)?

5 What are your plans to achieve your financial aspirations?

PLANNING AND ADMINISTRATION DIRECTOR

1 What are your short-, medium- and long-term goals for your life, personally and professionally?

2 On a scale of 1 to 10 (1 = low, 10 = high), how would you rate your 'self'-management?

3 How in control are you of managing your work/life balance?

4 How organized are you?

Wellbeing Director

1 How comfortable are you with your wellness plan?
   (This includes personal fitness, sleep, diet, relaxation
   and general check-ups.)
2 On a scale of 1 to 10 (1 = low, 10 = high), how would
   you rate your energy levels?
3 How comfortable are you with your work/life balance?

Learning Director

1 Do you have a learning and personal development
   plan in place or do you 'wing' it?
2 On average per month, how much time do you allocate to allow creative thinking?
3 When was the last time you had a new experience/
   learned something new? What was it?
4 How do you have fun in your life?
5 How do you achieve personal growth and stretch?

Communications Director

1 How effectively do you communicate with your team,
   your boss, your customers, your colleagues, your
   partner, your children and your family?
2 How effective are you at building networks and
   engaging others professionally?
3 How well do you communicate and build relationships outside work?

Insights gained

I've completed this exercise with tens of thousands of people
worldwide, and there are a number of themes and insights
that constantly emerge.

BITE-SIZED CHUNKS

There are many moving parts to success, with multiple things requiring your attention, all at the same time. This can sometimes feel overwhelming – so overwhelming, in fact, that there's always the temptation to do nothing as you try to figure out where to start.

To overcome this feeling, break down your objectives into bite-sized chunks. As the saying goes, 'How do you eat an elephant? One bite at a time.' Take small steps and find your natural groove, a rhythm that helps you focus and gain traction and positive forward momentum.

Adopting the seven directors approach allows you to split your life's goals and aspirations into bite-sized chunks and the multiplying effect of all seven roles working together results in constant small improvements and marginal gains, which can give an exponential uplift to your performance.

ARE YOU CATCHING YOURSELF DOING IT RIGHT OR DOING IT WRONG?

When I initially explained the seven director roles, what reaction did you have to each one? Did you instantly connect with one or two? As you read the role descriptor, did you say something like 'Yep, this one is definitely me! I have this one nailed', or 'I'm doing well in certain areas and could easily identify some quick wins to kick myself to the next level.'

What about the other roles? Were there some you didn't really care for one way or another? And be honest now: were there some that you thought were going to be painful just from reading the title? I've yet to find anyone who doesn't have reservations about at least one or two of the roles. (It's often the Wellbeing Director, the Finance Director or the Planning and Administration Director.)

I hear people make comments like 'Royston, my Wellbeing Director has gone AWOL', or 'I think my Finance Director has fallen asleep on the job.'

So when you're looking to create forward momentum and shift the performance of your life, where should you focus first? Is it the role that presents the greatest challenge; the one that will give you some quick wins; or the role that is already performing and in play?

Most people will instantly default to the underperforming roles that offer them the greatest challenge. And my response is always this: if you're the captain of a high-performing team, who do you pick first? Is it the worst player? Of course not. You pick your best player, the one that you know is consistent in their performance, truly committed, has a great attitude and will knock it out of the park every time with their performance.

It's the same with Me Unlimited. Think of it like a traffic light system:

- The director roles that are currently performing well are your greens. These roles are the ones you want working on your life first; they're already on the playing field creating the cadence and pace. These roles are your core, and once your core is strong you can start building out from there.

- Next come your ambers, the director roles that are there or thereabout. With some focus and quick wins, you can accelerate these roles to the next level in their wider contribution to the overall performance of Me Unlimited.

- And finally we come to the reds. Now here's some food for thought. If certain areas don't come naturally to you, could you seek outside help or 'outsource' them?

If you are consistently terrible with your finances, could you ask your partner to take this role, since they're a green in this area? If admin is not your thing, who can support you and fill this gap? Outsourcing can cost money, but it might be a worthwhile investment if it frees up your time for higher-value activities.

There is an important caveat to this. Outsourcing some of the activities and actions is about effective delegation of responsibility, not abdication. There are certain things that you must take absolute control over. For example, you cannot abdicate responsibility for your wellbeing.

A great exercise now is to go back and look at each of the seven directors you have scored and identify how many greens, how many ambers and how many reds you have. And then think about accelerating the performance of each area in alignment with the points above.

FREQUENCY OF REVIEW

People frequently ask me how often they should review their seven director roles and their progress. How regularly should you have what is essentially a 'board meeting'?

In a business, a board of directors tends to meet once per month, so why on earth wouldn't you run monthly 'board meetings' for the most important 'business' you will ever have – your life! If there is one action I would urge you to do right now, it is this. Go to your diary and from now on block out 'board meetings' for the start of every month.

Set aside 30 minutes and use the board minutes from the previous meeting (the template in the toolkit, the one you used to complete the exercise) to review each director role. Review where you were last month and where you wanted to get to, what your key actions were and whether they've been completed.

It may sound strange having a board meeting with yourself, but since you cannot fire any of your seven director roles because they're all you, this fundamentally means that they're with you for life. You have to get them to work at a high level and play to your strengths, or find ways to compensate for your weaknesses. You will need to work on those particular areas to achieve your goals, because I can guarantee that no one else is.

Test the process and, if you feel that monthly isn't frequent enough and you are losing focus and momentum, try bi-weekly or weekly until you find your groove and achieve maximum results. Whatever cadence and frequency you decide on, make sure you stick with it. Discipline and repetition are key to your sustained success.

MARGINAL GAINS

The whole concept of marginal gains is such a liberating, enabling and empowering concept. It refers to the accumulation of small improvements into a larger, more significant improvement.

Elite performance in business, in sport, and in your personal and professional life is not necessarily about doing major things differently. It's about the disciplined execution, repetition and relentless focus on doing the small things consistently and flawlessly. The aggregation and multiplying effect of these small things has an exponential, compounding effect on the end result and leads to an uplifted performance.

Marginal gains were made famous in recent times through the work of Sir Clive Woodward with his England rugby team and Sir Dave Brailsford with British Cycling and Team Sky. When Sir Clive took over the England rugby team in 1997 he set out to effect a wholesale culture change, restructuring the players' experience 'from driveway to driveway'. That is, from the moment the English players left home to play for their country to the moment they returned, everything would be considered, analysed and aligned with the team's values, purpose and strategy.

According to Sir Clive (in his book *Winning*),

> success can be attributed to how a team worked together under pressure, how they understood the importance of team work and loyalty and how they were willing to do a hundred things just 1 per cent better.

The final aspect Sir Clive called 'the critical non-essentials'. A fresh jersey at half-time, the same bus for every home game, a more inspiring locker room at Twickenham; every little thing, every marginal gain, helped Sir Clive's England team win the 2003 Rugby World Cup.

Britain's Olympic cyclists called it 'marginal gains'. In their preparation for the London Olympics in 2012, in which they won an incredible seven out of ten gold medals, the details included:

1 customized aerodynamic helmets
2 hot pants – worn to keep muscles warm between races
3 sweat-resistant clothing
4 alcohol sprayed on the wheels to enhance traction at the start
5 hypo-allergenic pillows to help stop riders catching colds.

The whole principle, Brailsford explained to the BBC, came from the idea that if you broke down everything you could think of that goes into riding a bike, and improved it by 1 per cent, you would get a significant increase when you put it all together. Just think what impact this could have if you did the same exercise in your personal life, on your business, and in your professional life.

Starbucks applied the principle when it focused on its exponential growth. The focus was 'To inspire and nurture the human spirit – one person, one cup and one neighbourhood at a time'. If your goal is to go to the gym three times a week, 12 times a month, 144 times a year, at the start of the year don't focus on the 144 gym sessions; focus on 'one session at a time'. The daily, weekly marginal gains will get you to the 144!

Formula One racing team McLaren F1 calls it 'tenths'. The entire team is galvanized by the idea of shaving tenths of a second off the lap time. All Formula One teams do it, of course, but McLaren makes it its central operating principle.

Marginal gains can be technical, physical, practical, operational and even psychological. In the film *Any Given*

Sunday, the Al Pacino character speaks about the same thing when he refers to the inches that are all around us:

> You find out that life is just a game of inches. So is football. Because in either game, life or football, the margin for error is so small … On this team, we fight for that inch. On this team we tear ourselves, and everyone around us to pieces for that inch … because we know when we add up all of those inches that's going to make the difference between WINNING and LOSING.

Where are *your* inches? Where are you going to find your marginal gains, both personally and professionally? To return to the million-dollar question from the beginning of this chapter,

If your life were a business, would you invest in it?

What would your answer be?

Your baseline

Having now completed the Me Unlimited exercise, you know your current state of reality and your baseline on which to challenge yourself. What a great position to be in: you know your capabilities, your effectiveness and even your success in each of the seven director roles.

In life, you don't know what you don't know.

Each of the chapters that follow will give you deeper insight into the seven roles. They are purposely designed to accelerate your awareness to a far higher level than you are at right now. And as you review your current baseline for each director, your mindset and thinking evolves and so does your score and committed actions.

That may feel like regression. It's not. A completely factual baseline is the point of origin for true growth. Hold your nerve and go with me on the journey. I have your back!

Take action: achieve more

If your life were a business, would you invest in it?

This chapter introduced the concept of your life represented as a business called Me Unlimited, with seven director roles collectively managing and controlling your life. This means that you alone have responsibility for all seven director roles. Throughout your life, as you pursue your goals, it's key to your success that each one of these director roles is doing the best job they can. Quite simply, this is your life and you're in charge.

I shared one powerful, transformational multi-part Accelerator exercise (4.1), using the Me Unlimited Template, available to download here: https://www.roystonguest.com/RISE-toolkit/

It asked you to rate where you are now in terms of the seven director roles, and then measure their position against where you want it to be. The gap will show you the focus you'll have to give each director role in order to achieve your desired position.

Here's a quick reminder of each director role to spur your thinking:

Your Chairperson – responsible for your vision and values and for setting the direction of travel, culture, environment and cadence and pace of your life.

Your Sales and Marketing Director – responsible for having a clear picture of how much money you're likely to generate (sales role) and for safeguarding and promoting your personal brand (marketing role).

Your Finance Director – responsible for the finances of your life, which include budgeting, maintaining accurate records and making sure you look after your money wisely.

Your Planning and Administration Director – responsible for setting audacious goals personally and professionally, working closely with your Chairperson role in translating your vision and purpose (planning role), and for maintaining control (administration role).

Your Wellbeing Director – responsible for ensuring that your physical and mental health, fitness, nutrition, rest and relaxation and other critical aspects of wellness are taken care of, keeping you in the performance zone.

Your Learning Director – responsible for your ongoing strategy of development, learning and maintaining your relevance.

Your Communications Director – responsible for how you interact with others and for how conversations are managed internally, with yourself.

It's time to put yourself firmly in the driver's seat of your life, program your satnav and become conscious and deliberate in the choices you make as the architect of your own destiny.

If your life were a business, would you invest in it?

How we're wired as human beings

'Anyone who devotes time and attention to understanding
what makes people tick, to me, is a smart person.'

Ron Silver

The subject of human motivation fascinates me. Over the
past two decades, part of my personal and professional
mission has been centred on developing a deep understanding of how we're wired as human beings. This journey
of discovery has resulted in a number of defining questions:

- What makes people tick?
- Why do people do what they do?
- How can you create lasting habitual change that
  truly sticks?

And for this last question, I mean change that truly, genu-
inely sticks – it's not just a 'hot bath' effect that wears off the
way that much externally driven 'motivational' activity does.

People reveal themselves in their patterns of behaviour,
and their reactions to similar external and internal influences. It doesn't mean we can simply apply a single brush
of paint to categories of people, because individuality is still
a very strong factor in making us who we are. But it does give
us a broad set of common traits.

Whether it is Maslow's Hierarchy of Needs, Tony Robbins'
Six Fundamental Human Needs or the formative work on life
coaching by Cloé Madanes, there is a shared clear obser-
vation of commonalities in our understanding of how people are wired and the drivers that make us tick.

Often, the starting point is commonalities that are referenced internally, not externally. More often than not, you can only be equipped to help others and to be the person you want to be for the people in your life if you have a strong understanding of yourself. You have to do the inner work first, as it's an inside job. It's the same thinking that applies to aeroplane safety demonstrations just before take-off, when the cabin crew say: 'Put on your own mask before you help with anyone else's.'

It's important to make a key distinction right at the start. Throughout this chapter, I am talking about both the internal and external work we need to undertake. Just as an understanding of yourself will enable you to be a better person, a deep understanding of others will enable you to be a better friend, leader, neighbour and partner.

The five interlocking human drivers

My research and work with thousands of individuals from every walk of life, as well as my real-world observations, have all prompted me to compile my own list of common traits to describe how we're wired as human beings. I call them the five interlocking human drivers.

As you read about these five drivers below, you'll identify aspects of your life where you achieve winning results by allowing a particular driver to come to the fore. But there are other aspects of your life in which allowing a driver to dominate your thinking and actions could derail your efforts. A greater understanding of yourself and others and how the drivers are playing out will enable you to regulate and become more conscious and deliberate in thought, feeling and action.

Driver 1: Certainty

'Certainty is the mother of quiet and repose.'

Edward Coke

This is the foundational human driver, which has its origins way back in the Stone Age when human beings had a survival need for certainty around shelter, food and heat – an individual's three most essential necessities.

Wind forward to today, and our needs haven't really changed: put food on the table, pay the mortgage and bills to keep the roof over our heads, and provide for our families and ourselves.

The need for certainty can lead you to make decisions that are well thought through and have predictable outcomes. But it can also lead to procrastination, analysis paralysis and attempts to control things and people too tightly.

Take a moment to think about this: in what areas of your life do you feel you have a strong foundational need for certainty?

- Is it a stable home or relationship?
- A secure job?
- A particular amount of money in the bank?

Is it a combination of these, or perhaps there are other triggers that are driving your need for certainty?

'My home is my castle'

Many people consider their home to be one of their key stabillizers and foundational blocks that meets their need for certainty. I am one of them. I travel a great deal for work, so my home fulfils an important need.

I can go and trail-blaze, setting the world on fire, knowing I return to the safe harbour of my home to re-energize, be still, reflect, think, laugh, play and spend quality time with my family.

I see in my young children how their confidence, self-belief and strong core are developing and I passionately believe part of this is because our home is a strong and stable environment, delivering on their own need for certainty.

A great life lesson

I didn't always fully understand the importance of certainty.

A few years ago, before my wife and I had children, my sister and her family came to stay with us. My nephew Tom was two years old at the time.

Imagine the following scenario: Jane and I were both young business professionals, working hard and playing hard with no inkling of what it meant to have children. I actually remember rolling my eyes at the level of bedtime routine my sister insisted upon for Tom: home by 5.30, bath, story, bottle and in bed for 6.30. It was a military operation.

Justine, my dear sister, let me apologize. How naive we were!

Fast-forward a few years to when we had our own children and the penny dropped. We learned quickly that routine and certainty are a basic fundamental need. The only triggers children have for signalling food time, bath time or bedtime are created around the certainty we set for them, through routines.

What a great life lesson it was.

Certainty in other aspects of your life

Think about other aspects of your life and how your need for certainty plays out. Do you have a boss who micro-manages everything you do? How does that feel? Perhaps it feels that they don't trust you or that you're not capable of doing the job. It could be that they enjoy being controlling, but it is also important to recognize that it might just be that they are acting out their need for certainty, and control is their default mode for fulfilling that need.

Consider these questions:

- How strong is your need for certainty in your life?
- In which areas of your life is certainty a must-have?
- Are there times in your life when certainty is less important and you're OK being a little more adventurous?
- What's the difference between those moments or scenarios?

Driver 2: Adventure

'The very basic core of a man's living spirit is his passion for adventure.'

Christopher McCandless

Picture this scenario: you know precisely what you are going to be doing every minute, every hour, every day, month and year from this day forth for the rest of your life. How does that make you feel? Bored? Comfortable?

As human beings, do we have the need for adventure? Do we have the need for mystery, the unknown and for surprise? You bet we do, because that is how we know we are alive.

- Does the notion of adventure resonate with you?
- If you could inject more adventure into your life right now, what would it be?

Entrepreneurs and intrapreneurs are absolutely wired for adventure, uncertainty and the unknown. It's innate in their DNA. They thrive on it. It brings out the best in them.

The younger generations, including the Millennials (born between 1977 and 1995) and Generation Z (born in 1996 or later), are wired differently from Generation X (born between 1965 and 1976) and the Baby Boomers (born between 1946 and 1964). They no longer see work as a job for life. They have an insatiable thirst for adventure, for variety, for 'stretch' experiences – and this is why today's average university graduate will have at least 15 jobs throughout their career.

How adventure links to growth

Adventure is closely linked to Driver 5: Growth, which is natural considering the interlocking nature of all the drivers. The following quote from the work of the French poet Guillaume Apollinaire demonstrates the point perfectly.

The Mother Eagle and Her Baby Chicks

'Come to the edge,' said the mother eagle.

'We might fall,' said the chicks.

'Come to the edge,' said the mother eagle again.

'It's too high!' the baby chicks wailed.

'COME TO THE EDGE!' the mother eagle repeated.

And they came.

And she pushed.

And they flew.

Of course, adventure can mean different things to different people. At one end of the scale are some of the greatest adventurers the world has ever seen: Captain James Cook, Sir Ranulph Fiennes, Roald Amundsen, Neil Armstrong ...

There's Richard Branson, who is always setting himself some crazy audacious goal, from trying to fly around the world in a hot-air balloon, to a successful attempt on the record for crossing the English Channel in an amphibious vehicle. One of Branson's legacies is undoubtedly his bold taste for adventure.

When adventure turns into uncertainty

However, as you approach the other end of the scale, adventure can change from being a positive enabler to something potentially unsettling ... because adventure is, by definition, uncertain. So what happens when the pendulum swings from adventure to uncertainty? Adventure may seem fun and exciting, but when we frame it as uncertainty, it becomes the opposite of Driver 1: Certainty. So now how do you feel about adventure?

For many people, the very idea of uncertainty is enough to freak them out, slamming the brakes on their need and desire for adventure. At this point they're between the rock and the hard place.

Imagine you're a leader in your workplace and one morning you announce to the 100 workers reporting to you that you're undertaking a restructure and everyone's jobs are at risk. Reactions would be at both ends of the scale. At one end would be individuals seeing it as an adventure and saying: 'About time, we should have done this 12 months ago. Where is the opportunity? Where can I add value, and where can I make a difference?' At the other end of the scale would be individuals feeling terrified. They'd be thinking: 'Am I going to have a job? Can I put food on the table? What will happen to my credibility with my friends and family? My pride is dented.'

US President John F. Kennedy once said: 'The only unchangeable certainty is that nothing is unchangeable or certain.' The reality is that change is one of the only real certainties in the world and the quality of your life is in direct proportion to the amount of uncertainty, adventure and change you can comfortably live with.

Consider these questions:

- Do you see change as your friend or foe?
- Do you see it as an opportunity or a threat?

- How can you embrace it and become an enabler of change and welcome it in all facets of your life?
- How can you think differently about change and challenge yourself to become 'comfortably uncomfortable' with the uncertainty it brings?

The battle between certainty and adventure

They say that opposites attract, but big differences can sometimes lead to friction, especially when the drivers are in conflict. Here's an example of this.

At a workshop I was running one of the delegates had an 'Aha!' moment when we were discussing the first two drivers, certainty and adventure. At the time, he and his wife were clashing constantly because halfway through the week she would ask, 'What are we doing this weekend? What are we doing on Saturday morning? Where are we going on Saturday evening?' And he would reply, 'I don't know, let's get to the weekend and decide what we want to do when we wake up.'

She interpreted his response as him not caring and being only interested in his work. But his perspective was very different. His mindset was that during the working week he had so much certainty around what he would be doing and that when it came to the weekend he wanted the freedom of adventure, the unplanned and the flexibility to decide in the moment. He craved the things he lacked during the week but his wife craved the certainty of making the most of their weekend together.

They shared the common goal of spending quality time together but were differently wired by their needs.

Think of examples in your life where similar scenarios may also be playing out.

Driver 3: Significance

'To consider meaning at any level implies a search
for the depth and dimensions of what is significant,
what truly matters.'

Anon.

Imagine walking into a room where all your friends are engaged in a debate and, as you walk in, a little cheer ripples through the group. Then one of them says 'Great, here's [your name], they'll sort this out once and for all,' as the other members of the group nod in agreement.

How would that make you feel?

Or if you have children, and as you walk through the door at home, they run and jump into your arms, delighted that you're now home as they show you pictures they've drawn at school, or share something fun that has happened that day.

How would that make you feel?

We all long for significance. We all want to matter, to be thought of as important, useful and valuable. We can be significant to our colleagues and bosses, to our friends who appreciate our support and care, and to our families who love us unconditionally and rely upon us as a critical part of their lives.

You may feel a high degree of significance when others praise you for your capabilities and achievements. Or you may feel significant when you know you've achieved something great regardless of the external validation you may or may not receive. The same need is met, just through different sources.

A feeling of significance can drive us to achieve amazing things: to be loving parents and partners, valuable friends, team leaders, to write books, build companies and run countries. But it can also drive negative behaviour, where we achieve significance by putting others down or being overly critical. Our need to feel important can lead us to become blinded to the needs of others as we attain significance whatever the cost.

It is no surprise that dictators, warlords and some of the worst characters in history are also those who had the most statues and monuments built to their own importance.

- How strong is your need for significance?
- In what areas of your life do you crave significance?
- What positive behaviours and negative or derailing behaviours does this need bring out in you?

Can you think of someone you know who may crave significance and act in really noble and admirable ways in pursuit of that? Can you think of someone you know who may crave significance and act in really unpleasant and destructive ways in pursuit of that? What's the difference in the way they seek the same end result?

Driver 4: Belonging

'Those who have a strong sense of love and belonging have the courage to be imperfect.'

Brené Brown

They say no person is an island and, in today's world, being aware of this is perhaps more important than ever. We're more connected than we have ever been, and yet human connections – real, genuine human connections – are becoming harder than ever to make.

This plays right to the heart of a significant phenomenon of social media groups. Individuals – myself included – love to join online clubs, groups or movements with people worldwide, the majority of whom we will never meet but who share our views, habits and fascinations.

In our need to meet the human driver of belonging, we don't seek to lead but to be part of a pack, to be a welcome member of something much larger than ourselves. It's the reason we join church congregations, associations and clubs, and the reason we feel an attachment to our place of work; that need to feel part of a team is huge.

As with all the five human drivers, the need to belong can lead to negative behaviours as well as positive ones. It is one of the reasons why young people may join gangs and do things the gang 'commands', potentially going against their very nature. This is significance working in reverse: a gang member doesn't want to stand out as the 'weak link'.

- In what areas of your life do you really need to feel that you belong?
- In what places or with which groups of people do you feel you really belong?
- What is different between the places or the groups of people with whom you are happy to just belong, and those where you feel the need to be significant?

Driver 5: Growth

'Without continual growth and progress, such words as improvement, achievement and success have no meaning.'

Benjamin Franklin

Few things feel worse than a sense that you're being left behind. And few things feel better than a sense that you're improving, advancing, getting better at something and increasing your value to your family, your work, your community and even to the world.

Your need for growth is certain to be one of the reasons you picked up this book and decided to read or listen to it. You want to know more, to improve and gain more control over the areas of your life where you know you can be absolutely great, and also the areas where you might need some help.

Growth is a key driver for us all. And there are very few limitations when it comes to learning and acquiring more skills or knowledge. The Internet is awash with tutorials, courses and quick solutions to any dilemma.

Nothing on this earth is standing still. It's either growing or it's dying, whether it's a tree or a human being. If you're not growing, you will be left behind! The opposite of growing is being in a rut, and there is nothing more soul-destroying than that.

Learn something new today!

One story that reinforces the point about growth and learning is a brilliant scene from a movie called *The Blind Side*, starring Sandra Bullock.

In the scene, she is dropping her birth son and adopted son at the school gates, and her parting words to them both are: 'Have fun and learn something new today.'

Now, while the 'Have fun' part is important, it's the second part that really struck me as being central to success: '… learn something new today'.

You don't need a formal education to learn something new. You don't need a library full of books. You don't even need access to the Internet. You just need a mind full of curiosity and a thirst for greater understanding.

- How focused are you on fulfilling your need for growth and what specific actions are you taking to achieve them – in the short, medium and long term?

- What steps are you taking in order to grow every day?
- How will you measure your growth?

Balancing and prioritizing the human drivers

Once you have a clear understanding of the human drivers, you can start to think about their importance, how they apply to you, and their influence on your thinking and subsequent actions. It will enable you to truly unlock a major part of your own individual blueprint.

Let me share some scenarios so you can start to see and feel how the five interlocking human drivers might play out. What you start to identify with will reveal how you prioritize the drivers in your own life.

Scenario 1: A restructure is announced at work

Imagine you're an employee and one Monday morning a restructure is announced that puts your job at risk. How would that make you feel? How would your need for certainty be triggered? Would it be an adventure for you, a challenge to rise to? Or would you be so full of uncertainty that you would panic?

What would happen to your feeling of significance and your ability to contribute? Would you see it as an opportunity to shine and prove your worth, or would you feel expendable and unimportant?

What about your sense of belonging? Would you feel your affiliation with the organization from that point on was broken, even if you kept your job, or would you be able to absorb the disruption and come back even stronger? What does it do for your need for growth that someone else could so easily take away your pathway to growth? Or would you see it as yet another opportunity to grow?

Scenario 2: Your house is flooded

Imagine that your home is in an area with a high risk of flooding. And the worst happens: your house is flooded and you have to move out for 12 months while they repair and renovate it.

- How is your need for certainty affected? If it's happened once, could it happen again? Could you live with that level of uncertainty every time there was a prolonged period of heavy rainfall?
- What does it do for your need for significance and contribution?
- What about belonging? How is the idea of 'My home is my castle' affected by this scenario?

Think about these questions one by one. Your responses will tell you a lot about your priorities and how the drivers play out for you in different scenarios.

Scenario 3: A friend splits from their partner

Imagine that a friend comes to you and she is absolutely broken. After ten years of marriage her partner has suddenly walked out, saying he wants a divorce. You have two roles: you need to be a shoulder to cry on but also a counsellor to help her rationalize what has happened.

Now think about how you would present the five interlocking human drivers to your friend as you try to see the world through their lens:

- What has just happened to their base need for certainty?
- What has happened to their need for adventure? Is it overridden by uncertainty, positively or negatively?
- What has happened to their sense of significance?
- What about their sense of belonging?

> - What impact does this have on their opportunity for growth and how can this be framed positively? How can they grow their personal resilience and ability to handle adversity?

How the drivers influence your thinking and actions

I encourage you to spend time thinking about the five drivers and how they influence what you do – and how you do it – on a daily basis. As you do this, you'll have breakthroughs in a number of areas of personal understanding. Remember, there isn't a right or a wrong here: only a right and a wrong for you.

You may be struggling in your office job (certainty) because you have a much greater taste for adventure (uncertainty). You may feel unfulfilled by your current status (certainty) and want to stand out (significance). You may feel you've had too much uncertainty in your life and long for the safe predictability of stable finances and relationships.

This is about raising your conscious awareness, and recognizing that some of the most important conversations we have are the conversations we have with ourselves, the ones inside our own heads. At the start of this chapter I stated the importance of 'putting on your own mask first', and how gaining a greater understanding of how you're personally wired, and using that knowledge and insight, will help you better understand and connect with others.

When you go about your daily activities, listen to the voice in your head as you face different scenarios and situations and start to think about how those five interlocking human drivers play out. The voices you hear and the silent conversations taking place are triggers for your subsequent behaviour and, ultimately, your actions.

The WEALTHY Process

The WEALTHY Process does not relate to financial wealth but is everything to do with a wealthy mindset – demonstrating the correlation between what you say and ultimately what you do.

Your ability to communicate effectively is an essential skill for maximizing your potential. Usually, however, this is about the external conversations and dialogue you have. The challenge we face is that our external dialogue is an extension and manifestation of what is happening internally, inside our own head, which usually follows a conversation you've had with yourself.

Figure 5.1 illustrates the whole process. The practical exercise below will bring it to life step by step.

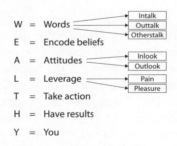

W = Words
        Intalk
        Outtalk
        Otherstalk

E = Encode beliefs

A = Attitudes
        Inlook
        Outlook

L = Leverage
        Pain
        Pleasure

T = Take action

H = Have results

Y = You

FIGURE 5.1 The WEALTHY Process

Accelerator exercise 5.1: Understand the power of 'otherstalk'

To get into the spirit of this exercise, as you read the words on the page I'd like you to use all your senses to bring it to life. You'll understand in a moment why I am asking you to do this. Trust me … it's going to be worth it!

I want you to imagine that I've placed under your chair a ripe, juicy lemon. Pick it up, lift it to your nose and have a good sniff of it. Wow, it's really fresh and juicy. Can you smell that?

Next, I want you to put the lemon on the table or whatever surface is near to you, and hold it firmly with your non-dominant hand.

Then, with your dominant hand, pick up a sharp serrated knife and cut through the lemon, from top to bottom. Be careful not to mark the table. Don't worry about all the juices that are running everywhere; we'll clean those up later.

When you've done that, put the knife down and pick up half of the lemon. Now, lift it up to your nose for a second time and smell the flesh. It's so fresh, and I bet from the smell alone you can tell this is going to be sharp-tasting, can't you?

Well, let's find out. I want you to take a big bite of the lemon and let the juice swirl around in your mouth. Really taste it. Wow, it's really sharp, isn't it? Let the lemon juice move around in your mouth, mixing with your saliva, reducing the bitter, sharp taste of lemon.

Now, take another bite and do it again. How does that taste?

OK, put the lemon down and answer this one question: do you have extra saliva in your mouth right now?

Now if you went with me on the journey and completed the exercise as per my instructions, if I were a betting man, I would say you did.

Let's look at how that scenario plays out against the WEALTHY process.

W = WORDS

We start with words, which can be one of three types:

1 **Intalk**, the little voices inside your head with which you have some of your most important daily conversations. In his book *The Chimp Paradox*, Dr Steve

Peters talks about your inner voice being your chimp, constantly talking away. It sometimes sets you up for success but on other occasions plants seeds of doubt in your mind, even sabotaging or derailing your potential. Yes, intalk is that important!

2 **Outtalk**, the conversations you have with others. Just imagine having a conversation with someone who is negative all the time. If that's their outtalk, imagine what the conversations are like with themselves on a regular basis!

3 **Otherstalk**, the things other people say. There's a great saying: you become like the five people you spend most time with. Choose carefully.

In the lemon example we observed the power of otherstalk, because it was my dialogue leading the conversation and building a mental image of the lemon in your mind using words.

E = ENCODE YOUR BELIEFS ...

The words – whether intalk, outtalk, otherstalk or, usually, a combination of all three – start to encode your beliefs about the world around you and how you perceive your life. The belief you acquired through the example was that you had a juicy lemon in your hand and in your mouth and, boy, did it smell and taste sharp!

A = WHICH AFFECT YOUR ATTITUDES ...

Your beliefs then shape your attitude, both internally about yourself, including your self-confidence and self-belief (your inlook), and also your outlook in terms of how you look and see the world. Do you see the opportunity in the difficulty, or the difficulty in the opportunity? In this case your attitude internalized the existence of the lemon and how it made you feel.

L = WHICH IN TURN CREATES LEVERAGE ...

Leverage is about one of two things: avoidance of pain or the gaining of pleasure. In this case the lemon was so sharp that your brain received a hotwired message from your nerve sensors that action was required.

T = LEADING YOU TO TAKE ACTION ...

The 'take action' in this exercise was to neutralize the acidity, and your brain triggered a chemical reaction in your body, resulting in your salivary glands producing saliva, which of course is an alkali, neutralizing the acidity of the lemon.

H = ... AND HAVE RESULTS ...

The result is more saliva, just as you experienced it. The increase in saliva was a real phenomenon, created by your brain, which reacted to the stimulus that was received only by reading the words on the page or hearing my voice on audio.

Isn't that incredibly powerful?

Y = ... AND WHO IS IT DOWN TO? IT IS DOWN TO YOU!

The WEALTHY Process is a clear demonstration of the connectivity of words, intalk, outtalk and otherstalk, and your subsequent behaviour and actions.

If you can trigger a chemical reaction from your brain by simply internalizing a message about a lemon, imagine how you can influence and take control of other internal programmes you're running. And it all starts with the intalk and words you use.

> Chapter 12: Programming your winning mentality, will give you a greater depth of understanding of this very topic plus a series of practical tools to use.

Creating leverage: pain and pleasure

I referred above to how we create leverage through two key levers: pain and pleasure. These two levers are fundamental to understanding how we're wired as human beings and what makes us tick.

Creating leverage is about uncovering what's most important to you as an individual in order for you to commit to making a change. To ensure that change is lasting, the commitment has to be overwhelming. It has to overcome the forces of inertia that hold your old behaviours and beliefs in place.

The catalyst for change is never a matter of ability; it's a matter of motivation. And what motivates people to do what they do is based on one of two things: the avoidance of pain or the gaining of pleasure.

If you ever find yourself in a 'no man's land' where you can feel yourself drifting, it's likely to be for one of two reasons. Either you haven't created a picture of the future, driven by a compelling reason and purpose that are going to pull you towards it (pleasure), or you haven't experienced enough pain to give you the impetus you need to take action (pain).

Which is the strongest lever – pain or pleasure?

If pain and pleasure are the two key levers for change, which one do you think creates the greatest leverage for most people? The following two examples will help to answer the question.

EXAMPLE 1: GIVING UP SMOKING

If you filled a room with a hundred ex-smokers and asked them why they gave up smoking, what reasons would they give?

- 'It's too expensive.'
- 'I fell pregnant so I had to give up.'
- 'I exercised for the first time in ages and was embarrassed about how unfit I was and how I couldn't catch my breath.'
- 'My child ran to me one day crying, saying "Daddy, I don't want you to die", because they had seen an advertisement saying that smoking kills.'
- 'I had a family member die of lung cancer.'
- 'I have recently been unwell and smoking made me feel worse.'

Do they sound like pain-driven reasons or pleasure-driven reasons? In nearly every case, when people give up smoking, it will be a pain-driven reason first.

Case study

My father-in-law had been a smoker all his life. One winter he had a really bad cough and cold and the pain was so bad that he decided to give up smoking. Interestingly, while pain was his primary driver and the motivational trigger for change, what drove him to ensure that he didn't start again was to treat himself (pleasure). He wanted a new camera for capturing special moments with the grandchildren, and the money he saved on cigarettes would pay for it. He created a goal born from his secondary driver, pleasure, which kept him on track and focused, ensuring no regression to starting to smoke again.

EXAMPLE 2: GOING TO THE GYM

Why do people visit the gym at the beginning of January? If you are an active gym user, you'll probably notice how the gym is suddenly full at the beginning of the year as people act on a resolution to get into shape. After Christmas most people feel that they've overindulged over the previous month (if not for longer) and feel overweight and unfit, so they decide to do something about it. They are responding to the need to avoid further pain.

Most people quickly give up and only a few see their resolution through. The pain isn't a strong enough lever to keep them focused and, at the point they decide to give up, they haven't quite experienced the pleasure lever yet. They haven't hit the tipping point.

But those who stay the distance tend to experience something else. While they are also trying to avoid pain at first, as time goes by they begin to notice that they are stronger and fitter. Their friends begin to say things like 'You're looking great!' 'You've lost weight!' 'That shirt looks amazing on you ...' Suddenly the lever of gaining pleasure has taken over, and their motivation steps up to another whole level.

Which is the biggest lever for most people: pain or pleasure? Most people make decisions based first on the avoidance of pain (their primary driver), not the gaining of pleasure (their secondary driver). Pain is the **catalyst** for action, but pleasure is the **continuation** of action!

The pain–pleasure levers as drivers of change

When someone is in pain, it is our natural human instinct to try to help take that pain away. Pain is usually considered bad. But as a human motivator – as a driver of change – pain can actually be a positive driver of change delivering positive results.

Do you think you are more driven by pain or pleasure? Does it actually change depending on the scenario or situation?

Remember, there is no right or wrong. There is only what is right for you and how you develop a deeper understanding of yourself, how you're wired and what makes you tick. Through that understanding you can act with pace, urgency and focus in unlocking your potential and living the life you were meant to lead.

Take action: achieve more

What makes you tick?

This chapter introduced the five interlocking human drivers: Certainty, Adventure, Significance, Belonging and Growth. Understanding why and how these five drivers play out in your life will give you invaluable insights into what makes you tick.

I shared one sensory Accelerator exercise (5.1) to demonstrate the power of the WEALTHY Process and the correlation between what you say and what you do. Your **w**ords ... **e**ncode your beliefs ... which affect your **a**ttitude ... which creates **l**everage ... to **t**ake you to action ... to **h**ave and achieve results, and – guess what? – it's all down to **y**ou.

Start to control and influence other internal programs you're running by recognizing the connectivity of your words – intalk, outtalk and otherstalk – with your subsequent behaviour and actions.

Create leverage by understanding what's most important to you in order for you to commit to change. Remember that the catalyst for change is never a matter of ability but a matter of motivation. And what motivates you to do what you do is based on either the avoidance of pain or the gaining of pleasure. These two levers are fundamental to understanding how you're wired and what makes you tick.

The value of values

'Values are like fingerprints. Nobody's are the same, but
you leave them all over everything you do.'

Elvis Presley

Among the often-unsung heroes of the modern age are the
ordinary men and women who blow the whistle on wrongdoing and bring down great institutions, from governments
to corporations. These whistleblowers almost never do it for
money, recognition or any of the other motivators human
beings lean into. What they see going on is simply at odds
with their values. They describe being unable to sleep, unable to eat and unable to focus because of their overloaded
consciences, and, ultimately, they find they have no choice
but to speak out.

Sherron Watkins was one of these people. She was an
employee of Enron who exposed the organization as a giant
financial fraud. Cynthia Cooper was another. She was an
employee at WorldCom who brought its accounting irregu-
larities to the attention of the FBI, which ultimately brought
down the company and saw CEO Bernie Ebbers go to jail
for 25 years. Coleen Rowley, an FBI agent, graced the front
cover of *Time* magazine alongside Watkins and Cooper as
'Persons of the Year' in 2002 for exposing botched investiga-
tive work around the 9/11 terrorists.

Perhaps the most famous whistleblower of all was Mark
Felt, another FBI agent who went by the code name 'Deep
Throat'. From late 1972 to mid-1973 he met *Washington Post*
reporter Bob Woodward in the dark shadows of underground
car parks late at night, to share details about the corruption
inside the Nixon White House, linked to Watergate.

The risks to Felt in exposing the Watergate scandal were so real that he felt his life was in danger. It wasn't until 2005, as he was nearing his death, that he finally confirmed he had been the legendary whistleblower. He had spoken out because his values forced him to.

You don't have to be tackling corruption or wrongdoing to exercise your values, of course. Values play an important guiding role in our everyday lives. One of the top three reasons why employees leave a business is that there is misalignment between their personal values and those of the organization.

On a much more personal level, if you're a parent you no doubt spend considerable time imparting your values to your children as a means of helping them live what you have defined as a good and purposeful life. In fact, the very values you hold dear today were likely given to you by, or at least deeply influenced by, your own parents, family, teachers and other people you knew in your formative years.

Values are your filter

Values are the filters that drive your decision-making. If *Rise* is about living with deliberate and conscious intent through the decisions and choices you make, then identifying your personal values and living through them is your highest priority. Only when you understand what it is that compels you to act can you begin to take real control of your life and live out an authentic and purposeful existence.

So here's a thought-provoking question for you: are you ultra-clear on the values you currently live by and the values you're going to live by throughout the rest of your life?

Company values

Organizations often put a lot of focus on identifying and articulating values, trying to get the kind of galvanizing impact on behaviour, thought and deed that comes as a result. It's not always a successful exercise, but when it is, and they get their values embedded in the hearts and minds of their employees, they often see high levels of performance and teamwork. Why? It's because, when people know what the values are, and believe in them and see them as important, they create one of the strongest bonds of culture.

The race is on for businesses to position themselves as trust brands, and values are the enabler that builds increased customer loyalty, resulting in increased customer retention and repeat business. A great example is Apple, which in the early days lived by the values 'Simplify, Perfect, Delight'. If you own an Apple product, you'll know Simplify, Perfect, Delight are values that Apple believes in. They're vivid and clear and come across in every element of the customer relationship. Richard Branson's Virgin group of companies demonstrates the values of 'Challenging, Disrupting and Delighting' and, again, they're traits you immediately associate with the Virgin logo.

There is such an expectation of authenticity when it comes to values that accountability comes as part of the package. Employees and customers alike will expect to see that your actions support your words. Companies such as Enron or Volkswagen, which positioned themselves as having admirable values but haven't lived up to them, have faced the wrath of customers, shareholders, regulators and employees alike. Failing to live and breathe the values can destroy the integrity of an organization overnight.

> 'Always do what is right. It will gratify half of mankind and astound the other.'
>
> *Mark Twain*

Personal values

Just as customers are drawn to companies that express and live out values they share, we are drawn to people, scenarios and situations in our personal lives where there is alignment of values.

You might hear yourself or others use statements like 'It just felt right' or 'My gut feeling was …' as they describe why they deliberately and instinctively chose a course of action. The reason it happens is because, consciously or unconsciously, our deep-rooted, firmly held values have acted as part of the filter for our decision-making process and the choices we have made.

But just imagine if you became even more conscious and deliberate about knowing and living your values? How would that drive and improve the quality of the choices you make for the rest of your life? Values have immense power to help you live the life you truly want to lead and show up every day being the authentic you.

But how does it all work and why do values have such immense power over our lives, our thoughts, our beliefs and our actions? Let me share one of my own observations about how we're wired and what makes us tick:

People never consistently do ... who they aren't!

That's not a grammatical error, by the way. It may be an interesting mix of words, but it is deliberate and it means something very specific.

If you ask a person to do something that isn't in alignment with their values and beliefs, will they do it? Well, they might in the short term, but certainly not in the long term.

If you flip the question over, and ask someone to do something that *is* in alignment with their personal values and beliefs, again, will they do it? The answer is that they always will, every day of the week. Why? Because people *will* consistently do ... who they are!

As human beings, we spend too much time trying to influence ourselves and others at a superficial level, without understanding what really makes us tick, what drives us to action and how and why we make the decisions we do.

People are like icebergs

In most businesses or organizations there will come a time when they're not delivering the results they want and the leadership team finds itself around a table trying to figure out where the problem lies. Collectively, they decide it's a behavioural issue, so they embark on a whole behavioural change journey, but after six months, when nothing has changed, they're back around the table, scratching their heads and wondering why it's not working.

Well, the simple reason is that they've only been playing above the surface, which as you can see from Figure 6.1 is only about a tenth of the game when it comes to the complexity of human beings, including you and me. Where they need to focus is beneath the surface, to understand what is

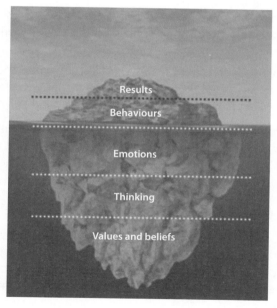

FIGURE 6.1 Most of who we are is below the surface.

driving the behaviour and subsequent results at the deepest level: the emotions, the thinking and – underpinning them all – the values and beliefs.

The difference between values and beliefs

Beliefs are based on learned information, which can be easily shaped as your knowledge evolves, and they are therefore an 'outside-in job'.

Values, on the other hand, are part of your core being, intrinsically aligned to what makes you tick, and as a result they are an 'inside-out job'.

Influencing values and beliefs in others therefore is complex because of two key challenges:

1 If the actions you want an individual to take are not aligned to their values and beliefs, then they are not consistently being who they are. This means that, particularly over the long term, it will never work.

2 The individual hasn't yet made the connection between the actions you want them to take and their values and beliefs, in which case the key to success is to align their actions to their values and beliefs.

Don't wait for people to do the alignment exercise themselves. Part of your role, as a great influencer and communicator, is to join up the dots for others. Find out who people are and what makes them tick. After all:

People will consistently do ... who they are!

If you uncover who you are, and your deepest-held values and beliefs, and take action aligned with those values and beliefs, you really can move mountains, accelerating your journey as the 'authentic you' in realizing your goals and ambitions.

If values are so intrinsically linked to behavioural change and subsequent results, that sparks an intriguing question:

can you change values and beliefs? It's a huge question and probably too big to answer in one go because values and beliefs are two different things; separating them into two questions makes it easier.

Can you change a value?

What is a value? The dictionary definition is that it is 'a moral principle or accepted standard of a person or a group'.

Where do values come from? They start in your formative years and are massively influenced by the important people in your life. Your parents taught you right from wrong, never to lie, to be honest and so on. Throughout school, your teachers taught you about effort and reward and the value of hard work. At the same time, society taught you about how behaviours are rewarded or punished. In the media, you saw celebrities and sportspeople and people with values you admired and values you did not, and those shaped you, too.

As you go through your life, from your formative years, through adolescence, to maturity and through the evolution of your life stages, as a student, as a young worker building a career and later in a relationship, your values will change in their emphasis. Your core values should always remain the same throughout your life – trust and honesty, for example – but your life stages will determine much of the flavour of the rest.

For example, when you're young and perhaps fresh out of university, your focus might be on building your professional career, travelling, having fun and being free of personal responsibility. Settling down is the last thing on your mind, and you tone up and down the emphasis you place on certain values as time goes on.

Your value set is constantly being tested, evolving and developing through all your life experiences, which is why constant reflection and review are elements of a fluid, dynamic and agile journey that never stops.

Can you change a belief?

A belief is something you accept as true or real – a firmly held opinion. How do you change a belief? By presenting factual information that contradicts the belief.

Let me give you a scenario: have you ever been out for dinner with friends, or in a business meeting, when someone shared with you a factual piece of information that gave you an 'Aha!' moment? It may have been something you had simply never realized before but which, as soon as you knew it, completely reshapes the way you thought about the topic at hand. You may have looked up the information later, in order to validate that it is in fact true, but once you did that, your beliefs and knowledge shifted for ever.

Very simply, what you believe can be easily changed when more information deepens the picture for you. To put this to the test, do you know what colour Santa Claus's clothes were originally? You might answer, 'Well, haven't they always been red?' Pre-twentieth-century pictures of Santa Claus in fact showed him wearing variously blue, green and yellow. It was only from the 1930s when Coca Cola started to use a red and white Santa Claus in their advertising campaigns that his clothing colour became fixed in the popular imagination – and he became the Santa we all know and love today.

That's a fun but perspective-changing new fact.

Or what about this? In the medieval period it was believed that the Sun and the planets revolved around the Earth – an idea known as geocentrism. While some ancient Greeks had proposed the heliocentric model – which had the Earth and the planets revolving around the Sun – it was not until the sixteenth century that Nicolaus Copernicus proposed this model mathematically, and this new belief found gradual acceptance.

How to determine your values

We've seen the important role values play and understand how they work. The next question is: how do you determine your own personal values? Or if you feel you already have them identified, how can you check that they are still relevant and on point and, perhaps most important, truly living today?

To start with let's talk about what *not* to do. When people hear about values, they often want to select them from a list of personal values. It seems easier to pick them from a menu. Avoid this at all costs, because values aren't selected; they're discovered.

If you start with a list of values, your conscious mind will evaluate which values appear 'better' than others. You will select personal values that 'sound good' based on your desired self-image.

> We don't choose our values. Our values reveal themselves to us.

Accelerator exercise 6.1: Create your own values

Here's how you create distinct and meaningful values that will serve you in every area of your life and work. Take out your journal, a notepad or tablet and let's get started.

To start with, get into the right headspace.

In order to do the deep digging this process requires, it is important to get into a headspace where you can identify and examine the preconceived notions life has thrown at you, so you can move them out of the way. They may be beliefs that have convinced you to act in certain ways, even though you've never challenged them to find out why. Or perhaps they are ideas you've lived by, perhaps even ones with which you've struck a regular, uneasy compromise but have simply allowed to persist rather than question.

The victory here is to get to a space where you're open-minded enough to freely explore how you feel, without being bogged down by logic. In the words of John Hunt, the founder of the renowned TBWA Hunt Lascaris advertising agency in South Africa, 'Logic is kryptonite, logic has the power to strip you of your ability to think freely in the same way kryptonite stripped Superman of his superpowers.'

Evaluate your life up to now.

Now that you're in the right headspace, it's important to create a context for your imagination and mind to do its best work. We are all born as empty vessels, subsequently shaped by moral values. So with all your current life lessons and experiences staying intact, if you stopped your life right now and started it again from scratch, what would you miss the most, what would you change, and what would you do differently?

Think of it as pressing a freeze button, allowing you to evaluate everything you've done in your life up to this point. Examine your decisions, what drove you to make them, and understand the filters through which those decisions were made. Remember, the things you're identifying here are things that already exist. You're not trying to invent anything new, but just trying to uncover them.

What things come to mind that made you feel calm and joyful? What were the moments when your behaviour made you proud or when you knew you did the right thing and felt you'd stood up for what you believe in?

What actions or behaviour have you displayed that fill you with disquiet, and perhaps disappointment or shame? This isn't an exercise in humiliation, but in understanding what drives you.

You might want to consider different aspects of your life to identify values that already guide you:

- **Individual values** reflect how you show up every day, the principles you live by, and what you consider valuable to be the authentic you. Among these, you might consider values such as honesty, passion, good humour and humility to be values you cherish.

- **Relationship values** refer to the way you relate to other people in your life: friends, family members, colleagues and other people you associate with. Among these you might consider values such as transparency, trust and caring.

- **Professional values** uncover the professional you, how you show up to the world. These values will have a profound impact on whether or not you can thrive in the environment in which you find yourself. Values here might include teamwork, integrity, growth and social consciousness.

- **Societal values** connect the people in your life, your work and the organizations to which you belong with wider society. Here, your values might be about being green, giving back, making a positive impact and sustainability.

Create a list as long as you like. Let your mind run free. Write your thoughts all down until you've got all the ideas you can come up with. What does the authentic you look like, feel like and act like?

If you go through this with real intent, it's likely that you'll have a long list of values, but usually some closely linked concepts can be folded into one stronger value. For example, if you have listed trustworthiness, integrity and honesty, could they be simplified into one overarching value? By grouping together closely aligned values you'll achieve clarity on your biggest and probably most important values, as they'll be the ones with the largest groupings.

How many should you be aiming for is a question I'm frequently asked. There is no right or wrong answer. It's how many you feel are appropriate for you. My only caveat would be that less is usually more. It's better to have three or four, or half a dozen maximum, that have real meaning to you.

You can have sub-values that sit behind a core value. For example, one of my core personal values is passion. Sub-values that underpin this include enthusiasm, dedication, commitment and positivity. This value is important to me because passion is infectious and life is too short to be wasting time. Do things that you truly believe in and are passionate about. Do what you love and love what you do!

Choose your top three values.

Now comes the crucial part. It's time to focus. Among the values you've chosen, which are non-negotiable? Which ones would you defend to your death? What are your top three? Remember that there is a world of difference between a deep-rooted core value and a preference, however strong that preference may be.

In order to grow, it is essential that at times you are uncomfortable. You should stretch yourself, extend your reach and try to build bridges between what you can do now and what you need to do to get to the next level. That's how you get better. Being out of your depth but grounded in the knowledge that you believe in what you're trying to achieve is rocket fuel for success. This feeling of discomfort is essential for growth.

But this type of discomfort is very different from the one you experience when your values are misaligned. Being out of your depth and out of alignment with your values is an equally potent pairing of forces, but one that is certain to lead to failure.

If you want real success, you'll have to push yourself out of your comfort zone now and then, with your values marking the edges of the brand-new untrodden path you head down. You may not know where you're going but, as long as you stay on the path, you're in a strong position to get to the other end.

Creating your values charter

Your values are your personal code, your values charter, so make them meaningful. Make them appeal to both head and heart, emotionally as well as logically. Make them into something that you can explain to others. Being understood in life is a great strength, and if others understand your core values, those which intrinsically drive you, you will build the foundations for quality values-based relationships. Too few people are able to articulate who they are and what they stand for, with the result that altogether too many relationships are strained. Be the opposite. Be clear. You'll be rewarded for it again and again.

When you're putting your values into words, use energetic, active words, not passive language. It will help hot-wire the values to the very essence of your being.

A 'thermometer check' against your definitions of success

You'll recall that, in Chapter 3: Why success is not an accident, I shared an Accelerator exercise (3.1) on defining what success means to you. Taking that insight, this is now your opportunity to complete a reality or 'thermometer check' between your success definitions and the values you've created here.

If there is real alignment, you should find that the values are a thread running through both your personal and professional definitions of success. Is this the case for you? Are there any glaring omissions? Are there any amends you want to make?

Living your values

'The true test of a man's character is what he does when no one is watching.'

John Wooden

Here's where the hard work begins. In order to start truly living your values, you need to interrogate your life, your decisions, your way of living, your way of earning a living and all the other things you're doing in between. Are your current actions and behaviours aligned to your values?

You're likely to discover that the areas in which you're seeing greatest success are the areas where you're most aligned, and you may now have a clearer understanding of why you're struggling in certain other areas.

The race is now on for you to achieve complete alignment between your values and not only what you do but also how you do it. Your values:

- inform your decision-making
- influence how you think, feel and act
- drive your behaviour
- are your conscience.

If you're being true to your authentic self and true to your values, you're either in or you're not. There's no halfway house. You cannot be honest 50 per cent of the time. You cannot be trustworthy on three out of seven days of the week and decide on the fly which three days it's going to be.

You're either in or you're out, living your values or not. Which choice are you going to make?

My personal values

Interestingly enough, my personal values came out of my professional values. You might think that that seems a half-baked way of doing it and you're right. I certainly wouldn't recommend you do the same. However, that's how it worked out for me because, for many years, before I met my wife and had my children, I was really only focused on my professional life and values, with very little thought for my personal values.

Years later, as my wife and I started our family, we began to think about what values we wanted to guide us. As you can imagine, Jane and I are closely aligned values-wise, which is why we chose each other in the first place. Here are the values we chose:

- Be passionate
- Be authentic
- Be caring
- Be trusted.

Our values have morphed into our family values charter that has pride of place on the activity board in the kitchen, alongside the timetables and weekly activity plans for the children.

Identifying and understanding your values is a challenging and important exercise. Your personal values are a central part of who you are and who you want to be. By becoming more aware of them, you can use them as a guide to make the best choice in any situation.

Take action: achieve more

The most important values to live by ... Do you know yours?

This chapter has focused on the importance of our personal values and beliefs, which drive our emotions, influence our behaviours and, consequently, help us achieve our goals. As part of Accelerator exercise 6.1 I asked you to consider the following question: Are you ultra-clear on the values you currently live by and the values you're going to live by for the rest of your life? To help you answer this question, I suggested five specific actions:

1 Determine your set of values using a process of discovery, identification and refinement.

2 Discover your preconceived notions and set them aside.

3 Identify your deepest values by asking questions such as: if I stopped my life right now and started it again from scratch, what would I miss the most, what would I change, and what would I do differently?

4 Refine your list to your absolute non-negotiables. Remember, some values can be sub-values of an overarching value.

5 Live them, always remembering that the true test of a person's character is what they do when no one is watching.

Some of life's decisions are about determining what you value most. When many options seem reasonable, it's helpful and comforting to rely on your values and use them as a strong guiding force to point you in the right direction to keep you on track.

Why you? The power of your personal brand

'Your brand is what other people say about
you when you're not in the room.'

Jeff Bezos

What do you think people are saying about you? Perhaps more importantly, what do you want them to be saying?

We live in the age of the brand – from the gadgets and devices we use for work and play, to the clothes we wear, the car we drive, the restaurants we frequent and the stores where we shop. We make conscious and subconscious choices determined not just by cost, style and quality but the 'brand values' that underpin those products and organizations.

While branding isn't a new concept, phenomena such as social media have stepped up brand interaction to a whole new level of intensity, so that today's brands extend far beyond products and services, to include people. For years, big brands have recognized the power of endorsements: when popular celebrities, sportspeople and businesspeople put their name and face to them, they can connect with people in entirely new ways.

These 'brand ambassadors' are expected to endorse the products through their messaging, and to live the spirit of the brand through their actions. TAG Heuer comes to mind, with its prominent watch ads featuring Leonardo di Caprio, Lewis Hamilton and Sarah Fisher, all of whom – the celebrities and the brand itself – share a deep commitment to excellence.

Similarly, George Clooney and Nespresso have aligned around the notions of taste, sophistication and old-school charm, which Clooney is known for and Nespresso wants to leverage. This partnership has very likely influenced the way you think about Nespresso.

In his 21 years as a football player, David Beckham represented Armani, Gillette, adidas and supermarket chain Sainsbury's. Now retired, he's the face of Breitling Watches, Haig Club Whiskey, H&M and UNICEF; all these brands are aligned to *his* personal brand, making the endorsements believable and authentic.

Santander pulled off a masterstroke when it signed a sponsorship agreement with Lewis Hamilton. While today he is a five-time Formula One World Champion, it wasn't always that way. Sometimes it's all about the right place at the right time, and Santander has certainly benefited from the brand association with Hamilton as his career has progressed.

Of course there is a downside, which brands need to be wary of. We've seen it go very wrong when the actions of a celebrity endorser go against the brand he or she is representing. Tiger Woods was once known for his clean living and respectability as much as for his golfing excellence – values that his sponsors aligned to. But when a series of personal scandals hit the headlines a few years back, Accenture, AT&T, Gatorade and others decided it was time to drop his contracts altogether.

Your brand can either work for you or against you!

Personal and professional brands

The concept of brand is not reserved for organizations or celebrity endorsers. It has total relevance to you and me as individuals. Personal and professional brands are not mutually exclusive, and the core of your brand values should be the same throughout your life. And, of course, the primary ownership for this entire concept sits with your Marketing

Director (see Chapter 4). It's time to explore how well that director is doing in creating and promoting your personal and professional brand.

Let's first examine *why* this notion of personal brand is so important.

In a rapidly evolving world, the ways we have to compete for our success are constantly changing. There is no longer such a thing as a job for life, and many job roles are simply disappearing altogether.

Today some mature countries have 25 per cent unemployment with 50 per cent of 16- to 24-year-olds unable to find a job. We're on the brink of a lost generation, and job transience is one of the realities of the future. Where once three generations of family members might have worked for the same employer, which offered them a job for life, today, according to US Bureau of Labor statistics, the average graduate coming out of university will have 12 to 15 jobs in a single career. That doesn't necessarily mean they'll work for 15 different employers, because it includes internal promotions or lateral moves, but it does tell you that change is the order of the day in the years to come. And that means you're going to have to stand out more prominently, and more often.

Just think about that number for a moment. You will potentially have to sit through as many as 15 job interviews over the course of your career, each time demonstrating to the interviewer why they should pick *you* over the other hundreds or even thousands of applicants applying for the same job. If you were being interviewed for a job, and the interviewer suddenly leaned in and said, 'I'm going to ask one question, and your answer will determine whether you progress to the next stage of the interview: Why you?', how well would you answer that question and with what degree of confidence, clarity and purpose?

Having a compelling personal brand that you can communicate in a simple and concise way gives you more choices in life, more freedom and more opportunities to live the life you truly want to lead. At its simplest, your personal brand is how others perceive you. In a professional context, that perception can affect your promotion chances or the likelihood of an application standing out from those of other applicants when you submit your CV or resumé for evaluation.

In a personal context, your personal brand will affect the quality of your relationship with your partner, your beliefs and qualities as a parent, your contribution to team sports and how you are perceived as a friend. Yes, your personal brand is that important!

A practical exercise

Imagine you're travelling to a conference early in the morning and are feeling hungry and fancy a special treat: a full English breakfast. At the side of the road, you see a sign for the Hilton Hotel and decide to pull off and go there for breakfast. How much do you think you'd pay in pounds sterling? When I share this exercise at conferences I often get a range of price points anywhere from £7.50 to £30.

Let's take a second example: imagine you drove past the Hilton and at the next turn off you see a sign for a trucker's cafe. What do you think you'd pay there for the same full English breakfast? Is it fair to say your pricing expectation has gone down? Most responses come in at less than £10 and 80 per cent of the audience guesses £5 or less.

In the third and final example, imagine you've had a great year and you decide to go away for a long weekend to Dubai. There are some great offers available to stay at the six-star Burj Al Arab. Unfortunately, the great deal does not include breakfast. How much do you think the same breakfast would cost you at the Burj Al Arab on the 56th floor overlooking Dubai? Is it fair to say that your price point has now increased to double figures, or even into the triple-digit price bracket? The conference audience will have price points ranging from £30 to £300.

The first important lesson of branding

Now comes the key part. What can you learn from these examples? Why did I share this exercise with you? What's different across the three scenarios?

It's branding and the perception of price and/or value.

There are a couple of key ways to use this lesson. The first, most obvious way, is to apply it in the context of business, that is, where your company or organization's business brand is positioned in the marketplace. Is it mid-range (the Hilton)? Is it at the lower end of the market (trucker's cafe) or at the premium end (the Burj)?

Whatever products and services you provide, the customer will have a perceived value of those goods based on the brand of your business, which underpins them. However, *Rise* isn't a business book, so I'd like to take you in a different direction.

If you're going to maximize the quality of your relationships with others in both your personal and professional life, do you think it is important that (1) they know who you are and what you stand for and (2) that they buy into you? I'm working on the basis that your answer is a resounding 'yes', in which case the next big question is about the position of your personal brand in the marketplace and the value you are placing on it.

Where is your personal brand in the marketplace?

Today you can't leave your personal brand to chance. Businesses and organizations don't, so why should you? They have entire marketing departments dedicated to the job: brand agencies, social media teams, customer focus groups … the list goes on. Companies don't leave brand associations to chance; they spend a significant amount of time and money ensuring that you think the things they want you to think when their brand enters your mind.

Since you are your own Marketing Director, you should have the same focus. To unlock your real potential and start living the life you were meant to lead, you must make it a conscious process to design, build and constantly develop your own compelling personal brand: identifying what you stand for, what you want to be known for and creating an engagement plan for how you are going to market the most important brand asset you own – yourself.

When people hear your name, what do they think? What are the characteristics and brand values that immediately come to mind? Remember the Jeff Bezos quote: 'Your brand is what other people say about you when you're not in the room.' Sometimes wouldn't you just love to be a fly on the wall and hear what people are saying about you? I know I would.

The powerful but very simple message is that you *can* greatly influence what others are saying about you by becoming conscious and deliberate in what you want your brand to stand for and making sure that it plays out through your body language, what you say and how you say it.

Where would your name appear on the team sheet?

When Manchester City football team manager Pep Guardiola is picking the team sheet for the next game, who are the first players to appear on the list?

Before he even commits to black and white or vocalizes their names, what thoughts are going through his mind? He's thinking: who are my trusted lieutenants? Who are the ones who deliver week in, week out? Who can I trust? Who has the personal resilience to handle the pressure? Who never lets me down and always gives me 100 per cent effort? Who will lead by example and, if things aren't quite going right, step up and take charge?

These are all brand traits which determine the sequence in which names will be called. Where would your name be on the list? Near the top? On the substitute list? Would you even make the bench?

Think of it from another perspective: imagine there is a restructure announced at work and the leadership team are locked away in the boardroom with a list of 100 employees, of which you are one. They are tasked with reducing head count by 20 people. As they call out the names, all six directors rank each person in terms of their value to the business on one of three lists. The first list is a definitive 'must keep at all costs', the second 'a nice to keep' and the third is the dreaded exit list.

Which list would your name appear on? How much value do you add? What difference do you make? And how is your brand perceived by others?

Building your personal brand proposition

If personal brand is so critical, is there a success formula to follow in designing your personal brand proposition? As you might have come to expect from this book by now, the answer is 'yes'. And this formula will allow you to avoid the trial-and-error pathway outlined in Chapter 3: Why success is not an accident, and will give you a real structure and a framework to channel your thinking.

The formula has the following six steps, which we're going to work through together.

Step 1: Identify characteristics you admire and those you dislike

The world is a university when it comes to personal brand. All day, we see aspects of personal character that we either love and wish to emulate or dislike and wish to avoid:

- The people in our lives: colleagues, bosses, customers, suppliers and partners

- The people we read about or see on TV and on the Internet: celebrities, sports stars and business personalities
- The people we know deeply, such as family members and friends.

Why reinvent the wheel when others are already giving us live-action case studies and success modelling to learn from?

Accelerator exercise 7.1: Write down the characteristics you admire

In the downloadable toolkit, https://www.roystonguest.com/RISE-toolkit/, you will find a Personal Brand Tracker that will help you with this exercise.

In the first section, brainstorm the personal characteristics you have observed in individuals you admire. Think of the person first and then think about three or four of their personal characteristics, or brand traits, that instantly pop into your mind.

For example, if I said the name Nelson Mandela, what would come to mind? On my list would be courage, resilience and humility. This is a man who walked out of prison and said: 'Hey, I know you locked me up for 27 years, but let's lead the country together.' That's an astonishing statement, which for many was the defining characteristic of this great man. What brand traits would you use to describe Richard Branson? On my list would be entrepreneurial, risk taking, visionary and charismatic. How about the singer/songwriter Lady Gaga? On my list would be eccentric, unique, fearless and consistent. For David Beckham, it would be athlete, family man, grounded, dedicated.

Do you have or want to have any of these characteristics in your own personal brand? Are they what you want to be known for?

Go ahead and pick your own list of ten people, and see if you can come up with 30 different traits. They can be from your personal or professional life as well as from the world of business, sport, music and entertainment.

This is not designed to be a one-off exercise, by the way. As you raise your conscious awareness of the importance of your personal brand and accept that building and shaping it is an ongoing journey, you should continually revisit this exercise. When you see a trait you admire in someone, add it to your list. Make it a habit to keep updating it.

Accelerator exercise 7.2: Write down the characteristics you dislike

Just as importantly, there are traits you see in others that you do not admire, and that may even repel you. These are traits you would like to explicitly ban from your personal brand. Some will be easy; some you'll have to really work at.

Brainstorm as many examples as you can of people who display characteristics you don't like. Use the same categories as before: people in your life, people you have heard of, and people close to you. Who was the worst boss you ever had? Why was that? What was it about them that you disliked, and what do you wish they had done differently?

Make it a habit that when you meet people, switch on the TV or scroll through social media, if any more characteristics spring to mind, keep adding traits you dislike, as well as traits you admire, to your list.

Step 2: Develop your personal brand

Now you have your two lists, here's the fun part: developing your personal brand.

Which characteristics from Accelerator exercise 7.1 do you feel naturally drawn to? Perhaps they're ones you already feel are an integral part of your personal brand, or perhaps ones you'd like to develop.

Also reflect on the characteristics from Acclerator exercise 7.2. These are the traits you'd like to make sure never manifest themselves in your personal brand or, if you recognize yourself in any, to eliminate fast. You know what I'm talking about here: the negative characteristics that you know don't serve you well but which may keep rearing their ugly heads, tarnishing the way people think of you.

For example, you might have a reputation for always being late for meetings, with others perceiving this as disrespectful. This might be a 'Stop doing' for you and something to work on urgently. Or you might consistently over-promise when making commitments. Your intentions are good and you mean well, but if you keep doing it, you'll give yourself a credibility problem.

Accelerator exercise 7.3: Use your Focused Five – where focus goes, energy flows!

In developing your personal brand, you are going to use Section 3 of the Personal Brand Tracker, titled 'Focused Five' – see Figure 7.1 opposite. This simple tool will allow you to identify quick wins and marginal gains in five focused areas: Stop, Minimize, Maintain, Do more of and Start.

Creating effective behavioural change starts with honing in on the things you already do well (the Maintain column) and then working out into the other four areas as follows; Minimize, Do more of, Stop and, finally, Start.

Now take the generic traits you identified in the earlier Accelerator exercises (those traits you admire and those traits you dislike) and apply them to your personal brand using the five headers detailed above. Figure 7.2 opposite shows a completed Focused Five to give you an idea of what yours could look like when finished.

'Your brand is what other people say about you when you're not in the room.'

Jeff Bezos

Stop	Minimize	Maintain	More	Start

FIGURE 7.1 The Focused Five

'Your brand is what other people say about you when you're not in the room.'

Jeff Bezos

Stop	Minimize	Maintain	More	Start
Over-promising and under-delivering	Saying 'yes' to everything and everyone	Enthusiasm and positive attitude	Time management	Monthly Me Unlimited board meetings
Procrastinating over tasks I don't want to do	Talking...more active listening	Monthly date nights	Being present	Risk taking
	Alcohol intake... weekends only!		Candid communication	Being courageous
			Work/life balance	

FIGURE 7.2 An example of a completed Focused Five

You'll see that not every box is full. The idea is not to fill the entire template but to draw out the key areas you want to focus on in order to build and develop your personal brand. You may have only one or two traits in each column, which is absolutely OK. But you must have at least one trait in each.

Over time, as you revisit the exercise, you'll find that some things come off your Focused Five and some new traits get added. You might find that some traits move between columns as you achieve your marginal gains. It is designed to be a fluid, agile process and, most importantly, it's fun and exciting as you take ownership for building the personal brand that you want to live and be known for.

Step 3: Align perception and reality

There's a great saying: 'Feedback is the food of champions.'

Your completed Focused Five is now the representation of the personal brand you are and the personal brand you want to be. However, at this stage it really only represents *your* view of the world and *your* perception of yourself. You now need to explore how aligned your perception is with reality.

The challenge in seeing the world through only your lens and your eyes is that, depending on your level of emotional intelligence and how honest you are prepared to be, you can end up with what I call reality distortion. At events, I use what I call the Brand Scale (Figure 7.3) to show how this works:

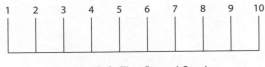

Figure 7.3 The Brand Scale

When I use this at events, I have some fun with the audience, positioning the purpose of the scale like this: 'In order for you to get maximum value from this session, what we've done in preparation for today's event is to solicit feedback from people who know you, by asking them to rate where they think your personal brand is on a scale of 1–10, with 1 being low and 10 being high. We've asked a cross section of peer colleagues, direct reports, your boss and a couple of friends, ten people in total, to give a balanced 360-degree perspective.'

It's amazing watching people's body language as they start to get a nervous twitch or start moving around in their seats. I then say: 'So, next step, I'm going to give you a couple of minutes to think about where those ten people, as an average, scored you on the scale, and then I'm going to invite you to place a dot on the point where you think they rated you. I will then place a second dot on the actual point where they have rated you and we'll see clearly how aligned perception and reality are.'

You can just imagine the audience now; some people are getting really anxious. I give them 90 seconds to think about it (which for some may feel like an eternity) before I let them off the hook by saying: 'I am of course playing with you. We haven't actually done that exercise. But if we had, where do you think the ten people would have rated you? And how accurate would the alignment be between your dot and theirs? In other words ... would perception (your interpretation) and reality (their combined views) match?'

There are three possible scenarios that help bring this concept of perception versus reality to life and that demonstrate why some people fall into the trap of reality distortion.

Scenario 1

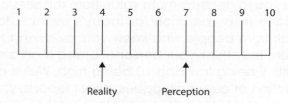

FIGURE 7.4 The reality/perception gap

In Figure 7.4 the individual has scored themselves as a 7 but feedback positions them as a 4. A perception/reality gap exists. It shows that he or she has a high perception of their self-worth and brand position, but that this is out of kilter with the feedback from others.

If I were to magnify the challenge and play with the extremities of the scale, self-perception could be an 8 or 9 and reality a 3. If this were a real scenario for an individual, you would describe them as delusional – clearly so wrapped up in their own internal view of the world that they are just not open to feedback, particularly the kind that might challenge them to change.

Do you know any people who fall into this scenario?

Scenario 2

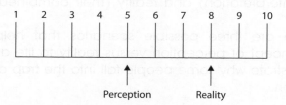

FIGURE 7.5 The perception/reality gap

In Figure 7.5 the individual perceives they're at 5, but feedback tells them they're actually much higher: an 8. There are two possible ways to interpret this result. The first is that this could be an individual with low self-esteem, self-belief or confidence. The second is that it could be someone who sets extremely high personal standards of excellence and therefore they are always going to score themselves lower than others because of the expectations they place on themselves. The latter can be a winning behaviour, but it can also be less positive due to the unrealistic expectations and pressure to be constantly better. Finding balance is key!

Scenario 3

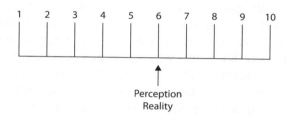

FIGURE 7.6 Perception and reality aligned

In Figure 7.6 we get to the real core of the perception-versus-reality quandary. If you are really in tune with who you are, what you stand for, the value you add and the difference you make, where should perception and reality be? The answer is that they should be aligned: there should not be a gap between perception and reality.

Creating the alignment of perception and reality requires commitment to confront the brutal facts. You need to be prepared to ask the probing, challenging questions and not just pay lip service to the answers. Be conscious of what you do well and know your strengths, but equally be balanced in knowing your weaknesses.

A clear view of your current state of reality is the platform from which you will be able to fast track your success in living the life you were meant to lead. Otherwise the only person you are kidding is yourself.

Accelerator exercise 7.4: Collect 360-degree feedback

I started this step by playing with the idea of receiving feedback from ten people, but now you must do it for real. You need to pick four or five people from both your personal and professional contacts and ask them for their help.

In your personal life they might be your partner, friends, family, neighbours, your gym instructor, members of a sports team you are in or associations or committees you belong to ... anyone who has had the chance to get to know you over time and who can give you valuable feedback and insights. In your professional life it could be your boss, a peer colleague, someone who works for you, a customer you're close to, a supplier or a partner. It might even be former co-workers and bosses you have a good relationship with.

Share that you are working on developing your personal brand and that you'd welcome their feedback. The key here is to emphasize that you want candid, honest feedback, identifying what they see as your strengths and what they see as your development areas. The key is not to pick people who you know are going to just sing your praises and tell you that you're wonderful at everything. As warming as that can be to the soul, it really isn't helpful in this exercise.

If you wish you can share with them your completed list of traits and characteristics in your toolkit. It might help stimulate their thinking and their valued contribution, but emphasize the need not just to stick to what's on the list ... They can be creative! Then give them a blank Focused Five template and ask them to fill it in on you.

Having a consistent approach to receiving feedback will make it easier for you to:

- compare the feedback, identifying commonalities, patterns and consistency, and also where differences exist

- understand how aligned the characteristics they identify in you are with the ones you identify in yourself

- answer the question of whether your perception (your interpretation) and the reality (their combined views) match

- identify any blind spots or reality distortions, positive and developmental, from which you can learn.

Understand the breadth and depth of thinking

If you've been careful in selecting your people, you know they will not just have paid lip service to the feedback they give. It will be thought through, constructive and focused on setting you up for success to be the best you can be. Speak with each person to understand the breadth and depth of thinking that underpins their feedback. The more examples and context they give, the more you will be able to work with the insights you're given.

Filter your feedback

Now, while feedback is the food of champions, there is another important skill that is critical to hone: filtering. Just because someone says you're bad at something, it doesn't mean you have to take that at face value. Just because someone sings your praises in a particular way, it doesn't mean you should consider yourself an expert in that area. Your self-knowledge is important here. Ask yourself whether their feedback is likely to help you achieve a more authentic 'you'. Is it going to help you be a better version of you? If not, filter it out.

Step 4: Create your brand essence

Your brand essence is your one sentence or strapline that clearly articulates who you are, what you stand for and what your personal brand is about. You may have several positive characteristics, but defining and packaging those traits into your one sentence demonstrates true understanding and authenticity of your personal brand.

This idea is championed by Daniel Pink, the author of the best-selling book *Drive: The Surprising Truth about What Motivates Us* and a globally renowned speaker and thought leader. Pink starts by saying that every great person is a sentence. He tells the story of a congresswoman named Clare Boothe Luce who went to see a young President John F. Kennedy in the early 1960s and said:

> Mr President, you don't understand something significant about leadership. A great person is a sentence. Anyone who has ever achieved anything in their lives isn't trying to do 97 different things, but one or two big transcendent things. Abraham Lincoln had a sentence. He preserved the Union and freed the slaves. FDR had a sentence. He lifted us out of a Great Depression and helped us win a world war. Mr President, you don't have a sentence, you have a muddled paragraph. You're trying to do 17 things and, as a result, you're doing nothing.

In a similar way, global brands work hard to convey the essence of who they are in a single sentence such as Nike's 'Just Do It' or McDonald's 'I'm Lovin' It'. They have a different application, but they are also designed to create a clear link in your mind about what it is they would like you to think when you hear their name.

And, of course, people can be global brands too. Love or hate TV personality Simon Cowell, he has consciously designed and built his personal brand around his one strapline: 'A plain-speaking music business expert, who shoots from the hip and is cruel to be kind.' This is his brand essence. He is consistent in living it.

Taking it a step further, when your brand is clear for everyone to see, your sentence can be something that even perfect strangers come to spontaneously. This is what happened with legendary Argentinian footballer Alfredo Di Stéfano, who is commonly thought to be one of the greatest players the game has ever known. When he passed away in 2014 at the age of 88, I was amazed to see how commentator after commentator, former teammates, friends, journalists, and everyone else who offered their insights about him, remarked on the exact same three things: his work rate, his winning mentality and his team spirit.

I would love to know whether those were conscious, deliberate characteristics that he worked hard on through his life or whether they were legacy characteristics that people latched on to after he died. And, in that context, I have a question for you: will you be described by the things you have consciously, deliberately worked on in order to build your personal brand in the years to come, or will the words people use be entirely accidental?

Pulling Steps 1–4 together

Now that you've completed Steps 1 to 4 of your brand journey, I urge you to stop and set aside some time to think about and create your one sentence. Don't be surprised if you acquire some brain ache and frustration as you make numerous attempts to carve out your sentence. It does take considerable time, effort and focus.

If you find yourself with writer's block or staring at a blank piece of paper, then maybe go back to the five or six people who gave you feedback as part of your 360-degree exercise and seek their ideas on what they see as your one sentence. Once you've developed your personal brand, road-tested it and validated it with external people to align perception and reality, and have really drilled down to the hub of your brand essence, it's time to live, eat, sleep and breathe it. This then leads nicely into Step 5: Communicate your personal brand.

Step 5: Communicate your personal brand

As we've seen from the examples throughout this chapter, communicating your personal brand is most effective when you're as conscious and deliberate about your messaging as Nike is, and as consistent in your words and actions as Alfredo Di Stéfano was. People are able to buy into your brand when they feel they can trust you. Here are some pointers to help you with this.

Think of your stakeholder groups

Your personal brand will be presented to different people at different levels and at different times, and how you communicate makes a huge difference in how it is going to be perceived and received.

Different audiences might include your boss, your customers, your friends, your family, your partner and your children. You may wish to demonstrate authenticity as a key brand characteristic, but the way you demonstrate authenticity through words and actions may be quite different.

To your boss, you may demonstrate yourself as an authentic team player, sharing your best ideas, being focused on details and seeing things all the way through to the end. To your children you may never miss a ballet recital, a parents' evening or a football match.

Imagine a lawyer who spends all day in court, locking horns with his opponents who then comes home in the evening and remains in that same mode with his partner and children. Clients and opponents may consider him to be focused and driven, but his partner and children think he's the opposite: detached and disengaged. Those are two very different brand statements.

To be consistent, the lawyer will do much better if he can think in terms of applying his brand traits to the specific situation at hand. If he can learn to change modes in order to suit the current situation, all the time remaining true to his personal brand, whilst emphasizing more relevant characteristics.

In all aspects of our lives we too must do the same. Map out your different stakeholder groups and become conscious and deliberate in how your personal brand is showing up for each one.

Don't be the best-kept secret

Having had literally thousands of conversations over the years about the concept of personal brand, there is one critical point I urge you to consider: you don't want to be the best-kept secret in the marketplace! It's the definition of insanity to have talent, experience or expertise that you never properly leverage or that others never have the opportunity to truly benefit from.

Please do not become the best-kept secret in the marketplace. You would be doing yourself a huge disservice. You may not be a natural self-promoter but other, lesser people are good at it, so through your Marketing Director you need to find the place where you are comfortably uncomfortable doing it.

I am sure you've met individuals who always seem to get their voices heard, irrespective of the quality of the point or message they want to make. Some people always seem to be promoted at break-neck speed despite others asking questions about their capability or 'fit' for the role. I have met hundreds of people like this and here's what I tend to find. These people never hang around for long! If you go back through their career, you see a pattern of both job and company movement on a frequent basis.

On the one hand, you could argue that their Marketing Director has done a brilliant job of 'selling' and promoting their personal brand. But if there isn't the breadth and depth of substance to be able to back it up, then one of two things happen. First, the individual jumps before they are pushed. And they will always have a compelling reason for doing so: they will say that the opportunity was not right for them (which usually has nothing to do with them). Second, they are pushed because they get found out. In essence, their Marketing Director might think they are doing a great job but it is all smoke and mirrors.

The key message is simply this: whatever shop window you create for the outside world, make sure you have the breadth and depth of substance to back it up. One way of doing this is by ensuring that there is only one version of the truth.

Tell only one version of the truth

You must communicate who you are as loudly as you can because there's no point in being the best-kept secret in the marketplace, but there is no benefit in being loud if you haven't got one version of the truth. Consistency is key.

In today's connected world, there is no such thing as 'off stage'. We are always 'on stage' and every interaction you have will either enhance or devalue your personal brand. Whether it's recruiters or customers, they will search across all your brand tools (CV, social media accounts, word of mouth) to sense-check consistency in how you are positioning yourself, personally and professionally.

This is where I recommend a clean sweep. Scrub down your social media platforms and perform a cursory search on your friends' platforms and remove any linked photos, videos or comments that don't align with your personal brand. Update your online business profiles, your CV, your professional bio; get that long-awaited haircut, clean your car, declutter the house and clear out your desk. Start as you mean to go on.

For example, you may want to consider replacing the email address you've had since your college days with something more in keeping with your current and future brand. boozy-billy@gmail.com was fun while it lasted, but it's time to move on. You're not only communicating your brand to the world but to yourself, every minute of every day.

Ever heard of the word 'verisimilitude'? It means having the appearance of truth. And in your personal brand you want the appearance of truth across all your brand assets, tools and in the physical you – what you say, how you say it and your body language.

Be a great storyteller

We live in a storm of stories. We live in stories all day, and dream in stories all night long. We communicate through stories and we learn from them. We collapse gratefully into stories after a long day at work. Without personal life stories to organize our experience, our own lives would lack coherence and meaning.

Brands play in an intensely competitive attention economy. The problem isn't just that attention is a woefully scarce resource relative to demand, it's that it's also shattered and scattered around. We can't blame our smartphones or other modern technologies for our short attention spans. The human mind is a wanderer by nature.

The most fundamental challenge we face in the attention economy is: how do we pin down the wandering mind? The answer is by telling great stories. In order to stand out and capture those wandering minds in the way a great movie or TV show might do, create great stories to explain who you are, what you do, what you believe and, most importantly, why. You can offer a list of characteristics, but a compelling story is always more memorable, and people who really stand out are those who are able to tell a compelling story simply and with passion, believability and authenticity.

What's your story?

Step 6: Protect your personal brand

The Japanese have a word *kaizen*, translated as 'never-ending continuous improvement', which some of the greatest organizations in the world, such as Toyota, have ingrained in their production philosophy. They know that if they keep trying to make things a little better, over time they will see significant improvements.

Deep within that thinking is the knowledge that you must be mindful every day of the impact of even small actions and ensure that they move you forwards, not backwards. Over time, the compound impact of small bad decisions can be catastrophic to your finances, your career and your relationships. The same goes for your personal brand.

One of the most extreme examples of a lack of mindfulness was that of Gerald Ratner, the CEO of Ratner Group, a mid-market jewellery chain in the UK, when he all but scuttled his 42-year-old company through a badly timed gaffe in a 1991 speech he made. In his speech, at a conference of the Institute of Directors, he said: 'We also do cut-glass sherry decanters complete with six glasses on a silver-plated tray that your butler can serve you drinks on, all for £4.95. People say, "How can you sell this for such a low price?" I say, "Because it's total crap."'

That wasn't all. He doubled down by referring to one of the popular sets of earrings his company sold as 'cheaper than a [Marks & Spencer] prawn sandwich but probably wouldn't last as long'. The comments cost the company £500 million in value and Ratner his job, and created the phrase 'doing a Ratner'.

The opposite of the concept of marginal gains, discussed in Chapter 4, is marginal erosion, a slow steady decrease in performance or results that, over time, compounds into a significant problem. No doubt that makes sense, but you may be wondering how vigilant and mindful you really have to be. Well, think of it like this: every day you meet new people, or are put into unique situations or experience different challenges, each of which puts your personal brand through a 'stress test'. On top of that, your personal brand is constantly evolving, which means being mindful should probably be something you practise until it becomes a natural part of who you are.

There are two questions to ask yourself to help keep this concept of personal brand alive and protected:

- What am I going to do today to be true to my personal brand, living with authenticity, purpose and focus?

- How am I going to enhance and protect my personal brand today through every interaction I have, whether online or offline?

Don't try to be someone you're not

Authenticity is about being the real deal. Your personal brand should be so authentic that everyone instantly 'gets it and gets you' when they put you and your brand together. Just as everyone 'gets it' when they think of Nike and 'Just do it', they should instantly link you and your personal brand with ease and see them as authentically linked to one another as one single version of the truth.

I remember speaking at a conference where I was delivering a session on personal brand and I was asked a great question: 'Royston, if you could only pick one brand trait, what would it be?'

It was a no-brainer and I responded with one word: 'Authenticity.'

Being authentic is about accepting who you are, warts and all, including the aspects you may prefer to be different, but accepting them anyway. When you can do that, you can also acknowledge the things that are actually special about you, that give you a special kind of personal currency in your relationships.

The importance of authenticity

Defining your personal brand is hard work and requires a phenomenal amount of energy and focus. Life is challenging enough with the pace we are all moving at, the multiple plates we're spinning and things we want to achieve, without adding more complexity by having to wear a cloak – a false façade – every single day.

In a world which has created so much uncertainty and where trust is broken between nations and individuals, the one thing people are looking for more than ever is connection; connection to individuals who are the real deal, who are authentic, who are values-driven with integrity and moral principles and standards. With these as the cornerstone of your compelling personal brand, you really can create a brand that will serve you in realizing your personal and professional goals, developing rich and fruitful relationships and living a life where you realize your full potential.

Just think about the people in your life whom the previous paragraph might describe. These are probably the greatest people in your life, your closest friends and most honoured members of your family. But how many of these are there?

For most of us, there are only ever a few people who we can really rely on throughout our lifetimes. Although the individuals may change as relationships evolve and new people come into our life, the number of people we can depend upon without question is always going to be very small. As we get older, our tolerance for people and their behaviour changes so that we have less and less time for people whose brands don't align with ours and a greater appreciation, perhaps even a craving, for those whose personal brands truly do.

Authenticity is therefore critical in all your brand thinking, whether that is personal or professional. You can't say one thing and do another. You can't make claims about how you are and then act in a totally different way – not if you want to be believed.

Think about these two final important questions:

- Where is my personal brand in the marketplace?
- Would I buy me?

If you can honestly, hand on heart, look in the mirror and answer a resounding 'yes' to the latter question, 'Would I buy me?' ... then you are well on your journey to living the life you were meant to lead.

The Man in the Glass

This is one of my favourite poems and it is a fitting end to this brand chapter. It needs no tee up!

When you get what you want in your struggle for self
And the world makes you king for a day,
Just go to the mirror and look at yourself
And see what that man has to say.

For it isn't your father, or mother, or wife
Whose judgment upon you must pass,
The fellow whose verdict counts most in your life
Is the one staring back from the glass.

You may be like Jack Horner and pull out a plum
And think you're a wonderful guy,
But the man in the glass says you're only a bum
If you can't look him straight in the eye.

He's the fellow to please – never mind all the rest
For he's with you, clear to the end
And you've passed your most difficult, dangerous test
If the man in the glass is your friend.

You may fool the whole world down the pathway of years
And get pats on the back as you pass
But your final reward will be heartache and tears
If you've cheated the man in the glass.

Dale Wimbrow, 1934

Take action: achieve more

Why you?

This chapter started by asking what you think people are saying about you – or, more importantly, what you want them to be saying. In this age of brand, we make powerful decisions based on what we associate with a brand, how we feel about it and what we believe it stands for. The same power applies to your personal brand. You cannot leave your brand to chance.

I shared six steps for building your personal brand, broken into four brand-building Accelerator exercises. Use the Personal Brand Tracker as you work through each exercise, available to download here: https://www.roystonguest. com/RISE-toolkit/

Step 1 focused on identifying the characteristics you admire and the characteristics you dislike in others. You completed two Accelerator exercises (7.1 and 7.2), to list individual characteristics you admire and individual characteristics you dislike.

Step 2 moved on to developing your personal brand. With the help of Accelerator exercise 7.3, you completed the Focused Five, a simple tool to help you create effective behavioural change, starting by homing in on the things you already do well (Maintain), the things you want to Minimize, Do more of, Stop and finally Start.

Step 3 asked you to align perception and reality. By collecting 360-degree feedback in Accelerator exercise 7.4, you developed your brand scale by assessing where you believe your brand sits on a scale of 1–10 and then asking others where they believe your brand sits on the same scale.

Step 4 asked you to create your brand essence, your one sentence that describes you.

Step 5 reviewed the components for communicating your personal brand. It considered your stakeholder groups, how not to be the best-kept secret, how to keep to only one version of the truth and how to be a great storyteller.

Step 6 was about protecting your personal brand. It described the importance of being mindful every day of the impact of even small actions and ensuring that they move you forwards, not backwards. Ultimately, the key to your personal brand is authenticity, being the real deal and not trying to be someone you're not.

Your personal brand is what people say about you when you're not in the room. What do you want people to be saying about you from this point on?

8

Mortality motivation

> 'Life's only certainties are death and taxes. But do you
> know when the first one is likely to catch up with you?'
>
> *Benjamin Franklin*

When I was younger and starting in my career, the last thing I wanted was a conversation about mortality. It seemed a morbid, even depressing subject to talk about and, in my youth, I wondered why I should be bothered about it. I felt I was immortal, or at least that the end, if it dared to come, would be a very long way off.

Today, as I write this book, the lens through which I see the world has changed. While I'm not predicting my death any time soon, I am intensely aware of the value of time – a fleeting commodity that is irreplaceable and that will pass no matter what I, or you, do with it. Maybe it's because I'm now older, or a parent thinking about the legacy I wish to leave for my children, or maybe because I've seen first hand how life, without warning, can send you reminders of who's the boss and that in an instant your world, your priorities and your focus can change.

I don't know if that sounds like a bleak idea to you but, to be absolutely clear, I don't see it that way at all. I see my emerging awareness, which has grown increasingly prominent over time, as a wonderful, galvanizing positive. I call it mortality motivation and it's a powerful driver for creating context, meaning and focus in what you do, why you do it, and how you can become the best version of yourself. Realizing that we are not immortal is a great leveller, a reality check that we all need to embrace in order to maximize our time on planet Earth, no matter how old or young we are.

One common theme throughout this book is the undisputable truth that each of us is born with the potential to achieve greatness. But many of us do not realize our full potential. Instead, some people go through life with an aching feeling that they haven't lived life to the full, that they're now too old or have wasted too much time, or perhaps have tried and failed and don't feel they have the time, energy, belief or confidence left to try again.

Well, to all those people I would say simply this: you have absolutely no control over the length of your life ... but you do have absolute control over its breadth and depth. You have the power to ensure that you make every day, every minute and every interaction count. Don't waste your energy sweating the small stuff.

I want you to imagine a scenario that may make you a little uncomfortable, but which, by the time you get to the end of it, will give you a solid reference for building your mortality motivation.

Start with the end in mind

Picture this scenario: you walk into a church full of your friends and family. The candles are lit and the sound of the church organ vibrates through your whole being. As you approach the coffin at the front, you get the fright of your life because the person lying in the coffin is you!

Next, you hear a voice reading your eulogy. You realize, with another jolt, that the voice is yours, telling your story. What story will be told?

Will it talk about the mountains you have climbed, the friendships you have forged and the successes of your life, both personally and professionally?

As you hear this story played out in your own words, questions start forming in your mind. Was your life what you wanted it to be known for? Was it a fulfilled life? Was it a life you were proud of?

168

Please don't think of this as morbid. I'm not asking you to consider your own death – quite the opposite. I want you to embrace the days ahead when you've got so much life left to live. You can get to the end and have lots of 'would haves', 'could haves', 'should haves' or you can recognize that the time you have to create and live your dreams is limited, not guaranteed and, as a result, we should all pay it the respect it deserves.

Now is your chance to define the life you want to live, in order to feel fulfilled, motivated and inspired to be the most successful you. Your mortality motivation should be a driving force when you are setting your goals, focusing your mind and energy every day to pursue them.

Our average life expectancy

For the period 2010–15 the United Nations World Population Prospects: 2015 Revision reported that the average life expectancy at birth, worldwide, was 71.5 years (68 years and 4 months for males and 72 years and 8 months for females). The 2016 World Factbook reported something similar: 67 years for males and 71.1 years for females, for an average of 69 years. While these life expectancy figures are averages and we all know that other factors come into play – lifestyle, diet, weight, genetic make-up, wealth, plus a variety of other things (including luck) – the numbers do at least give us a benchmark.

You might be wondering why life expectancy is different for men and women, and we're not entirely certain why girls born today will live just under four years longer than boys on average. Historically, scientists assumed that this was because men worked more physically intensive and dangerous jobs. Another theory was that men are more likely to drink and smoke heavily, but a far more likely explanation is down to evolution, and our hormones in particular. Testosterone may cause men to burn out slightly faster than women, who have the biological advantage of the healing benefits of oestrogen, the female sex hormone, which naturally mops up poisonous chemicals.

Regardless, the message to take away is this: your chrono-logical age is what it is, but you can manage all the other things around it. You have no control over the length of your life, but you do have control over its breadth and depth.

We all know people who already seem old in their thirties, and perhaps you're lucky enough to know people who still seem young in their seventies or eighties. 'Old' 30-year-olds tend to have very poor mortality motivation. They forget that, while they're wasting their breath complaining, someone else is taking their last breath and wishing they had many more. 'Young' 80-year-olds tend to have very good mortality motivation. They know they're potentially nearing the end of their days and want to make sure they enjoy what is left of them. They have learned to control the controllable.

> The length of our lives is out of our hands. But its breadth and depth is not.

The lesson of Wally Hayward

South African Wally Hayward had a lifelong love of the annual Comrades Marathon, an ultramarathon of 90 kilo-metres in South Africa.

In 1930, when he was just 21 years old, he became the youngest entrant in the race and won it on his first attempt. Clearly, this was a young man with great drive. It was 20 years before he attempted it for a second time in 1950. And he won again, this time at 41 years of age. He continued to win every year until 1954, as a 46-year-old competing against people in their twenties and thirties. He held the record for the oldest man to win the race until 2004, when Vladimir Kotov from Belarus took the title.

But the story doesn't end there. In 1988, at the age of 80, he returned. He wasn't anything like his former self, of course.

He wasn't as strong or as fit. He didn't have the same stamina. But he still beat more than half the pack of runners in that year's race, proving that, if you want it, age doesn't matter – just your motivation.

While many people his age were sitting around getting old, and many people much younger than him too, for that matter, Wally Hayward was out proving that while he couldn't control the fact that his body was 80, he could control his version of what being 80 looks, feels and acts like.

The lesson of Roz Savage

Consider the story of Roz Savage, a young woman who had a perfectly good career as a management consultant from her early twenties to her mid-thirties, until she began to realize that she was on a road to nowhere in comparison to her own goals and dreams.

She gave a very influential TED Talk in April 2010 called 'Why I'm rowing across the Pacific', the title of which gives you an immediate insight into how she turned her life around and put it on a totally different track. She describes it like this:

> For a long time I didn't believe I could have a big adventure. The story I told myself was that adventurers looked like [strong bearded men]. I didn't look the part; I thought there was them and there was us and so, for 11 years, I conformed. I did what people from my kind of background were supposed to do. I was working in an office in London as a management consultant. I think I knew from day one that wasn't the right job for me, but conditioning just kept me there for so many years, until I reached my mid-thirties and I thought: 'You know, I'm not getting any younger. I've got a purpose in this life and I don't know what it is, but I am pretty certain that management consulting is not it.'

So fast-forward a few years; I had gone through some changes to try to answer that question of what am I supposed to be doing with my life, when I sat down one day and wrote two versions of my own obituary: the one that I wanted, a life of adventure, and the one I was actually heading for, which was a nice normal pleasant life, but wasn't where I wanted to be.

And I remember looking at these two versions of my obituary and thinking: 'Oh boy, I am on totally the wrong track here. If I carry on doing what I am doing now, I am just not going to be where I want to be in five or ten years or at the end of my life.'

I made a few changes, let go of some of the trappings of my life and through a bit of a leap of logic, decided to row across the Atlantic Ocean.

That was the start for Roz Savage, who went on to become a Fellow of the Royal Geographic Society, the subject of a TV movie, a published author, and to be honoured by Queen Elizabeth II. She couldn't do anything about being 34, or about the fact that she had spent her twenties in a career that didn't fulfil her. But she could control what came next, which is exactly what she did.

And so can you.

> What you do today is important because you're trading a day of your life for it.

All of this talks to the idea that we should make the most of our time on this earth and get the most out of each of our days ahead. But how many days do you have exactly? And what does it matter if you squander some and only make the most of a few?

Let me share a personal story about a guy called Mike (not his real name) who I used to train with down at the gym.

Mortality motivation in action

I thought of Mike as a friend, but during a particular period of about six weeks it bothered me that he was in a negative spiral and always complaining about what was going wrong in his life. I would walk into the changing room and ask him how he was and he would pour out chapter and verse of all the things that were bothering him and how unfair it all was ... and believe me, the list was long. This guy could have challenged J. K. Rowling for storytelling if he'd decided to capture all that he was disgruntled with.

It eventually got to the stage where I would hide behind the locker on the other side just so I didn't have to train with him that day. But then I realized that if I was a good friend I needed to help him, interrupt his thought pattern and this negative spiral he had got himself into, and create context for his thinking.

So, next time I saw him, I asked: 'How are you?'

And off he went. This was wrong and that was wrong, so eventually I put up my hand and stopped him. I suggested a beer after we'd both trained to which he agreed, probably because he saw it as an opportunity to continue this conversation later.

So there we were in the pub and I said to him, 'It strikes me there are a few things which you're not happy with in your life right now, and this has been going on for a few weeks. I'd like to give you something to think about.'

And then I posed the question: 'How old are you?'

'I'm 43,' he replied.

'Do you know what the average life expectancy of a man is in the UK?' I asked?

'No idea,' he said.

'Well, I do. It's 79. And by my reckoning that means if you're 43 and you die at the average life expectancy age, you've got 36 years left. That's only 13,140 days.'

There was a deathly silence, which I played with before kicking in with the final piece of my jigsaw.

'That's not long when you think about it in days. You've already lived for 43 years, which is 15,695 days, so you're in the home straight already,' I said. 'So there's something I'd like you to think about,' I continued. 'There are obviously things in your life that are not working for you currently or things that you're not happy with, so you can do one of two things. First, change the way you're thinking about things or second, change what you're doing. Because the simple truth is today is another trade-off, and it strikes me that you're not happy with the trade you're currently making!'

To cut the story short, it made a massive difference to him. He did change a few things and he also changed the way he was thinking, which in turn created a fresh perspective and context. For most people, it's usually a combination of both.

Making the most of what you have

Someone who has strongly influenced my outlook on life, and who passed away during the writing of this book, was the eminent, ever brilliant Stephen William Hawking CH CBE FRS FRSA. My reason for paying tribute here is that Stephen Hawking, almost more than any other person, embraced the challenge presented by his own mortality and, more than that, used it to maximize his extraordinary gift.

We all know the iconic image of Stephen Hawking in his wheelchair, his computer screen always nearby, through which he explained to the world the incredible ideas – ideas that had literally never been thought before by any other human being – that ran through his brain. What you may not know is that his physical disability began in 1963 when, as a graduate student at Cambridge University, he learned he had amyotrophic lateral sclerosis, a neuromuscular wasting disease also known as Lou Gehrig's disease, and was told he would never live beyond the 1960s.

It's incredible, then, that, thanks to medical care, he lived to develop what his thesis adviser at Cambridge called 'the most beautiful paper in the history of physics' in 1974. It's even more incredible that he lived to write the 10-million sell-ing book *A Brief History of Time: From the Big Bang to Black Holes*, published in 1988.

But what is most incredible to me is what he did with what he had. Stephen Hawking was blessed with one of the most brilliant minds of all humanity, which was locked inside a disabled body. Perhaps that was a curse. But perhaps it was a blessing because it caused him to focus on nothing but what went on within the walls of his brain. And in his daily race against the clock, Stephen Hawking changed our understanding of the universe.

None of us know our check-out date, but I marvel at the neat symmetry that the greatest physicist of the modern age died on the same day that the previous title holder, the equally brilliant Albert Einstein, was born: 14 March. It's almost as if he meant it to be.

The blessing of Great Ormond Street Hospital

I am blessed to have spent time at Great Ormond Street children's hospital in London, a few years back. Great Ormond Street is the largest centre for child heart sur-gery in the UK and one of the largest centres for heart transplantation in the world. I have the upmost respect and admiration for the team who work there. They do the most valuable and amazing work.

I was asked to give a talk to the doctors and nurses and, before I spoke, I had the privilege to go on a hos-pital tour, meeting staff and also some of the sick chil-dren. It was one of the most enlightening and grounding experiences I have ever had. To see some of those young children, some of who were really unwell but with phe-nomenal attitudes, optimism and resilience, was some-thing to behold. Even writing about it now puts a lump in my throat. If you are a parent, you will know what I mean.

> Boy, did it stop me in my mental tracks and reload the importance of mortality motivation. Even more importantly, it gave me the spur to make sure I wasn't sweating the small stuff and was deliberate and conscious about the choices I was making with my time.

I appreciate that you may not be able to draw on an 'Aha!' moment like this one that makes you sit up and take notice, and that may be a good thing. But I've come up with this simple exercise to get you to start thinking with the end in mind. It's split into two parts.

Accelerator exercise 8.1: Develop your mortality motivation

Part 1

Based on the average life expectancy where you live, how many days do you have left? (To find the specific life expectancy for where you live, simply type into your search engine and then do the simple calculation.) Then, with that number, ask yourself the following:

1 How good is the trade of time you're making each and every day?

2 Are you happy with the trade?

If the answer to question 2 is yes, then keep doing what you're doing. But if it's no, what do you need to do differently or how do you need to change the way you're thinking about things in your life right now?

Let's make sure every day is a good trade.

Part 2

1 Imagine a standard tape measure (or use a real one if you have one to hand). You'll want one that is at least as long as your average life expectancy in centimetres, where one centimetre represents one

year. Open the tape measure at the point where you discovered the life expectancy for a person of your gender, in the country where you live.

2   I am a male in the UK, so my life expectancy is 79. So I'll open and set my tape measure at 79 centimetres. Since I am now 45, the statistics say I've got 34 years left. The next step is to wind the tape measure back in so that there are only 34 centimetres showing, representing the years I have ahead of me to pursue my personal and professional goals. What is it for you? Wind back the difference so you are only showing the years left ahead of you.

3   Now, since we need to sleep for roughly eight hours per day, or one-third of each 24-hour cycle, we must also 'delete' that time from the years we have left. In my case, that's 11.3 years of sleep, so let's wind the tape measure in once again. I am now left with 22.6 years, roughly one half of which I will spend at work pursuing my professional goals and the other half pursuing my personal ones. That's 11.3 years for each. That's the time I have left to work with. How much is it for you?

It's an indication of the time each of us has left to achieve our goals, pursue our dreams and live the life we want to live. That's the time we have left to ensure our obituary is the one we want people to read.

Even the most strident optimist can see that time is precious and using it deliberately and consciously is critical if you are to achieve your greatest ambitions. That's the important benefit of developing your mortality motivation.

Playing the second half

I am tuned into my mortality motivation in a positive way, aware that I am playing the second half of my life. At 45 years of age. I feel young, I am healthy and strong, thank goodness, but the reality is that with average life expectancy in the UK at 79.4 years for men, I have lived more than half my life. Converting it into days really focuses the mind:

- 79.4 years = 28,981 days
- At 45.1, I've already burned 16,461 days, leaving only 12,520 days left (if I live to the average age).

The great thing about numbers is that they don't lie. They help you face reality. 12,520 is not a big number and for me this timeline is a great mortality motivation, which helps me create high levels of ownership and focus about what I'm going to do with my time.

I am an older parent, having had both my children in my early forties. Eloise is five years old and Ethan is three, and I think about all the things I want to do with them and, perhaps most importantly, how I want to have all my faculties about me to do those things.

I have always been a big skier and I want to be able to fly down the slopes trying to keep up with them. I want to play football and roll around on the beach or the lawn. I want to be there to help them do their homework, to laugh, to cry, to support, and be the rock for them as they grow into their own personalities and lives. I am so serious about this that when each of them was born, I signed a pledge to them, called 'Daddy's Promise', written by David Teplow.

Daddy's Promise

I promise to love you – unconditionally.

I promise to protect you – for your pain hurts me more than my own.

I promise to guard and to guide you – materially, mentally and morally.

I promise to foster soundness and strength – in your health, your head and your heart.

I promise to catch you doing things right, and let you do things your way, no matter how messy.

I promise to applaud your accomplishments – whether they be anonymous, for nobody's eyes, or world famous, for the Nobel Prize.
I promise to be a good example always – for there's no telling what act or attribute you might emulate.
I promise to be honest, open and direct.
I promise to be a pillar of courage and a pillow of comfort.
I promise to explore the world with you, explain the world to you, and expect the world of you.
I promise to be a fortress in which you can hide, a friend in whom you can confide, and a father in whose heart you'll find love and in whose eyes you find pride.

Do I always get it right? No. But the positive intent and focus to live by these principles is there 100 per cent.

I have a professional legacy I want to fulfil. I have personal goals to achieve. And I know this for sure: if it is to be, then it is up to me. Taking control of your life, your thoughts, your actions and results is the whole point of *Rise*.

Those 12,520 days I have left aren't just days for kicking around without a care, and neither are yours. A few days lost here and there because of a lack of focus may not appear to matter, except that those are days you can't take back.

And please don't misunderstand me, I'm not talking about living a life of rigid discipline, as I personally don't believe that's what living is. It's about moderation and making good choices.

Make your choices carefully because, ultimately, your choices make you.

Life is back to front

As you get older, it's not just important to recognize that your finite number of days is decreasing all the time, but that each of those days left is increasingly precious.

You see, life is back to front.

When you're young you have your health, boundless levels of energy, a positive innocence and naivety and a hunger to make your dent on the world. But you are spinning the plates; forging a professional career, building a family, managing the tensions of work–life balance and paying all the bills. And then when you're older you probably have the financial resources and more time, but do you necessarily have your health? This one is close to home for me because I see this challenge with my own parents every day.

My father is 75 years old and has been on a kidney dialysis machine for 18 months. That's eight hours every night, 365 days a year. As I write this, he has just recovered from cancer and been given the all-clear. His knees are gone and he has gout in his foot. And yet he is one of the most positive, upbeat people you'll ever meet, despite the challenges of his health. My mother is 74 and suffers from Alzheimer's and is on so much medication that she always seems to be taking something throughout the day.

> Don't fall into the trap of banking everything up, thinking you'll do it later in life. Why wait? Some day may never come. Find the balance between living your dreams right now and living in the chapter of your life you're in.

The lessons are out there

My parents' health has been partly responsible for my being so focused on my mortality motivation, but you don't have to have personal stories of your own to get in touch with yours. I hope you don't, but I do want you to have the opportunity to dig deep and focus, so I'd like to share some of the greatest, motivating examples I can think of, which I believe will add enormous value to your own mortality motivation.

Henry Fraser

There have been a number of books published in recent years that I have found incredibly motivating. They include *The Little Big Things: A Young Man's Belief That Every Day Can Be a Good Day* by Henry Fraser (2017). The book includes the motivational quote 'Being challenged in life is inevitable, but being defeated is optional', and the story it tells will not let you down.

Henry Fraser was 17 years old when he severely damaged his spine in what would, on any other day, have been a minor incident. On holiday with his friends in Portugal, he dived into the sea and hit his head on the seabed, dislocating the fourth vertebrae in his neck and emerging, after six months in hospital, paralysed from the neck down.

That would have been it for many people but, as Fraser says: defeat is optional. Through his recovery, and to focus his mind, he has emerged as a recognized and talented 'mouth artist,' painting pictures by holding a paintbrush between his teeth. Fraser is now in his mid-twenties, and he has developed for himself a career that many able-bodied people would envy but never try to create for themselves. His story is inspirational, and must make you sit up and ask: 'If he can achieve what he has, what excuse can I possibly have?'

Paul Kalanithi

Paul Kalanithi was a talented neurosurgeon who had his life in front of him when he was diagnosed with cancer at just 35 years of age; this illness ultimately led to his death at just 37. Through his treatment, his wife and he conceived their only child, who was born just before he died. His story is laid out in his best-selling book, *When Breath Becomes Air* (2017), in which he covers topics such as what to do when your life is catastrophically interrupted and what it means to have a child as your own life fades away.

Paul Kalanithi's message is one everyone needs to hear for the clarity of focus he has around the important things in life. The very things we ignore are the things he realized mattered most.

Holly Butcher

The story of Holly Butcher went viral after she posted her dying letter on social media in early 2018. She was just 26 and was honest and thoughtful about what it meant to 'accept your mortality at 26 years young', in her own words:

> It's just one of those things you ignore. The days tick by and you just expect they will keep on coming, until the unexpected happens. I always imagined myself growing old, wrinkled and grey, most likely caused by the beautiful family (lots of kiddies) I planned on building with the love of my life. I want that so bad it hurts. That's the thing about life: it is fragile, precious and unpredictable and each day is a gift, not a given right.

As her words of wisdom unfold, she offers round after round of sage advice:

> Those times you are whinging about ridiculous things (something I have noticed so much these past few months), just think about someone who is really facing a problem. Be grateful for your minor issue and get over it. It's okay to acknowledge that something is annoying but try not to carry on about it and negatively effect other people's days.

How guilty are we all of that?

I recommend you seek out her full letter and read it thoughtfully.

Don't sweat the small stuff

Neither Holly Butcher nor Paul Kalanithi are with us any longer unfortunately, and Henry Fraser is living a new life after his first was shockingly disrupted.

But what about you? How guilty are you of slipping into autopilot on a daily basis, choosing to play the victim, or losing sight of the big picture? I would bet you're sometimes fairly guilty of that; it's a common human fault.

The stories in this chapter, and others like them, reveal a common thread: in the end the big important things are usually the small, seemingly unimportant things that you put off while you get on with your life or don't pay attention to because you're too 'busy'. These are simple things such as cuddling your little girl or boy, playing with your dog in the garden, going for a walk and enjoying the sunshine.

I hope it's now clear to you that mortality motivation isn't depressing or bleak; it's a rallying cry for you to get out there and do something remarkable with your life, in line with your own definition of success. And it's a warning that you ought to start doing that right now.

Your legacy

- We should all remember that no matter how big our house is, how new our car is, or how much money we have in the bank, we all end up the same way, so stay humble. As you waste your breath complaining about life, someone out there is breathing his or her last breath, so remember to appreciate what you have.

- Know that true and lasting success is not measured by the amount of money you make but the number of lives you affect. Holly Butcher may not have made a fortune, but the insight she shared at the end made her life a valuable contribution to all of us.

- What is the positive dent you are going to make in the world? What will your legacy be? What will you be remembered for?

- What will be in your obituary, your eulogy?

Take action: achieve more

You'll look back at this point and thank yourself you started today.

This chapter considered the value of time, and how the length of our lives is out of our hands, but that its breadth and depth are not. It's a rallying cry to live to the full while you're alive and to do the work now to make your dreams come true. What you do today is important because you're trading a day of your life for it.

I shared one eye-opening Accelerator exercise (8.1) to bring home the point that time is precious and using it deliberately and consciously is critical if you are to achieve your greatest ambitions. It asked you to calculate the number of days you have ahead of you based on your average life expectancy and where you live, and then asked:

- How good is the trade of time you're making every day?
- How will you use your time to realize your full potential?

Don't sweat the small stuff. Don't waste your final breaths complaining about life; appreciate what you have. If you want to make the most of what you have available, you must make the choice to do so. Today.

Wellbeing: why the greatest wealth is your health

'Health is like money. We never have a true idea of its value until we lose it.'

Josh Billings

I couldn't write a book about how to set yourself up for success and be the best version of you without including a chapter on wellbeing – not least because wellbeing is one of the seven directors of Me Unlimited.

I'd argue that it's actually the most important director role of them all. I don't make that statement lightly, and here's why I believe it to be true. Without your health you limit the performance of the other director roles and, in fact, any of the other ideas and strategies covered in this book.

I've experienced this first hand. A good friend of mine in his mid-fifties has suffered two heart attacks that have affected his health significantly. When I speak with him about it, the one thing that is most striking is the level of remorse he feels for how he lived his life prior to those significant interruptions to his health. He was single-minded about success, about building his business, buying and selling properties, working long hours and claiming (I heard him say this more than once) that he could handle massive amounts of stress.

The constant pressure and the coping mechanisms he used – regularly drinking too much, smoking, not getting enough sleep, overeating, never finding time to exercise, allowing his blood pressure to shoot up and up as he vented his daily frustrations – ultimately were too much and his body simply said 'Enough'.

He's alive. He's one of the lucky ones, all things considered. But he has to take it easy, avoid stress and therefore the business pursuits that used to define him can no longer be his driving purpose. And this struck me most of all: he is under such strict instructions from his doctor and his wife to take it easy that even basic exercise needs serious consideration. Gone are the skiing holidays and rigorous pursuits, which they both enjoyed.

Sharing his story provides us all with a key life lesson. By his own admission, he's reasonably well off in terms of money but the poorest person he knows in terms of his quality of life. And the thing that pains him the most is that he knows he is the cause of his physical weaknesses and he knows he could have avoided almost all of them.

Protecting your health

If you have your health, look after it and do whatever you can to keep it. Once it's gone or been damaged, it can be almost impossible to get it back, certainly to the same level you experienced previously. If the day comes when you have to start thinking about your health in terms of how to try to get it back, you'll find that so many avenues are already closed to you. At that point you'll wish more than anything that you hadn't made some of your previous lifestyle decisions.

That's the best reason of any to work on your health right now. The great news is there are preventative measures you can take immediately to protect your health and even strengthen it while it's good, to earn yourself more longevity and greater quality of life throughout your life.

While nothing is certain or guaranteed, and illnesses and disabilities beyond our control can happen at any time – even to the most health-conscious individual – you can put yourself firmly in the driver's seat of your life. This is the focus of this book and so my challenge for you is simply this: control the controllable – those things that are within your immediate circle of influence.

Can you honestly say you are currently doing everything within your control and influence to lead a healthy lifestyle, one that sets you up to turn your future dreams into reality?

I don't profess to be an expert

I write this from the point of view of a male in his mid-forties who has always been pretty focused on health. I have never smoked, drink only in moderation (though my doctor might still say too often!), make time for exercise and generally keep a watchful eye over what I eat. I try to keep in touch with how my body and mind are feeling because I know how important it is to note the warning signs.

However, that does not make me an expert on health, only a very keen guardian of my own. It does make me an extremely attentive student, though, which is why I feel compelled to share my thoughts and experiences on this topic.

Just as I rely on specialists in other areas of my business and life, I seek help and support in this area too. A personal trainer is as important to me as a strong accountant; they're just focused on a different set of numbers: those for cholesterol, blood pressure, glucose and BMI.

When I introduced the seven director roles in Chapter 4, one of them was the Wellbeing Director. When you are performing that specific role, you are responsible for the health and wellbeing of your body and mind, which will propel you to success. You've only got one body and one mind, and your goal should be to enhance and improve what you have.

Wellbeing includes fitness, exercise, diet, relaxation (including healthy sleep), mindfulness, building your personal resilience plus the more general check-ups. I'll explore each of these in turn so you can audit how well you're currently performing against each, recognizing that, if you don't get this game plan right, the more appropriate name for your business might be Me *Limited*!

My focus here is on the 'why' and 'what' of achieving and maintaining wellbeing. I will leave the specifics of the 'how' to the specialists, who have a great deal more knowledge and expertise than me in these areas.

Mindfulness and wellbeing

'Wherever you are, be there totally.'

Eckhart Tolle

Mindfulness. It's a pretty straightforward word. It suggests that the mind is fully attending to what's happening, to what you're doing, to the space you're moving through. That might seem obvious, except for the annoying fact that we so often veer from the matter in hand. Your mind takes flight and pretty soon you're engrossed in thoughts about something that happened previously or fretting about the future. And this can be a source of great anxiety.

Yet no matter how far you drift from the present, mindfulness can snap you back to where you are and what you're doing and feeling. Since it's hard to nail down in words and you'll find slight variations in the meaning in books, websites, audio and video, here's my all-purpose definition that treats mindfulness as a quality that you already possess rather than something you have to conjure up.

Mindfulness is the human ability to be fully present, aware of where you are and what you're doing, and not overly reactive or overwhelmed by what's going on around you. While mindfulness is innate, it can be cultivated through proven techniques – short pauses you insert into everyday life and merging meditation practice with other activities such as yoga or sports. When you're mindful, you reduce stress, enhance performance, gain insight and awareness through observing your own mind, and increase your attention to others' wellbeing.

Professor Mark Williams, former director of the Oxford Mindfulness Centre, says that mindfulness means knowing directly what is going on inside and outside ourselves, moment by moment. He says:

> It's easy to stop noticing the world around us. It's also easy to lose touch with the way our bodies are feeling and to end up living in our heads; caught up in our thoughts without stopping to notice how those thoughts are driving our emotions and behaviour. An important part of mindfulness is reconnecting with our bodies and the sensations they experience. This means waking up to the sights, sounds, smells and tastes of the present moment. That might be something as simple as the feel of a banister as we walk upstairs.

Being present and in the moment

Let me share with you an example that highlights this concept perfectly. An area manager working at one of the big mobile telephone companies was attending a living**your**future™ programme. In one of the sessions I was talking about being present and in the moment, and she put up her hand and said: 'Royston, this happened to me recently.'

She shared the story whereby one Saturday morning, just after 6.00 a.m., she was sitting in her living room while her three-year-old was playing around her (he was an early riser!). At the same time, and thinking nothing of it, she was on her phone reading and responding to emails. After some time, her son stopped her and said: 'Mummy when are you going to get off your phone and spend some time playing with me?'

She was mortified. It became a defining moment for her, centred on the importance of 'being present'.

Three practical strategies for being more mindful

Just like many of the concepts in this book, mindfulness could be a book in its own right. But what I share with you here are my top three strategies that you can instantly apply to start benefiting from mindfulness right now. This might act as the catalyst to spark your curiosity or take further action and delve into the world of mindfulness.

1 Mindfulness immersion

A while back, as I was taking the rubbish bin outside my gate for collection, a task I had done thousands of times before, I didn't notice that one of the bricks in the path had moved slightly, and as the bin hit it, it twisted and flipped on to its side, spilling rubbish all over the ground. The last thing I wanted to do there and then, when I was thinking about the day ahead and preparing in my mind for an event I was about to speak at, was stop and pick up rubbish.

But the spilled rubbish was a direct consequence of the my thoughts being elsewhere. If I had been more focused on the simple task of taking the rubbish bin out and doing it right, I'd have spotted the problem before I got to it.

Silly mistakes become part of every day when you're not being mindful. You've probably slipped into autopilot when you're doing something simple you've done a hundred times before. But have you ever had an unexpected accident when you weren't paying attention?

Ever had a bumper-to-bumper bashing in peak hour traffic? You know what I mean: one of those silly, avoidable, embarrassing accidents where your car connects with the car ahead because you lost concentration for a moment, while you thought of something else and drove into the back of them. That's a classic case of a lack of mindfulness.

Or have you got into the car with the intention of driving to the shops, but ended up heading in the opposite direction, to your office instead? If you have, you may have laughed it off as another case of autopilot, but what it was really was a lack of mindfulness.

Ending up in the wrong location because you weren't thinking in the moment may be mildly annoying, but it is much more serious than that. While you were driving and not paying attention, there were other cars, cyclists and pedestrians all around you who were operating on the assumption that you were. A lack of mindfulness can lead to dangerous situations.

Leonardo da Vinci said this in 1592 and it's still as relevant today as it was back then:

> The average person looks without seeing, listens without hearing, touches without feeling, smells without awareness, eats without tasting.

In the general busyness in which we lead our lives, we've stopped living fully through our senses. Think about it for a moment. How many times have you missed the fact that your partner has had a haircut because you're not truly paying attention (looks without seeing). Have you eaten on the go, using food merely as a functional means to an end (eats without tasting)?

The intention of mindfulness immersion is to cultivate contentment and to be truly present in the moment. Now you're beginning to practise mindfulness.

2 Mindful breathing

This is my favourite mindfulness strategy because it works, it's simple, you can do it anywhere, at any time, and you get immediate results.

If you feel yourself heading down a pathway you don't want to go (to a place of anger, resentment or conflict), through conscious awareness you can slam on the brakes and almost immediately channel yourself down a more productive pathway as you apply mindful breathing. Within three breathing cycles, you'll feel that you are back in the driver's seat with your hands firmly on the controls.

Research has shown that practising mindful breathing can help you become more aware of what you are feeling and thinking in the 'present', in a non-judgemental way. Mindfulness is linked to improved health, lower anxiety and stronger resilience against stress. Studies have also shown that people who participated in a 15-minute mindful breathing exercise recorded less negative emotions when shown a series of negative images, compared with those who didn't engage in the mindful breathing. This suggests that focused breathing can enhance your ability to modulate your emotions.

How and why mindful breathing can help you

Mindfulness helps you to detach from your thoughts, feelings and emotions, allowing you to work through and understand those feelings, instead of allowing them to consume you. Mindful breathing offers you an 'anchor' – your breath – on which you can focus whenever you feel you are struggling with negative thoughts. Mindful breathing assists you in being 'present' in the moment, instead of worrying about the past or stressing about the future.

To help understand how mindful breathing can truly help, it's worth understanding how we experience 'stress'. When you are in a stressful situation, the most 'primitive' part of your brain (the amygdala) triggers what is known as the 'fight or flight' response. This causes changes to your heart rate, muscle tone, blood pressure and concentration. You stay in this heightened state until your brain perceives that the 'danger' has passed.

This primitive response is vitally important when you need to react quickly, such as when you need to escape the path of an oncoming vehicle. However, it is not advantageous in ongoing stressful circumstances that cause anxiety, where there is no time for rest and recovery – such as constant demands in your workplace or relationship problems. This is when 'chronic stress' does not allow your brain to return your body to its resting state, which affects your mental and physical wellbeing, both in the short and long term.

How you manage stress is crucially important. Even if, as a short-term approach, you use mindful breathing in any perceived stressful moments during the day, taking your attention from what is occurring and focusing only on taking new breaths, you will significantly improve your ability to manage stress.

Think of chronic stress as affecting your brain in a similar way to how simultaneously running too many programs on your computer can reduce its performance. Your brain is your computer and can become overloaded. Pausing and taking a few mindful breaths focuses you on a short single task to clear your mind, allowing you to refocus, make better decisions and 'reboot'.

Accelerator exercise 9.1: Practise mindful breathing

Have you ever said to someone just at the point they are about to explode: 'Just breathe.' Well, that was you sharing the mindful breathing technique in its simplest form.

Mindful breathing should ideally be practised for five to ten minutes daily for at least a week. It can be practised standing, but it is easier when you are sitting or lying comfortably. You can have your eyes open or closed, but it's usually easier to keep your focus if you close your eyes.

1   Begin by taking an exaggerated breath – particularly if you are trying to stay calm in a difficult situation – then take a deep inhale through your nose (on a count of 3), hold your breath (on a count of 2) and finally take a long exhale through your mouth (on a count of 4).

2   Continue with this breathing pattern, focusing on the rise and fall of your chest and the sensation of the breath through your nostrils.

3 As you work through a cycle (inhale, hold, exhale) you will become more relaxed. Try to extend the length of the cycle by inhaling through your nose on a count of 5, holding your breath on a count of 3 and exhaling through your mouth on a count of 5. The optimum cycle to work towards is 7/7/7 – a 21-second cycle.

You may find, particularly in the beginning, that your mind becomes side-tracked by various thoughts. Don't be harsh on yourself; just notice when you are distracted and gently bring your attention back to your breath.

Breathing techniques, coupled with other activities such as tai chi or yoga, can induce a relaxed state of mind that is invaluable in reducing the body's response to stress.

'Whoosah'

A technique that started out as a joke in my family and which has now stuck is called 'Whoosah'. The term was used in the 2003 movie *Bad Boys II* starring Will Smith and Martin Lawrence. Lawrence's character attends an anger management course where he is advised to stroke his ears and say 'Whoosah' in moments of stress to help him pause and take breath.

It is so comical watching five-year-old Eloise say to her three-year-old brother, 'Ethan, calm down, remember Whoosah', as she demonstrates the technique to him, including the all-important stroking of ears. It has become the family trigger for mindful breathing.

3 Mindful thoughts

When you enter a new situation – a meeting, a party where you don't know anyone or, more specifically, something that you believe you could not possibly enjoy, such as a crowded bus, a train or a long queue at an adventure park with the children (I have recent personal experience of this one) – ask yourself the following questions:

- What is good about this?
- What do I appreciate here, right now in the moment?
- What is fun and funny about this?
- How can I make a positive difference to myself and others right now?

Waiting in line in a two-hour queue at an adventure park to meet and greet 'Princess Ariel', accompanied by my own 'Princess', turned my daughter's dream into her reality. Yes, I could have focused on the queue being too long (which it was) and the room being too hot (which it was) but instead I chose to focus on the positive things, and seeing my daughter's excitement as she tried to guess whether she would meet 'Mermaid Ariel' or 'Human Ariel' was priceless. (We met 'Human Ariel', in case you were wondering!)

Mindfulness is about picking your thoughts and focal points deliberately. It isn't difficult … you just need to remember to do it.

Fitness and wellbeing

'No matter how slow you go, you are still lapping everybody on the couch.'

Anon.

We all know that being physically active is good for your body. But your physical wellbeing and mental wellbeing are closely linked, so physical activity can be very beneficial for your mental health and overall wellbeing too. Being fit can do all the following:

- **Reduce the risk of some diseases.** Being more active can reduce your risk of heart disease, stroke and some types of diabetes.

- **Reduce the risk of physical health problems.** The stress hormone cortisol can be a killer, but as you get fitter, your body is better able to regulate it.

- **Promote healthier organs and bones.** A stronger heart and bones are among just some of the many physical improvements you can experience by being more active.

- **Reduce weight, increase energy.** Losing weight doesn't just make you feel better; it improves your stamina and energy too.

- **Improve sleep.** If you want to sleep well at night and have more energy in the morning, few things work as well as daily exercise.

- **Reduce anxiety and stress and create happier moods.** It's all about the chemicals: more endorphins (those feel-good hormones produced by your brain) and less cortisol are natural responses to exercise.

- **Improve your emotional state.** As you exercise, you clear your head and are able to think more clearly by stepping back from your immediate concerns.

- **Increase your self-esteem.** It feels good to feel good. You'll have a lot more confidence when you feel energetic, positive, strong and healthy.

- **Reduce the risk of depression.** One study found that exercising three times per week can reduce the risk of depression by almost 20 per cent.

- **Connect you with people.** Many forms of exercise are social activities, which help you make beneficial and positive connections with like-minded people.

- **Be fun!** If you're thinking of exercise as hard work and even torture, try doing something else. Running may not be your thing. Try tennis. Find something that suits you and you'll have a ton of fun getting fit.

Turning positive intention into committed action

Even though I know and accept all this and have experienced the benefits first hand, I get very frustrated with myself when I allow other demands on my time to interfere with my fitness routine. It happens often despite my best intentions. I know that when I do prioritize the time – note the word 'prioritize' – it really makes a difference. I feel more alive, sharper and more on my game. I sleep better and I'm definitely more productive and focused and I have higher levels of concentration. At those times, I'm really in the groove and, although I'm busy and focused, fitness training is a non-negotiable because it's one of the enablers that allows me to play my 'A game' in the performance zone.

If you ever catch yourself falling into a similar scenario to me, you'll love the next three ideas.

Idea 1: Unpack your personal 'why'

Be crystal clear about your reasons for doing it: your 'why'. If the why is compelling enough, you'll figure out the 'what' and the 'how'. For me it's simple. I want to be present to see my children grow up, start their careers, get married and build their best lives. I've got a lot to look forward to if I can manage and look after my health.

What's your why?

Design your fitness programme around your 'why' and your lifestyle. Your 'why' is a great guide to motivate you to focus on your wellbeing, but what to do and how to do it are huge considerations in ensuring your success. You have to take your 'why' and use it as fuel to create a 'what' and a 'how' that fit into your lifestyle in order for it to be sustainable.

There's no one-size-fits-all. I have friends who regularly run marathons and commit to significant amounts of training time. I personally couldn't do this because I wouldn't want to dedicate the time I have available to this one activity. While it may align with my 'why', it doesn't align with my lifestyle. Instead, I have a goal to run a minimum of four 10-kilometre runs a year, each one in under 55 minutes. For me, this is a practical goal. I can train for 10-kilometre runs anywhere and at any time and it doesn't consume big chunks of the day.

The key to success is to make your fitness programme a fixed part of your lifestyle, not merely an 'optional extra' which can be easily swapped or dropped.

Idea 2: Block out sessions in your diary and stick to them!

Simply block out fitness session slots in your diary, just as you would for any other meeting, event or party invitation. This will be how you spend some of your best time ... sessions with your Wellbeing Director. Think of them as non-negotiable and never to be missed. Treat them with respect and stick to them.

Idea 3: Set specific fitness goals

Fitness is a lot like most things: consistency and common sense rule the day. You can go all out for the extremes now and then, such as training for an ultramarathon or getting ready for a tournament, but generally your body will respond optimally if you train consistently, on a regular schedule, with a view to achieving marginal gains that lead to excellent health over time.

I am convinced that the power of consistency over time will get you from average to excellent in absolutely anything. But I'm equally convinced about the power of marginal erosion. If you stop your fitness routine, your body will slowly lose its strength and power over time, to the point where average becomes the new normal.

Many people tend to drift in and out of fitness, perhaps never really reaching a peak but never reaching a low either. You may train regularly and be in great shape, but then your schedule is disrupted. Six months later you've put on a few pounds and feel a little less energetic as that marginal erosion starts to take its toll.

If you take the decision at that point to step back into your fitness regimen, you can rekindle the process of marginal gains and get back to excellent health again. No matter what, a consistent and steadily increasing pace is the way towards greatness in anything, especially fitness.

If you're struggling to take action with this one, know you're not alone (not by a long shot). Find a fitness training 'buddy' from work or a 'virtual trainer' online, or join a local gym or hire a personal trainer, all great ways to keep you accountable. A cursory Google search will help you find a training programme for anything, and there are a broad range of apps that can assist you in setting goals and tracking progress in any kind of fitness activity.

Nutrition and wellbeing

'Every meal is a short-term investment in how you feel and perform, a mid-term investment in how you look, and a long-term investment in your freedom from disease.'

Alan Aragon

The saying goes that you are what you eat. If you eat unhealthily, you cannot expect good health to follow. If you eat well, good health becomes a much more likely outcome. As I said before, I am not a nutritionist but a student of health, and in particular my own. If I'm being honest, nutrition is the area where my Wellbeing Director needs to pay more attention.

I *could* spend this part of the chapter sharing top tips and ideas for your nutrition plan; the importance of drinking enough water, eating your five a day, why small meals on a regular basis are better than a big meal, especially late at night, or a whole host of other thoughts and ideas. But I'm not going to. My goal in getting you to think about your nutrition as an integral part of your overarching wellbeing is to simply shock you. Yes, you read that right; I want to shock you into action – in these three ways:

- First, by firmly imprinting the importance of nutrition on to your radar
- Second, by stacking the business case for why this is such an important area
- Third – if I have achieved the first and second goals – by strengthening your motivation enough for you to feel compelled to take action in creating your nutrition plan.

The obesity epidemic

There is a growing public health crisis that is global in scope, and it isn't another emerging infectious disease. It concerns being overweight and the adverse health consequences of obesity, which include type 2 diabetes, high blood pressure, heart disease and strokes, certain types of cancer, sleep apnoea, osteoarthritis and kidney disease.

Facts are a great leveller as they give you a real-time view. These are the facts as of October 2017:

- Worldwide obesity has nearly tripled since 1975.
- In 2016 more than 1.9 billion adults, 18 years and older, were overweight. Of these, over 650 million were obese.
- In 2016 39 per cent of adults aged 18 years and over were overweight and 13 per cent were obese.
- Most of the world's population live in countries where being overweight and obese kills more people than being underweight.
- There are more obese US adults than those who are just overweight. According to a study in *The Journal of the American Medical Association* (*JAMA*), the obesity rate among adult Americans was estimated at 32.2 per cent for men and 35.5 per cent for women.

- The UK is not in great shape either and is the most overweight nation in Western Europe, with levels of obesity growing faster than in the USA. The Organization for Economic Cooperation and Development (OECD) said that Britain was the sixth-worst country in its 35 member states, coming behind Mexico, the USA, New Zealand, Finland and Australia.

The stats for children make even more unpleasant reading:

- In 2016 41 million children under the age of five and over 340 million children and adolescents aged five to nineteen were overweight or obese.
- One-fifth of children aged ten to eleven are obese.
- The statistics for more than 1 million pupils across England show that 32.4 per cent of girls and 36.1 per cent of boys in the final primary school year are overweight or obese, while the figures for reception are 22.1 per cent and 23.1 per cent respectively.

It's no wonder the World Health Organization is calling it the obesity epidemic.

The solution

Obesity is preventable. Being overweight is preventable. It is entirely possible to reduce the incidence of diabetes, heart disease and cancer.

Fast-paced living does not have to equal junk food, eating on the go or missing meals. You have an obligation to yourself to create a healthy and balanced diet that includes a daily mix of fresh fruit and vegetables, and a mix of carbohydrates, fats and protein. The discipline is to stick to it until it becomes habitual and your default mode for how you eat and fuel your body.

Maintaining your wellbeing

'It's easier to stay well than to get well.'

Anon.

Common sense and making good decisions are a common thread throughout this chapter. Yet most of us don't take the time to do these things because we're busy, caught up in the stuff that is 'urgent' but not necessarily good for us. The challenge we have is that the world isn't structured for good decisions; it's structured for convenience. And convenience usually comes at a price.

- It takes time and effort to make a healthy salad, but just seconds to phone for a pizza to be delivered to your front door by a guy on a motorbike. It's obvious which is the easiest decision, but it's also crystal clear which is the best one.

- It takes discipline to go to the gym and work out as a means of unwinding and easing your mind and body out of a stressful day, but it's easier to just go home, flop on to the sofa and flick on the TV.

- It takes effort to wake up early and go for a run, meditate or read a few pages of a book before the day surges forward with all its demands.

Many of us have all the right intentions, but we somehow never manage to put these things at the top of our 'to do' list and translate them into meaningful actions.

Do you own a car, or have you owned one in the past? What do you do when it's due its service? Do you decide to leave it for a while longer or book it in? If you're like most people, you'd make the booking as the service comes around, without a second thought, because common sense says that is what is required to keep your car running smoothly.

And yet most people haven't been for a dental check-up or eye-test in years and will only go to see a doctor when something is broken. The reason is that most of us just don't value ourselves enough, putting others first and not making the time for ourselves. The result is bad health decisions.

If you've ever experienced poor health or someone close to you has, you'll understand why I am so fanatical about this. What if there are genetic problems in your family? What if there were something you could do right now to protect your future health?

Relaxation and recovery

'There is virtue in work and there is virtue in rest. Use both and overlook neither.'

Alan Cohen

One final suggestion to round off this chapter is to make sure you structure some downtime into your life. It's good to be focused and driven and to push yourself to excel – but it's also good to just do nothing. Being busy all the time is not sustainable. In fact, it's a perfect recipe for burnout, and burnout isn't just a metaphorical thing. If you've ever experienced it or witnessed anyone else hit the proverbial brick wall, it's very real and it's very difficult to recover from.

For me, there are two ways to unwind and recover from hard work: there is rest and there is relaxation, and the two aren't entirely the same. Rest and relaxation work hand in hand and it's important to invest time in both, in order to optimize your mental and physical health.

Rest

Rest is defined as where you cease work or movement in order to sleep or recover your strength. You rest when you are tired and when you go to sleep at night. Sleep and rest refresh your mind and repair your body. Most adults require between seven to eight hours of sleep each night. Without sufficient sleep, our bodies suffer a variety of physical and psychological impacts, including:

- impaired memory
- poor concentration and judgement
- lowered stress threshold
- reduced sociability and optimism
- changes in vital signs and slower tissue repair
- weight gain.

Relaxation

Relaxation, on the other hand, is the act of relaxing, and can be defined as the release of tension and the refreshment of the mind or body. Relaxation differs from rest in that relaxation is your mind's way of rejuvenating and ridding itself of stress.

Relaxation occurs while you are awake, and involves you engaging in activities that you enjoy. Relaxing has been shown to improve your mood and cognitive functions, such as decision-making and memory, and it lowers the risk of depression, anxiety and other heart-related issues.

> In order to give your best, you have to be at your best. If you do not look after yourself, who's going to do it for you?

The resilient you

Resilience determines whether you succeed or fail in life. It's true in sport, in business, entertainment, and it's true in your life.

Many of the early theories about resilience stressed the role of genetics. Some people are just born resilient, so the argument went. There's some truth to that, of course, but empirical evidence today shows that resilience can be learned. The reality is that sometimes in life you don't realize how much resilience you actually have until you are tested. As the saying goes: cometh the hour, cometh the man.

Developing resilience: three critical ingredients

There are many arguments around what makes one individual more resilient than the next. In my experience it comes down to three things;

- A unique ability to confront reality head on
- An unwavering belief that life is purposeful
- An uncanny ability to improvise and adapt.

A UNIQUE ABILITY TO CONFRONT REALITY HEAD ON

Individuals who possess a strong bias and a rich reservoir of personal resilience live their life in a constant state of reality. They don't bury their head in the sand when faced with challenging times. They don't go into denial hoping that a situation or scenario will just sort itself out. And they're never delusional about the magnitude of opportunities or challenges facing them. They simply have a unique ability to confront reality head on. They are what I call 'pragmatic optimists'.

A common belief is that resilience stems from an optimistic mindset. While that's true up to a point, it applies only when optimism doesn't distort reality. In extreme scenarios and situations, rose-tinted thinking can actually spell disaster.

When researching his 2001 book *Good to Great*, Jim Collins wanted to determine how companies transform themselves out of mediocrity. Collins had a hunch (a wrong hunch!) that resilient companies were filled with optimistic people. He tested out his thinking on Admiral Jim Stockdale, who was held prisoner and tortured by the Viet Cong for eight years.

Collins recalls:

> I asked Stockdale: 'Who didn't make it out of the camps?' And he said, 'Oh, that's easy. It was the optimists. They were the ones who said we were going to be out by Christmas. And then when that day passed, they said Easter, and then Fourth of July and out by Thanksgiving, and then it was Christmas again.' Then Stockdale turned to me and said, 'You know, I think they all died of broken hearts.'

In the business world, Collins found the same unblinking attitude shared by executives at all the most successful companies he studied. My own personal experiences, whether in business or personal life, show this too. Like Stockdale, resilient people have a sober and down-to-earth view of those parts of reality that matter for survival.

Now this is not to diminish optimism. When you're turning around a demoralized team or helping an individual going through a difficult time, a sense of optimism and possibility is a powerful tool. But for bigger challenges, a cool, calm, almost pragmatic sense of reality is critical to your success. This is why I see the resilient high achiever as a pragmatic optimist, where both characteristics work in positive tension to the benefit of each.

- Do you truly understand and accept the reality of your situation and scenarios you face both personally and professionally?
- Do you confront reality head on?

We all have a tendency to slip into denial as a coping mechanism. Facing reality is gruelling work. It can often be draining and emotionally wrenching. But once you're prepared to confront your reality, then you have a solid platform on which to build.

An unwavering belief that life is purposeful

In his book *Man's Search for Meaning* (1946), Viktor E. Frankl, an Austrian psychiatrist and Auschwitz survivor, described a pivotal moment in the concentration camp when he developed meaning therapy. He was on his way to work one day, worrying whether he should trade his last cigarette for a bowl of soup. He wondered how he was going to work with a new foreman whom he knew to be particularly sadistic. Suddenly he was disgusted by just how trivial and meaningless his life had become. He realized that, to survive, he had to find some purpose. Frankl did so by imagining himself giving a lecture after the war on the psychology of the concentration camp, to help outsiders understand what he had been through. Although he wasn't even sure he would survive, Frankl created goals for himself. In doing so, he succeeded in rising above the suffering. 'We must never forget that we may also find meaning in life even when confronted with a hopeless situation, when facing a fate that cannot be changed.'

This dynamic of meaning making and creating purpose is, most researchers agree, the way resilient people build bridges from their current state of reality to a compelling future state.

An uncanny ability to improvise and adapt

In one word, it's bouncebackability. Yes, you read that correctly. It is a real word, albeit a recent addition to the English dictionary. Its official definition is 'the ability to be successful after a period of failure'. It was first coined by ex-footballer Iain Dowie, when he was manager of Crystal Palace Football Club, who famously described his team as showing 'great bouncebackability'.

Behind any great success is years of dedication, trial and error, mistakes, successes and setbacks. Achievers don't always get it right and, yes, in some situations they might actually fail (or experience what others perceive as failure). I know in my life I have experienced stunning successes and some fantastic failures. But I view the failures as learning opportunities, stepping stones to the ultimate goal. And if plan A doesn't work, the great news is that there are 25 more letters in the alphabet.

Imagine bouncing a rubber ball; the harder the ball hits the ground, the higher it bounces back. That's bouncebackability!

You're going to take knocks, some days are going to feel like a train crash, and you will go down blind alleys. But if you have an ultimate destination in your mind's eye, a focused goal and purpose coupled with drive, determination and motivation, then, when you do fall over, you'll pick yourself up, dust yourself off, improvise, adapt and refocus on your goal.

That's personal resilience in action!

Being the whole package

Life really has two meaningful dimensions: length and quality. How long you live may not be in your hands, as we discussed in Chapter 8: Mortality motivation, but that doesn't mean it's out of your hands entirely. You can't be sure of lengthening your life, but you can certainly do things not to artificially shorten it.

Your quality of life is something you can control in so many ways. It's enough to make you feel really powerful. And who wouldn't want that feeling? Whatever you choose, please be sure you're willing to pay the worst price for it. Don't ever find yourself in the position of appreciating something only once it is gone.

Take action: achieve more

If you want it, make it happen

This chapter has explored the concept of wellbeing, digging deep into your Wellbeing Director role. This director is responsible for keeping your mind, body and soul in optimum shape as you pursue your definition of success.

Your health is fuelled by a number of critical components, including mindfulness, exercise, diet, relaxation (including healthy sleep), building your personal resilience plus more general maintenance and check-ups. I'd therefore argue that your Wellbeing Director is the most important director role of all. Without your health, you limit the performance of the other director roles and all the other ideas and strategies covered in this book.

I shared one Accelerator exercise (9.1), a mindful breathing technique designed to induce a relaxed state of mind, invaluable in reducing your body's response to stress:

1 Deeply inhale through your nose (for a count of 3), hold your breath (for a count of 2) and then exhale through your mouth (for a count of 4).

2 Try to extend the length of the cycle by inhaling through your nose (for a count of 5), holding your breath (for a count of 3) and then exhaling through your mouth (for a count of 5).

It isn't difficult ... we just need to remember to do it.

Your ability to overcome setbacks and get back into the game comes down to the resilient you. If you have the ability to confront reality head on, have an unwavering belief that your life is purposeful coupled with an uncanny ability to improvise and adapt, then you are building a resilient you – able to live the life you were meant to lead.

Financial freedom

'The philosophy of the rich versus the poor is this: the rich invest their money and spend what is left; the poor spend their money and invest what's left.'

Jim Rohn

It's true that money doesn't buy you happiness. But it does play a significant role in making it possible for you to enjoy the best the world has to offer.

Imagine you a few years from now, when most or even all of your financial goals have been achieved:

- You've bought your dream place in the sun to retire to. And it's mortgage free.

- You have no debts. Your money is yours to spend and invest as you see fit.

- Your children are at university, or have already completed their studies. Tuition fees are fully paid up at the beginning of each year because they were planned and budgeted for.

- And this morning, after breakfast, you and your partner will head off and strike another item off your bucket list of 'must see' places.

- Best of all, you've got the lifestyle you want and you'll never have to work again to maintain it. All thanks to great financial choices made over your lifetime.

Does that sound like you?

Your version might be slightly different, but I am sure you understand where I'm going with this. When you achieve a level of financial comfort where money is no longer a daily worry, life becomes an entirely different game.

It all starts with a plan, of course. And that plan begins with a clear definition.

What does financial freedom mean to you?

Financial freedom is a very personal thing. Just as you uncovered your personal definition of success in Chapter 3, Why success is not an accident; your definition of financial freedom is dependent on your particular aspirations and goals, your vision of the life you want to lead and why you want it.

When you created your definition of success, what part did money and finances play? This is your opportunity to carry out a reality check and make sure there is alignment. It's a virtual certainty that strong, stable finances are a key enabler to you living out your broader definition of success, both personally and professionally.

What does financial freedom look like to you? Is it:

- working because you want to, not because you have to?

- being so financially secure that you forget when payday is?

- having the freedom to choose a career you love without worrying about the salary or package it comes with?

- taking an international holiday every year without it straining your budget?

- responding to the needs of others with outrageous generosity, because you can?

- retiring a whole decade early?

- paying off your student loans/credit cards/ overdrafts so you're not being crippled by monthly interest payments?

- dropping the second job because your promotion covers the difference?
- scheduling the maternity/paternity leave you actually want off, not what you can afford to have off?

My definition of financial freedom is simply this: the ability to live the lifestyle I desire without having to work for or rely on anyone else for money.

> Living your life according to your own definition of financial freedom brings with it financial independence and options.

According to a 2018 Go Banking Rates survey, one in three Americans have no retirement savings, and among those who have saved, 56 per cent have less than $10,000. Given that most retirees cannot survive on social security payments alone, that paints a pretty bleak picture.

Figures from pension provider Royal London suggest that a 25-year-old wanting to retire at 65 on an income of £19,000 (including state pension) would need to save £370 per month. A 45-year-old would need to save £900 per month to achieve the same result.

Earning financial freedom for the future requires planning and discipline today, and the sooner you begin the better. Start early for less pain and more gain. Unless you win the lottery or come into an inheritance, the chance of you waking up one morning with the financial freedom you desire, with no planning or thought, is extremely low. If you're not conscious and deliberate in the choices you make today, you will have little or no understanding of how those choices can affect you tomorrow and into the future or – more importantly – whether they will bring you closer to your definition of financial freedom.

Confronting reality: the headwinds to navigate

Life is full of headwinds:

- People are living longer (average life expectancy in the UK is now 81.6 years), so you need to plan your finances so they stretch further.
- The cost of living is rising, at a rate of around 2 per cent year on year.
- Many families face the additional cost of supporting elderly parents or grandparents, reducing their ability to save.
- Pensions are always under threat and in many countries are being reduced. In 2018 the weekly pension paid by the UK government is £164.35, not enough to live on without being supplemented by additional income.
- Common investments are increasingly out of reach. The average property price in the UK is £226,351. With an average base salary of £27,200 (UK) that's more than a 12x multiplier, making it difficult for many to get on to the property ladder in the first place.
- We are paying for more things, such as university fees, as subsidies or allowances are reduced.

But the biggest headwind to face is your own relationship with money. A lot of what makes people 'good' with money or 'bad' with money is their mindset and their sense of worth.

Mindset and worthiness

Why do so many lottery winners end up doing nothing meaningful with their newfound wealth? Or worse, why do they allow it to ruin their lives, and end up broke just a few years later? The statistics are absolutely jarring. Lottery winners in the USA are more likely to declare bankruptcy within three to five years than the average American. The reason for this is twofold:

- **Mindset:** Bad spending habits mean they over-extend their cash flow and end up defaulting on commitments and repayments.

- **Worthiness**: Deep-rooted guilt that they don't deserve their sudden windfall means they succumb to every friend, relative and neighbour who comes to them with an extended hand.

You don't have to look very hard to uncover one story after another of how winning the lottery has ruined people's lives, caused unhappiness and depression and even increased the incidence of suicide.

Single mother Sharon Tirabassi won more than $10 million in 2004. She spent it all on a mansion, exotic cars, designer labels, entertaining her friends and family with sensational parties and expensive holidays, as well as giving cash gifts and loans to family and friends. Within a decade, all the money was gone and she was back to taking public transport to her day job to earn her rent.

William 'Bud' Post won $16 million in the Pennsylvania lottery in 1988. He found himself more than $1 million in debt just 12 months later, and describes the experience as a total nightmare. Bad investments, lost relationships, lawsuits and even the loss of his brother who took out a contract on his life, caused a year of turmoil for Post. Today he lives on food stamps.

It's not just lottery winners who struggle with mindset and worthiness around money. There's a long list of the once rich and famous who fell on hard times, through bad spending and money habits.

Shane Filan, lead singer of boy band Westlife, declared bankruptcy in 2012 after he lost more than £18 million in bad property deals. At one point, while he appeared incredibly successful, playing for crowds of 80,000 people, he had less than £500 in his bank account.

Mike Tyson, the legendary world heavyweight boxer, made more than £300 million in his career, but by 2003 he had turned it into a debt of more than £21 million and was unable to pay his bills. Sanford Ain, who represented Tyson's wife in a divorce battle, described Tyson's spending as 'inappropriate at best', adding that his troubles could be attributed to a lack of willpower and to allowing people to take advantage of him.

And the famous MC Hammer, of 'Can't Touch This' fame, went bankrupt when tax authorities caught up with him for lack of payment of nearly $800,000.

The list of others is long and distinguished: Sarah Ferguson, the Duchess of York; tennis legend Boris Becker and even Lady Gaga have at times had significant financial challenges due to overspending, bad investments and bad associations.

The lesson is that money isn't the solution to anything unless you have the right mindset and sense of worth because, as these stories show, you can easily end up sabotaging your own life and success.

What is worthiness?

We often confuse worthiness with being deserving. Are you worthy of the life you imagine in your definition of financial freedom, or are you deserving of it? Are you worthy of being wealthy, or deserving of it? Perhaps more directly, are you worthy of being loved by your soulmate, or are you deserving of it?

We're all worthy. Let's put that part to bed right away. Every one of us has the right to live a healthy life and to decide how we define success and financial freedom.

But are you deserving? That's a different conversation altogether. Worthiness is a birthright but being deserving is something you have to earn. You deserve wealth by making smart choices, being disciplined, and putting in the extra effort it takes to acquire wealth in the first place.

If you squander your wealth, no matter how much money you have made, you are no less worthy of the opportunities life has given you, but perhaps not deserving of them. To deserve something, you must be willing to take it seriously, work at it, be thoughtful and in tune with it, and willing to adapt and make hard choices.

Unfortunately, we often attribute the wrong measurements to determine whether or not we are deserving, many of which can negatively affect our ability to really achieve our goals:

1 **The people who surround you**

Some people define themselves by who they know rather than who they are. While there are tremendous benefits to being in a strong, supportive relationship, and it may be exciting to have rich, powerful or even famous friends, ultimately your value is measured by who *you* are, not who you associate with.

2 **What you do**

Some people define themselves by their career and, when you ask them about themselves, the first thing they'll talk about is their job. They run the risk of negative changes in their career bringing their own perceived status down with it. What you do is only one component of your whole being.

3 **How much money you have**

The whole focus of this chapter is financial freedom and defining what this means to you. If your quest is to simply have more and more, I doubt you'll ever be satisfied. With that mindset, even a billion pounds isn't enough if someone else has 10 billion.

4 **What you achieve**

Achievements are among the things that make us bountiful and complex beings, but they can be fleeting as someone else inevitably will do what you did faster, better or for longer. The pursuit of a big achievement can mean many failures along the way, and if achievement is your only measure, that can eat you alive.

5 **How you look**

It's no secret that the world celebrates beauty, but if achievements can be fleeting, youthful good looks go for double. Looks fade as time goes by and, ultimately, substance trumps beauty every time.

How what you feel affects your choices

How you measure your worth will greatly influence the decisions you make.

You can see the world two ways: as one of scarcity or one of abundance.

If the money lesson you learned growing up was one of scarcity, then it doesn't matter how much you earn, you perceive the act of 'buying things' as making you feel better. So we have this phenomenon of individuals living from pay day to pay day, stressed out because they are literally one pay day away from financial catastrophe. If they lose their job, the weight of their debts and commitments could be enough to leave them destitute.

On the other hand, an attitude of abundance often has precisely the opposite effect. When you focus on what you have, not on what you don't have, and appreciate the inherent value of money, you're less likely to spend it so casually.

It's one of the reasons the 'poor stay poor', as scarcity leads to poor money management as overcompensation, and why the 'rich get richer', as abundance leads to an appreciation of the value of money, not just the things it can buy.

Managing your money

The path to financial freedom and independence isn't achieved through a get-rich-quick strategy.

Most of us know what we're supposed to do when it comes to basic money management: spend less than you earn, save an emergency fund, and invest for the future and retirement. That's most people's entire financial strategy in 16 words. But – and it's a big but – establishing your own person-alized financial strategy, developing good money habits and sticking to them are always easier said than done.

How you manage, spend, and invest your money will have a profound impact on your life, and yet even though the basics are fairly simple (the 16 words in the previous para-graph), very few schools teach these important life skills. While this may be a missed opportunity for school leavers, it doesn't have to be this way for you.

If you're not on the pathway to great money manage-ment yet, here's how to get started.

Accelerator exercise 10.1: Manage your finances

One of the questions for the Finance Director role in your Me Unlimited exercise is: do you have too much month at the end of the money or too much money at the end of the month? You won't get ahead if you don't have a plan for your money. Instead, you'll find yourself wondering where your money went at the end of every month.

That's not financial independence; that's a recipe for financial disaster. If you're married, get on the same page as your partner about your budget. If you're single, find an accountability partner to help keep you on track.

Track your spending

First, focus on *how* you spend, not *how much* you spend. Give every amount you spend a name to allow you to track your spending. For example, this amount is for rent/mort-gage, this amount is for food, this amount is for electricity and insurances, this amount is for school fees or child care, this amount is for trips out and so on.

Once you've labelled every item of expenditure, you can now create groupings or categories of similar items, for example household running costs, entertainment, education/child care. These categories will be a combination of fixed monthly costs and variable/discretionary spend.

Create a budget

Now you know what you're spending your money on within each category, you're in a position to start creating a budget.

Budgeting is important to get your finances on the right track, but it doesn't end there. No matter how much money you have, you need a budget and you need to review it on a regular basis. This regular review will allow you to identify any overspend or underspend in a particular category, identify any challenges and make any required adjustments to either your budget or your expenditure.

This is where the discipline of Me Unlimited can serve you well. The key monthly report that you as the Finance Director should be making is your performance against your financial budget and what your expenses for the month are.

You won't achieve financial independence by accident. Budgeting, sticking to your plan and frequent review are the first step to *building your wealth*.

Accelerator exercise 10.2: Clean up your finances

In the process of managing your money, you may realize that you've made some past mistakes with your finances. That's OK! But if you're striving for financial independence, you have to clean up the mess. It won't simply go away on its own.

If you have short-term debts such as credit cards, student loans or car loans, it's time to get serious about kicking them to the curb. This is because, while you owe money, your pay cheques have someone else's name on them. If you want to reach your financial freedom goal, you need your full income at your disposal, not bits and pieces that are left over after paying credit card and loan interest.

Paying off these types of debt helps you lay a foundation to build wealth that will last. And once you're debt free, stay there for good! Having debt undermines your ability to build wealth and puts your financial freedom at risk. It's simple. Steer clear of debt, particularly the kind with high interest charges that you never seem to be able to get on top of.

Attack your debt with discipline and rigour with any extra cash, until it's gone. Discipline here is the key word as it is so easy to 'treat yourself' – to a new outfit, an additional night out or some other discretionary spend. No, paying off your debt should be your highest priority.

Paying off debt is hard work, but there's nothing like the feeling of actually keeping the money you bring in every month!

Audit your outgoings

Deep dive into each category of expenditure you created in Accelerator exercise 10.1 to get a real understanding of what it is and why you're paying it. Are you paying a monthly gym membership that you haven't used for the past six months? Are you paying for a yearly subscription that auto-renews and have long since forgotten? What standing orders or direct debits are still on your account that need cancelling? Many of us have one or more scenarios like these draining our finances, even if only in small amounts. This is money that could be put to better use.

Clean sweep your finances

Monitor your outgoings. Pay off your short-term debts. Set a realistic monthly budget. The powerful idea is this: when you clean sweep these things – put them in order or delete what needs to be eliminated from your life – you will feel lighter and happier and your mind will experience more calmness and peace. Why? Because you are in control of your finances. While they might not give you your definition of financial freedom yet, you now have a solid foundation on which to build.

Most people feel as if they have got a pay rise when they start budgeting. Suddenly, as your money starts to be used in the most constructive way or you begin challenging what you spend it on, it goes further.

Once you have got a grip on your finances, start to save small amounts each month and put to one side a contingency/emergency/rainy day fund – whatever you want to call it. Nothing derails a financial budget like an unexpected expense. When the washing machine suddenly stops working or your car's gear box packs up, you've suddenly got to find money, and if you don't have any cash to hand, you know where it's going to come from, don't you? Yes, a loan or a credit card, with interest attached, so your unexpected £500 expense is actually £600 or £700 by the time you've paid it off.

Saving a small amount each month will soon mount up and it will act as your buffer if and when an unexpected cost raises its ugly head.

Accelerator exercise 10.3: Stop comparing yourself to others

What I've shared with you in the first two Accelerator exercises are skills relevant to your money management. However, they would not be complete without addressing your mindset.

In this age of social media, reality TV and celebrity magazines, it's far too easy to get sucked into making comparisons and trying to 'keep up with the Joneses'. You don't know the intimate details of the other person's finances or broader life. Someone may appear to have a fantastic life filled with fabulous clothes, vacations and other fun stuff, but it could be fueled by credit card debt, or worse. If you need a real-life example, check out the *Real Housewives of New Jersey*. All that glitters is not gold.

When you expend unnecessary energy making comparisons, you divert attention away from focusing on your own finances and aspirations. Create attainable goals for yourself and compare yourself only to those goals and how you are doing in relation to those. Celebrate your wins and update your goals as you reach them.

> The only person you should focus on and who should hold you to account is your future self. If you can make that person feel proud of who you are becoming, then you've made a significant step on your journey to success.

Aligning your definition of success and your financial goals

You'll undoubtedly need to know the level of financial resources required to turn your definition of success into reality. The next important step is determining what your financial goals need to deliver in order to realize it.

For example, if you want to retire at 55, you would need answers to three questions to help you validate the alignment between your financial goal and your current reality:

1 What amount of money will you need to enable you to retire at 55?

2 What are your current financial projections for getting you there?

3 Is there a gap and how realistic is it that you will be able to bridge that gap?

In reading this, I know that Jane, my wife, would say 'Royston, there is no way you're going to retire at 55; you love what

223

you do too much.' And she is probably right. But knowing the answers will give me financial freedom and choices. I might not retire fully, but I might decide I want to take more holidays, or work four days a week or play more golf. I want the choice to decide to continue to work because I want to, not because I have to.

Paul Armson wrote a great book entitled: *Enough? How Much Money Do You Need for the Rest of Your Life?* In the introduction he talks about the fact that the majority of people have no idea where they are heading financially. They may have assets, investments and/or high levels of income, but most people have no idea what it all means or what sort of financial future awaits them.

On the one hand, you don't want to retire too early, only to discover that your money runs out. On the other hand, you don't want to retire too late and end up working when you could have been playing. And the one thing you definitely don't want is for the taxman to take a huge chunk of your hard-earned money on your death because you were naive and didn't take the necessary steps to protect your wealth.

We all need to be able to answer this question: How much money do you need for the rest of your life? And the secondary question would be 'And for what?' And a third question: over what timeline?

- At what age do you want to retire?
- What are your base living costs?
- At what age will you repay your mortgage?
- What dependants do you still have/will you have (children, parents)?
- What one-off costs might be coming your way? (It might be a deposit to help your children on to the property ladder, to pay for weddings and bringing up grandchildren.)

- What education fees will you need to help pay for and for how long?

- What if your health declines and you need care? What if you need to stop working earlier than intended?

These are just examples to get your mind thinking, but they only skim the surface. If you don't know how much money you need for the rest of your life, your number, your key action from this chapter is to work it out.

Accelerator exercise 10.4: Determine your number

Paul Armson shares a powerful financial model, simplified as a bucket with a series of inflows at the top and a series of taps, representing outflows, at the bottom. The model walks you step by step through how to calculate your number.

With his permission, we have created an extract of this model from his book *Enough?* which is available for you to download in the *Rise* toolkit: https://www.roystonguest.com/RISE-toolkit/

Of course, you can also seek other external support, a financial adviser or pensions adviser, who will ask the right questions to help you determine your number.

Once you understand your number, ask yourself these questions to work back from the end goal:

- What provisions do you currently have in place?

- If you project them forward will they meet your number?

- If not, what are you going to do to bridge the gap?

This is where your money mountains come into play.

Your four money mountains

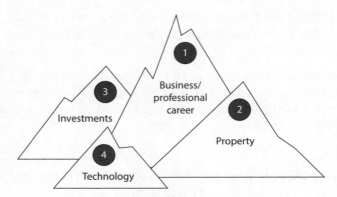

FIGURE 10.1 The four money mountains

Figure 10.1 shows the framework and approach I have been using for over a decade and it helps me shape my financial thinking. It comprises four mountains, which represent the four biggest influencers of wealth creation, and which together form a rounded, balanced and integrated financial plan.

Money mountain 1: Business/professional career

There are a number of different approaches you can take here, and the great news is that your strategy doesn't have to be confined to just one. You could be full-time or part-time employed, self-employed as a sole proprietor, or a business owner with ambitions to grow and scale your business and employ multiple people.

You could start out on a pathway of being employed, but make the switch to self-employed or building a business further down the line. Let's look at the different options in turn.

EMPLOYED

You need to be smart about your career choices. Since your biggest wealth-building tool is your income, the career you choose with have a direct correlation to the amount you earn and can potentially earn. Some careers have income ceilings – the maximum amount you'll ever be able to earn irrespective of how good you are. Others operate with uncapped bonus potential.

Of course, in an entry-level position you may not always have the luxury of choice, but as your career progresses you should benefit from growth in your income. There is absolutely no good reason to be stuck in a dead-end job over the long term, because ultimately you're trading your time every day you turn up there. Time is precious, and you need to get the most from your days.

For that very reason, although this is a chapter on financial freedom, money shouldn't be the only consideration when choosing a career. While a high salary or exceptional bonuses will directly contribute to your wealth creation in the short term, you also need to take into the account the trade-offs you'll make over the longer term. If there aren't any, then congratulations, you've just found your dream job.

So what should you look for? Here are a few things to keep in mind:

- **Where do you want to be in ten years?** Start with the end in mind. Does this job align with your overall goals?

- **Is there income-earning potential?** Even if you're not making your dream salary from the start, make sure there is opportunity for your income to increase as your value and contribution increase.

- **Can you grow?** Are there opportunities for you to move up and grow, personally and professionally?

- **Do you enjoy the work?** Don't spend a career at a job you hate. Find something you're passionate about that allows you to use your gifts and skills.

- **Do the benefits support your goals of financial freedom?** Your options for retirement savings and

health insurance can dramatically affect your
ability to build wealth.

- **Will it give you the work/life balance you desire?**
Your choice of career will have a big impact on
your long-term financial goals, so take it seriously.

Self-employed and sole proprietor

You may opt to start out on your own. The obvious challenge
with this is that when times get tough, which they will, being
on your own can be a daunting, overwhelming and often
lonely place. You're working all the hours, weekends and holidays for some crazy boss – you.

But, of course, the benefits outweigh the challenges
because otherwise why would you do it? Being in control of
your own destiny, being in a position to make the final decisions or all the decisions, avoiding office politics, and ultimately
knowing you have flexibility in your working day are all the
draws which pull people towards becoming self-employed.

Be mindful of the discipline required to manage your time
and where you draw your lines in the sand. You may find
you've got a tougher job on your hands, with less freedom
and less money than you would have if you simply took a job.

That said, those who manage self-employment well say
there are many benefits, so it's definitely worthy of consideration.

Building a business or two ... the entrepreneurial itch

Entrepreneurship is living a few years of your life like most
people won't, so you can spend the rest of your life like most
people can't. As a result, it's not for everyone.

In my business growth book, *Built to Grow*, I reference the
phenomenon identified by management guru Michael Ger-
ber of the technician with an entrepreneurial seizure. This is
an employee with high-level technical skills who believes they
could do as well or even better if they started a business offering services that capitalized on those skills. On the surface

it seems like sound thinking, but you don't have to dig very far to discover a fundamental problem: the world of business and the application of technical skills are very different things.

It's also common to underestimate how hard it is to build a business. Where motivational gurus will tell you that going out on your own is about freedom and control and commanding your own destiny, many entrepreneurs discover that the initial stages are about loneliness, anxiety, sleepless nights, pressure, and perhaps even keeping a growing army of debt collectors at bay. The broad and diverse facets of building and running a business can be brutal and, unless there is a compelling reason to put yourself through it, it may be impossible to stay the distance.

But in terms of building real wealth, growing a business is, hands down, the most effective method. Some of the richest people in the world have achieved their wealth through growing their business:

- Jeff Bezos founded Amazon
- Bill Gates co-founded Microsoft
- Warren Buffett grew Berkshire Hathaway
- Bernard Arnault grew LVMH
- Mark Zuckerberg co-founded Facebook
- Amancio Ortega founded Inditex fashion group.

Substantial wealth comes from building a business that can scale.

Money mountain 2: Property

Your home should be part of your plan for financial freedom, not something holding you back from achieving it. It's so important to make wise decisions about the kind of home you purchase and how you choose to finance it. If you buy a home that is a good investment, it will continue to grow in value over the years.

In the UK, if you take a snapshot from January 2005 when the average UK house price was £150,488, to January 2017 when it was £218,255, that's a whopping 45 per cent return over the 12-year period. Property can and does yield healthy returns and significant capital growth, so choosing one that helps you build your financial freedom is just good sense.

Here are four golden rules for ensuring that property is an integral part of your financial freedom plan.

RULE 1: LOCATION, LOCATION, LOCATION

There's a UK TV programme called *Location, Location, Location*. The programme, presented by Phil Spencer and Kirstie Allsopp, helps people find their perfect home and it's all about the property location.

Buying your home should be a head as well as heart decision. Your home is much more than a simple financial decision; it's the source of so many memories depending on what life stage you're in: your brand-new starter home or where you'll raise your children or where you'll live out your days.

In the past I have bought new properties on new developments and in great locations, in the early phases of development. Yes, there has often been the downside that I lived in what felt like a building site, but I was always able to lock in great value at the beginning by getting the property at its lowest possible price with all the potential to come when the site was complete.

RULE 2: SPECULATE TO ACCUMULATE

I have a builder friend who, with his wife, buys houses that need serious renovation. And I mean *serious* work. They almost take them back to a shell and virtually start again. They live in them while the work is going on, and spend their evenings and weekends working on them. Having renovated four houses, and each time increasing the value of a property by an average of £200,000, they have been able to afford their forever house.

If you have the energy, the time and the vision, speculating to accumulate is a great way to increase wealth!

Rule 3: Pay down your mortgage

Paying off your mortgage is a huge milestone in your journey to financial freedom. Providing you're able to pay additional lump sums without incurring any fees, you should use any extra money coming in to reduce your mortgage by either the monthly amount or the years remaining.

Rule 4: Build a property portfolio

Owning properties that generate rent, or which are likely to increase in value, is a great way to increase your wealth. But just as there are upsides, there are downsides which need careful consideration: you need liquid capital to invest so you're not simply building a large debt, you need cash flow to cover any shortfall in rent, and you need to decide whether to commission a letting agent or do it yourself.

Also, with tenants (or letting agencies) to manage, properties to maintain and fix when things go wrong and legal obligations to comply with, there are many challenges you should be ready for. Only enter this route if you have your eyes wide open.

Money mountain 3: Investments

Make your money make more money. The skill of achieving financial freedom is your ability to convert earned income into passive income and/or portfolio income. I am not a financial adviser; in fact, I hire financial advisers to advise me, so what I'm offering here is simply my perspective.

Make your money work for you – it does not sleep, get tired or go on vacation. Properly invested money earns more money over time. Don't lock all your cash away in a low or zero-interest savings account. Invest your money so you earn more than you had before. Sometimes that's an investment account, but sometimes it's starting a business, or investing in that business or getting qualified to be able to get a better-paid job.

They say that the best time to start investing, however you choose to do it, is ten years ago. The second best time is right now.

One of the best pieces of advice I can offer you is to find a great financial adviser or specialist expert who will help you create your plan. An expert will be able to explain a financial strategy that even a layperson can understand. They'll be able to advise you on the best strategy for your future, with fixed goals in mind, no matter where you are right now.

A great financial adviser will also raise the importance of having a will. Do you have one in place? If you are single and it's just you, it may not matter too much because if anything happened to you, there are no dependants. But it's a real risk for those who depend on you if you don't have your affairs in order. The lack of a will can throw your affairs into total chaos and reduce the financial security and freedom you have worked to achieve.

A financial adviser or specialist expert will advise on all these things and much more: maximizing tax allowances, preparing for tax charges (inheritance, capital gains tax, and so on), protecting your current income from critical illness or death, setting up a child's university fund, and the list goes on.

Money mountain 4: Technology

This may seem like an unusual addition to the money mountains, but there's no doubt that technology can be a significant wealth creator for anyone who embraces it. It's certainly a massive playing field leveller.

My daughter Eloise, five years old at the time of writing, watches video blogs of several different youngsters who have their own YouTube media channel. Eloise, along with thousands of followers worldwide, watches these youngsters open and play with toys that the 'advertisers' have kindly sent them, they discuss the latest 'toy' trend and demonstrate how to play with it. It's insane when you actually think about it.

Today you can create a business in the back room of your house, and over time turn it into a global business that makes money while you sleep. There has never been a time like this for aspiring entrepreneurs.

I have a school friend who is a lawyer today. When GDPR (General Data Protection Regulation) was coming into force in the European Union at the beginning of 2018, she saw an opportunity and turned it into something really spectacular. Recognizing that GDPR represented a burning platform for many business owners, in particular small business owners, my friend decided to set up a Facebook group to advise, guide and support business owners on this topic. She committed to a daily video, either live or recorded, every single day from early February to 25 May 2018.

Within three months, she had acquired 36,195 Facebook group members. She offered for sale a GDPR toolkit, containing templates, policies and other supporting documents. I asked my own lawyers how much they would charge for a similar thing and it was in excess of £4,500. My friend sold hers for £197 (It started out at £97). While I don't know the actual numbers, I'm a businessman so can easily guesstimate some conversions. I would say, as a conservative measure, that over that 12-week period, sales were probably over £1,000,000. That's from scratch!

If you had any doubts about the importance of technology in this mix before, hopefully they have now been laid to rest. There are so many opportunities today where using technology can help generate secondary revenue streams.

Airbnb is another great example. As we have seen, the greatest asset many people own is their home. Airbnb has made it possible to generate a secondary income stream when you are away on holiday or out of town on business or have a spare room. Some people are making a serious amount of additional income through this platform.

While it's not for everyone, what it demonstrates is the need to think differently about how you can maximize and capitalize on opportunities available to all.

I am so passionate about the whole technology revolution that I have already asked how soon my young children can start to learn coding. I want them to learn the skill as early in life as they can. It's going to be a game changer for those who can code. And I fear that those who can't will be left behind.

Achieving financial freedom

Financial freedom is much more than just being able to cover unexpected emergencies without breaking a sweat. It's about doing the things you want to do, visiting the places you want to see and leading the life you were meant to live.

It's also about having enough to leave a legacy for your family, your children and their children. To get to that point in the future, you have to think and plan for it today.

Take action: achieve more

How much money do you need for the rest of your life?

This chapter has examined the role financial freedom plays in helping you achieve your goals and the importance of making good money choices. It is much more than just being able to cover unexpected emergencies without breaking a sweat. It's about doing the things you want to do, visiting the places you want to see and leading the life you were meant to live.

I shared four money management Accelerator exercises to help you think and plan for your future today:

Accelerator exercise 10.1 Examine your spending patterns and create a monthly budget to help you manage your money.

Accelerator exercise 10.2 Clean up your finances and take charge of any waste and inefficiencies in your spending.

Accelerator exercise 10.3 Stop comparing yourself with others. Set goals for your own life, making your finances only about you, aligning them with your definitions of success.

Accelerator exercise 10.4 Determine your number – the amount of money you need for the rest of your life, for what and over what timeline.

Shape your financial thinking using the money mountains concept, the four biggest influencers of wealth creation: business/professional career, property, investments and technology, which together will form the bedrock to helping you achieve your financial freedom goals.

Transformational visioning and goal-setting

'The tragedy of life doesn't lie in not reaching your goal.
The tragedy lies in having no goals to reach.'

Benjamin Mays

Where do you want to be by the end of this year, personally and professionally? What about in five or ten years, or perhaps by the time of your next milestone birthday? Wherever it is, whatever you want to achieve, your success is inherently based on actively working towards it in a structured and systematic way, with passion and drive and with the ultimate goal clearly in your mind.

Earl Nightingale, author of *The Strangest Secret* (1976), called it the progressive realization of a worthy accomplishment. In a nutshell, that's what this chapter is about.

A fresh perspective

I'm going to take an educated guess that you may not be overly enthusiastic about a whole chapter focused on goal setting, particular since this very topic is well covered both in print and online. If that is the case, I've got some great news. I have a number of fresh, original and challenging insights to offer, which I know are going to add real strength to your toolset, your determination and, ultimately, your success.

The approach I've taken over the years is to ensure that the practice of goal setting is steeped in massively transformative energy, not just a tick-box exercise with a little guilt attached because you think it's the right thing to do. Instead, you'll approach it as a discipline that propels you to success by the sheer scale of its conscious and subconscious power.

By this I mean that, while many goal-setting techniques are technically accurate, they often lack a few critical elements which I've discovered lead to real tangible and sustained success. The *Rise* approach is different because it will enable you to hotwire your goals to the absolute essence of your being; to think about them from an emotional, not just a logical, perspective so that every conscious and subconscious decision you make is linked to the attainment of your goals.

Many goal-setting techniques will advise you to revisit your goals regularly to keep them on track. I believe it's immensely more powerful when your goals live inside you, not outside you. That's the importance of the additional component: 'transformational visioning'.

What else is different?

I'll share a hot new take on the traditional concept of SMART goals, going deeper and adding more energy and commitment to the process. I call it C-SM²ART and I'm excited to explain this latest thinking with you in this chapter.

Few success practices are as important as articulating your most closely held goals and then reviewing them daily. Becoming an expert at setting and then considering your goals on a consistent basis is essential to a life of greatness. And yet most people don't spend more than an hour a year doing this. It's true. People spend more time planning their summer vacations than they do designing their lives.

As the architect of your own destiny, it's the Planning Director's responsibility to paint a compelling picture of your future. This in turn sparks all the other director roles into action towards its attainment.

So let's start with the 'why' of transformational visioning and goal setting.

Seven reasons why setting goals is critical to success

In the Lewis Carroll classic *Alice's Adventures in Wonderland*, there's a telling exchange between Alice and the sinister Cheshire Cat:

> One day Alice came to a fork in the road and saw a Cheshire cat in a tree.
> 'Which road do I take?' she asked the cat.
> 'Where do you want to go?' was his response.
> 'I don't know,' Alice answered.
> 'Then,' said the cat, 'it doesn't matter.'

Having a direction gives you something to aim at; a purpose and meaning to your actions and a means of measuring whether you're on track and how much progress you're making.

Without one, as the Cheshire Cat says, you can just walk in any random direction along any pathway.

1 Goals create focus and direction

Where focus goes, energy flows. As human beings, we have an abundance of latent potential just waiting to be unlocked. Focused goals are the magic key to unlocking the door to the source of power: all your resources, including your mindset, physiology and whole being, hotwired to the attainment of your biggest, boldest dreams and goals. Goals breed focus.

2 Goals give your life meaning and purpose

The first question you ask yourself in the morning, and every subsequent question during the day, is answered for you when you have goals. Why am I getting up? What am I going to do first? What is the order and attitude of the day going to be? Why does it matter?

Goals infuse your life with purpose and meaning, giving you the knowledge that you're on the right path to the attainment of your biggest ideals.

3 Goals challenge you to grow

Goals are the enabler for personal growth. They take you outside your comfort zone. I challenge you to set goals that make you feel 'comfortably uncomfortable', stretching the boundaries of your own possibilities and allowing you to become the best you can be.

4 Goals drive you to take action

It's easy to drift in life and sleepwalk through your days. If you don't act on life, life has a habit of acting on you. With goals fixed, you dictate the pace, the cadence and the rhythm. Whether it's billionaires, entrepreneurs, captains of industry, elite athletes or anyone else at the top of their game, one of the primary traits of great people is that they are action oriented. They just make stuff happen. Their days are consumed with thinking about their biggest, boldest goals, *and* a relentless drive to take daily actions that turn them into reality.

5 Goals allow you to keep score

What's the difference between Lewis Hamilton achieving pole position in a Formula One race and ending up on the second row of the grid? Or Usain Bolt winning Olympic gold in the 100-metre race rather than coming second, or even fifth? It's often no more than one-tenth of a second.

In sport and in life, tiny fractions of time or distance make the difference between a medal and no medal. Achieving success is often about zeroing in and managing those tiny fractions, hunting out places where you can make marginal gains. To put it simply: people who keep records break records.

In life, you've got to keep score. It enables you to measure the distance between your position today and the point at which you began. These quantifiable milestones will build momentum and continue to motivate you towards your end game.

6 Goals allow you to replicate your successes

In Chapter 3, I introduced the concept of success formulas; a formula that is replicable will allow you to deliver predictable, repeatable, sustainable results every time. The great news is that there is a formula for setting goals, too, and it's a formula that, as I'll demonstrate later in this chapter, I can guarantee you will have used at least once in your life already. The moment you raise your conscious awareness of it, you can start replicating it in other areas of your life for accelerated success.

7 Goals offer inspiration

Goals breathe life into your days. We all have days when we wake up a little groggy, where everything feels like the movie *Groundhog Day*, and when our enthusiasm and motivation just haven't kicked in yet. But the moment you switch your attention to your personal 'why', your definition of success, your goals, you press an ignition switch that sparks you into action.

The very act of articulating your goals on a crisp white piece of paper causes you to step into a whole new world of possibility for what your life can become.

- Setting your goals is a statement that you refuse to be ordinary
- Setting your goals is a bold play for your best life
- Setting your goals is an act of heroism because you are reaching for the potential sitting inside you. As Mark Twain noted: 'If everyone was satisfied with themselves there would be no heroes.'

Even stacking all the benefits and creating the 'why' for goal setting fills me with nervous excitement, pricks my conscious mind and ignites my energy levels to make my own goals happen. And that's even before we've covered the 'what' and the 'how'.

Thinking from your goals

Let's keep the pace with this chapter and talk about transformational visioning – the critical component of your entire goal-setting journey, but so often missed.

The key guiding principle is aptly captured in this expression:

Don't think of your goals ... think from your goals.

What does that mean? Read it a few times and give it some thought.

I consider myself to be fortunate as this principle was drilled into me from a young age. At 16, I left school for an apprenticeship in construction. I always remember the first project I worked on, a brand-new hospital in the North-west English city of Liverpool. On the day we 'cut the turf', as the ceremony was known, I stood on a green field with the architect, the structural engineer and the client. I held in my hand an artist's impression of what the hospital was going to look like two and a half years into the future when it was finished.

All construction projects are created that way, with a diagram, a plan, a blueprint and a drawing of the finished building. And what happens every day after is a step-by-step execution of the plan to create in exact detail the reality depicted in the picture. The hundreds of people responsible for the project are not thinking of what it could look like when it is done; they're thinking of what it already looks like and working backwards to ensure that future reality comes true.

They're not thinking *of* their goals; they're thinking *from* their goals.

Just imagine if you had that level of clarity and focus – that you had a clear picture of what your life looks like, feels like and acts like at a defined future moment in time. And with that new level of focus and belief, you return to your current reality with a detailed plan for precisely how you're going to bridge the gap between where you are now and where you want to be.

That's the difference between thinking *from* your goals, not *of* your goals.

Goals

From the golf course ...

Star golfer Jack Nicklaus, revered as one of the greatest golfers of all time, used to tell the story that, with every single shot he played, whether it was a practice round or a critical shot in a Masters, he would imagine a series of movie clips of what was about to happen. First, he'd see the ball rolling towards the hole and then dropping in. Then, in his second clip, he'd see the contours the ball was moving along and the speed it was moving as it traversed the green in order to drop into the hole. The third clip was the trajectory that the ball took from the fairway in order to land softly on the green. The final clip was the swing projection he would need to create in order to get the ball to fly right into the optimum part of the fairway for him to approach the green.

He would work backwards from the goal, covering the various steps one by one, in reverse order until he knew exactly how to begin. He wasn't thinking *of* his goal; he was thinking *from* his goal.

... to Silicon Valley ...

Microsoft founder Bill Gates is another who thought *from* his goals, even though his vision wasn't even technically possible when he started out in the mid-1970s. His vision from the early days of Microsoft was a home computer in every house across the world, operating a Microsoft operating system.

That big vision is an example of transformational visioning and goal setting: thinking *from* your goals, not *of* your goals.

... to music

Music superstar Ed Sheeran is one of the best-selling artists in the world. You may look at this young artist and see an overnight success, but what may surprise you is that he's been focused on his music career since the age of four. He found his direction after listening to an Eminem album at the age of ten, dropping out of school to pursue a music career in London at just 14. He left behind a school experience characterized by relentless bullying over his red hair, his big glasses and his lazy eye and speech impediment, the results of an operation gone wrong.

This artist, who today is friends with the likes of Taylor Swift and Jamie Foxx, wins music awards and accolades and has a worldwide fan base, was sleeping in the London Underground and on park benches at the age of 15.

He says he was often asked why he didn't go and get a proper job to earn money rather than sleeping on park benches, and his answer may challenge you to sit up and think about the energy and focus you put into your own goals. He says: 'I never wanted to lose the hunger and focus to make it in the music industry, that's all I ever wanted to do and be, a musician who could move people through lyrics and music.'

Ed Sheeran had a transformational vision of his future. He was thinking *from* his goals, not *of* them. Today we all know him and appreciate his talent. His transformational vision has become his reality, through relentless focus, self-belief and, most of all, brave and consistent action.

You get to visit the future

The really exciting part in *thinking FROM your goals* is that you get to go and check out your future. It's a kind of 'try before you buy': you build a crystal-clear picture in your mind's eye of what it looks like, feels like and acts like. It's your opportunity to reconnect with your dreams and jumpstart your personal transformation.

Transformation, however, doesn't just happen. It takes a plan and a support system. It needs the 'what' and 'how' of transformational visioning and goal setting.

The 'what': your bucket list

A bucket list is, by definition, a list of things you want to do before you die. The term was made popular by the 2007 movie *The Bucket List*, where Morgan Freeman and Jack Nicholson (both of whose characters are dying of cancer) travel around the world with a wish list of things to see and do before they die. If you've seen the movie, you may have had a poignant moment when you realized that the main characters were only making a real effort to achieve their biggest goals because they had been diagnosed with terminal illnesses and time was running out.

There is a really important life lesson here for all of us. You know my passionate belief on this subject from reading Chapter 8: Mortality motivation. You shouldn't wait until your doctor tells you that you're running out of time. This should not be the catalyst to start to achieve your goals or make your dreams come true.

Unfortunately, though, life is sometimes lived backwards. When you're young and have your health and a long road ahead of you, you're often so busy building your career and trying to earn money that you put off your dreams until later. When you're older and you have the money, you may not have the health or the time to pursue them.

You don't have to be in the last months or years of your life to put together a bucket list and start pursuing it. In fact, that's the worst time to do it. If you start writing down the goals you truly want to achieve while you have the luxury of time to execute them, you can start chasing your dreams right now.

Creating perfect moments

While *The Bucket List* movie was fiction, there are many real-world examples that really add urgency and weight to the idea of pursuing your dreams right now, rather than putting them off.

What if you suddenly found yourself having to chase daylight? At 53, Eugene O'Kelly found himself having to do just that. As Chairman and CEO of KPMG (US), O'Kelly was in the full swing of his life, enjoying a successful career and drawing happiness from his wife, children, family and close friends. His mind was consumed with vibrant, lively matters such as his next business trip, the firm's continued success, weekend plans with his wife, and his daughter's first day in eighth grade. But after a three-month tour of KPMG offices worldwide, he returned feeling unwell. He initially put it down to stress and jetlag, but when it didn't improve, he went for a check-up with his doctor.

On 24 May 2005 everything changed. Eugene O'Kelly stepped into his doctor's surgery with a full calendar and a lifetime of plans on his mind. He walked out having discovered he had an inoperable brain tumour that would end his life within the next 100 days. The morning after, he wrote a bucket list of all the things he wanted to do, the conversations he wanted to complete with people, the friends he wanted to visit, the holiday he wanted to take with his wife and the quality time he wanted to spend with his family.

Six days later he resigned as CEO of KPMG. His lifetime of plans was concentrated into just 100 days, just enough time to complete his bucket list. *Chasing Daylight* is O'Kelly's honest, touching and ultimately inspirational memoir, completed in the three and a half months between his diagnosis with brain cancer and his death in September 2005. The book's haunting, yet extraordinarily hopeful voice, reminds us to embrace the fragile and fleeting moments of our lives, such as the time we have with our family, our friends and even ourselves.

What if you suddenly found yourself chasing daylight, with only 100 days left? What would you do? I know that the only 100-day plans I'm used to creating are business plans but this is a stark reminder that life is for living in the now, and the one thing you can never take for granted is life and, in particular, your health.

If you were to create a 100-day plan of all the things you want to do, people you want to spend time with, and things you want to say, what would be in it? It doesn't matter how big or small they are, just make sure you do them now.

My big takeaway from *Chasing Daylight* was something O'Kelly called Perfect Moments; waking up to see the sun rising, the sound of the birds, the gentle breeze blowing against your face, the conversation with a loved one, the laughter with a child, the air of excitement for what the day has in store. It resonated with me because it highlights that, in a world where the big things make little difference, it's the little things that make a big difference.

What's on your bucket list?

Making a bucket list is easy. You simply write down the things you've always wanted to do but that you've never got around to doing, things like bungee jumping, skydiving, travelling to Rome or learning Spanish. Things that for whatever reason you have put on hold until 'some day'.

It doesn't have to be just a list of things you want to do. Your bucket list can also include Big Hairy Audacious Goals (BHAGs) as James Collins calls them in *Built to Last*, like playing the top 12 golf courses in the world, visiting Lapland at Christmas, setting up your own business or climbing Mount Everest.

When I share this exercise with clients, I'm often asked: 'Where do I start? How do I know what to put on my bucket list to make it meaningful and personal to me?' I have two answers to this:

Get into the right mindset

A bucket list should be something that propels you to achieve success because it presents a compelling view of the future. The ideas you capture are exciting and just reading and reviewing them should trigger your enthusiasm to immediately start taking action to make them a reality.

To get into the right mindset, suspend your disbelief and take away your mental limitations. Recall how you thought as a child, when you seriously believed you could be anything you wanted: an astronaut, a fighter pilot, an explorer, an artist, a gymnast or the owner of your own ice-cream van. Imagine the mindset you were in when you were a child writing your Christmas list to send to Santa Claus. You knew no limits; whatever you wanted went on the list.

Once you have created the right mindset, allow all possibilities to stream through you to your fingertips and write or type them up. Nothing is too big or too small as long as it is something you really want to achieve.

Google bucket list examples for ideas and inspiration

You'll quickly find hundreds that will inspire your own thinking and that may trigger a desire you had pushed deep down. This process will help you create your personalized bucket list.

Accelerator exercise 11.1: Write your bucket list

I would like you to start writing your own bucket list right now. You can either use the Transformational Visioning and Goal Setting Tracker, which you can download from the *Rise* toolkit https://www.roystonguest.com/RISE-toolkit/ or you can write or type. The key is committing the items on your list to black and white.

I'm often asked whether it is necessary to create one personal bucket list and one professional list. The answer is that it doesn't really matter. Personally, I prefer not to be too prescriptive by creating categories, but rather let my thoughts and desires flow naturally.

There's also no ideal length for a bucket list. It should include all the people, experiences, adventures, achievements, qualifications and everything else you would like to complete before the end of your time, whenever that may be. It could be 20 things or 127. It doesn't matter, as long as they're all the things you really want to shoot for.

If you already have a bucket list, here are some questions to consider:

- When was the last time you looked at it?
- How well are you doing at completing your bucket list items?
- Is it time to update it or rewrite it, based on some of the pointers we've talked about here?

Turning your bucket list into tangible goals

Think of your bucket list as a 'visionary wish list' containing all the aspirational things you want to achieve. Reading it should fill you with excitement as you think and see yourself achieving those things.

But your vision only has real power if it has action behind it. As Joel A. Barker, the first person to popularize the concept of paradigm shifts, so eloquently described it, 'Vision without action is merely a dream. Action without vision just passes the time. **Vision** with **action** can change the world.'

So let's change your world by setting some tangible goals. Before we dive into the goal-setting model, there are two 'golden rules' to consider. These golden rules are the science and psychology behind goal setting, and help explain why so many people fall into the trap of their goals becoming nothing more than a pipe dream.

Golden rule 1: Write your goals down

Goals must be written down in black and white. This is important: the process of writing down your goals is the first step to creating a hard-wired message to your brain saying: 'These are real'. Psychologically, that's when your conscious and subconscious minds start to work in unison to help you achieve your goals. It's incredibly powerful.

It amazes me when I speak at a conference or hold a workshop and I ask the audience how many of them have set goals. Typically, about 30 per cent put up their hands. But when I ask who among them have written their goals down in black and white, easily half the hands go down.

Not writing them down takes away their power to galvanize your thinking and really ignite all your senses to fire at their full potential.

Golden Rule 2: Write your goals in the present tense

Goals must be written in the present tense. In my experience, of the two golden rules, this is the one people miss the most. It is so critical to the process, simply because of the psychological power involved.

Let me give you some context. If you write your goals in the future tense, where do they stay? That's right, they stay in the future. Writing your goals in the present tense aligns with the guiding principle I shared at the start of the chapter:

Don't think of your goals; think from your goals.

If you are thinking *of* your goals, you'll write them in the future tense. But when you're thinking *from* your goals, you must write them in the present tense as if you've already achieved them. The way you say them, think about them and, yes, write them is designed to align your subconscious mind with the idea that they're already in place so that it works with your conscious mind to drive actions which will ultimately make them a reality.

The 'how': creating C-SM²ART goals

With your goals written down and in the present tense, let's look at the 'how' – the specific action of turning those goals into what I call C-SM²ART goals.

If you've had any experience of writing goals, you've probably come across the concept of SMART goals, which are:

Specific

Measurable

Achievable or **A**ctionable

Realistic

Timely.

I believe there is an additional component that adds some extra firepower to your goals and makes them really transformational. Goals also have to be:

Challenging.

You'll recall that one of the five interlocking human drivers covered in Chapter 5, How we're wired as human beings, is growth. Life begins at the end of your comfort zone. Add *challenging* to the front of your goal-setting model and you get C-SMART goals. This is a powerful, disruptive addition that instantly challenges you to stretch beyond your comfort zone and explore the sense of possibilities. How high is high?

Remember Accelerator exercise 2.1: Raise the bar from Chapter 2: Setting your standards of personal excellence? In thinking about your personal and professional goals, where are you going to set the bar – at 6 feet or 100 feet? So now our goal-setting model is **C-SMART:**

Challenging

Specific

Measurable

Achievable or **A**ctionable

Realistic

Timely.

But there is one other change. Where C-SMART goals are always measurable by definition, I firmly believe they have to be measurable not just at the end but along the way. In other words, they've got to be measurable twice, hence the **M²**.

Goal setting isn't just about the destination; it's also about the journey and the key milestones along the way that reconfirm you're on the right path, moving at the right pace, heading in the right direction. So I believe goals should always be **C-SM²ART:**

Challenging
Specific
M²easurable
Achievable or **A**ctionable
Realistic
Timely.

Bringing C-SM²ART and transformational visioning to life

I was coaching a client who had the opportunity to participate in a Mount Kilimanjaro charity climb. She had two windows of opportunity, since they were planning on doing the climb in March and October that year. March was only two months out, but the October one would give her ten months to prepare.

Her natural instinct was to opt for the March expedition, but through conversation we naturally decided that wasn't **realistic**, considering the training and preparation she would need to do, and considering that she hadn't made fitness a priority in her life to that point. So this was already going to be a **challenging** goal.

After the conversation, we agreed that ten months was a **realistic** and **timely** goal to aim for, so we set her sights on October.

In order to set a compelling vision that would enable her to think from her goal, not of her goal, the next thing we did was a visioning piece in which I asked her a series of questions. This is how it went:

I asked her to close her eyes and imagine standing at the top of Mount Kilimanjaro, having just completed the climb.

- What did it look like?
- What could she see?
- What did it feel like?
- What sounds could she hear?
- What could she smell?
- What could she taste?

This is how she answered the questions, and how we shaped her vision and goal:

It's 27 October 2016 at 06h34, and I have just finished a climb to the top of Mount Kilimanjaro. I am standing at the top of the mountain looking out as far as the eye can see, as the sun rises and the night changes to day. The wind is gently whistling through my ears, but otherwise the silence is breath-taking.

I feel amazing as this was one of my biggest goals, to stretch my comfort zone even though I am not a natural athlete. The smell of the air is so fresh and clean, and I can almost taste the champagne, which we'll be cracking open to celebrate the achievement of our goal. I feel alive and so proud of myself for achieving this goal ... it was challenging but I feel like I've grown in confidence and belief about what I can and can't do in my life.

Now that she had a compelling vision and a **specific** goal, she found a picture of the summit of Mount Kilimanjaro, superimposed herself on to it with the words to her goal. She put it up on her wall like a visioning board so that she could look at it every day.

We then created her training programme – the 'how'. Rather than reinvent the wheel, we researched Google for 'training programmes for climbing Mount

Kilimanjaro' – success modelling in action. A whole host of training programmes came up, we picked the best one, personalized it for her and worked out what she needed to do week by week, right up to the point of departing for her trip. She now had an **achievable** and **actionable** plan with the appropriate **M**²easurables.

The visioning board and goal were her anchor. If she ever felt her enthusiasm waning on a dark, cold wet morning, a quick peek of herself standing on the top of the mountain was enough to reconnect her with her 'why' and her purpose.

The final part of the exercise was to audit her vision, her goal and her training plan against the C-SM²ART model. You'll see highlighted throughout the example the specific components of the model, the vision and the goal written in the present tense and the sensory experience coming to life.

This is how you set C-SM²ART goals. Just imagine the impact you could make if you applied the formula to all areas of your life.

Accelerator exercise 11.2: Create C-SM²ART goals

Now I've walked you through a real-life example on how to write a C-SM²ART goal, I would like you to revisit your bucket list and pick one personal goal and one professional goal that you want to complete in the next 12 months.

Using the same process as above, translate them from being items on your bucket list into C-SM²ART goals. Creating a visual board is an option. If you're visually based it might work for you, but it's not mandatory. You'll see quickly how a rather static item such as 'Climb Mount Kilimanjaro' can become a vibrant, lively, compelling spur to take action and make the goal a reality.

Your Transformational Visioning and Goal-setting Tracker

I've created a Transformational Visioning and Goal-setting Tracker tool for you. You can download this from the toolkit, https://www.roystonguest.com/RISE-toolkit/, if you haven't done so already. How to use it is self-explanatory, with instructions provided for each stage. However, there are some points worth mentioning here:

- First, the headers align with the directors of Me Unlimited. This is deliberate in order to create consistency and to allow you to use the two in unison. Clearly, we are working with the Planning Director role of Me Unlimited for this exercise.

- Second, a key step of completing the tool is inserting your personal and professional definitions of success. Naturally, a number of your goals will be driven from these definitions, so to include them in here will ensure alignment.

- The third key point is about timeframes for achieving your goals.

Meaningful timeframes

One of the questions I'm frequently asked is over what time periods should goals be set? At the front of your goal-setting tool, I've broken it into three timeframes:

- Short-term goals, coded ST, are anything you are going to achieve in the next 12 months

- Medium-term goals, coded MT, are for one to three years

- Long-term goals, coded LT, are for more than three years.

Now you're off on the road with a vision of your future, an action plan for getting there and a timeline with milestone measures for when you'll arrive. You're in the driver's seat like never before, creating certainty and personal growth.

A FINAL REALITY CHECK

The last component of the Transformational Visioning and Goal-setting Tracker is the reality check. This is a series of critical questions that are essential for making sure your motivation and your 'why' remain strong, and that you've really thought through how to work on your goals and turn them into reality.

1 Where am I now?
2 How did I get here?
3 Where am I going?
4 Why do I want to get there?
5 What are the possible obstacles?
6 What am I going to do next? (What are the solutions and the actions?)
7 How will I know whether I'm on track? (What are the review periods, daily focused questions and so on?)
8 What if I don't achieve my goals (the pain)?
9 What if I do achieve my goals (the rewards)?

The last page of the Transformational Visioning and Goal-setting Tracker is where you sign and date your 'psychological contract' with yourself. By doing this it becomes more than just a set of words; it's a firm promise to yourself. If anyone deserves your authentic commitment, it is you.

Accelerator exercise 11.3: Keep track of your goals

Your next step is to book an appointment with yourself to ensure you block out time to personalize and complete your tracker. Trust me, this will be one of the most important meetings you'll have this year, and one you'll be glad you took the time to have.

Set your schedule for reviews so you can keep track of your goals and add momentum and inspiration to them daily, weekly and monthly, to ensure that you remain on track for their realization.

Implementing your goals

You might have heard the saying that most people overestimate what they can do in a year but underestimate what they can do in a lifetime. Implemented goals are the bridge between your current reality and your future vision. It is one of the most liberating, empowering feelings when you know your life has purpose and direction and daily you're taking actions to turn your goals into reality.

There's one final thought I feel compelled to reinforce, which is simply this: 'It's not the attainment of your goal that is the critical part ... it's what and who you become on the journey.'

So often, I hear people making statements like: 'I'll be happy when I am rich' or 'I'll make a change when spring comes around.' It's always some day, some day, some day. Don't fall into this trap. Make sure you squeeze the enjoyment out of every second, every minute, every hour and every day of your life, and that you're not banking up your happiness for some day.

Most of your life is spent in pursuit of your goals. The attainment of the actual goal for most is only a fleeting moment in time, before you recalibrate and set other goals and catapult yourself forward into the next exciting chapter of your personal growth journey.

Take action: achieve more

Where do you want to be by the end of this year?

This chapter explored how achieving your definition of success is inherently based on a structured and systematic approach of transformational visioning and goal-setting, coupled with an abundance of passion and drive to make it happen.

Goals create focus and direction, give your life meaning and purpose, challenge you to grow, drive you to take massive action, allow you to keep score, and allow you to create a formula to replicate, while at the same time offering you inspiration to continue on your journey.

I shared three goal-setting Accelerator exercises so that you don't think *of* your goals but think *from* your goals. Use the Transformational Visioning and Goal-setting Template, available to download here: https://www.roystonguest. com/RISE-toolkit/

Accelerator exercise 11.1 Write your bucket list, your visionary wish list of all the things you want to do, visit, see and achieve.

Accelerator exercise 11.2 Create your C-SM^{2}ART goals from two of the items (one personal, one professional) on your bucket list. These goals must be **C**hallenging, **S**pecific, **M**^{2}easurable, **A**chievable or **A**ctionable, **R**ealistic and **T**imely and written in the present tense.

Accelerator exercise 11.3 Simply book time out to complete your tracker and get your C-SM^{2}ART goals down in black and white. If you don't, who will?

Living the life you were meant to lead starts out with a vision and a plan to turn it into reality. Now is the time to create your powerful, meaningful, actionable goals to propel you to success.

Programming your winning mentality

'Whatever your mind can conceive and believe, it can achieve.'

Napoleon Hill

Here is the key to success and the key to failure: 'You become what you think about.' Let me say it again as it's the pillar principle of this entire chapter: 'You become what you think about.'

Throughout history, great teachers, philosophers and prophets have disagreed with one another on almost every major point about human existence – except for one. The one thing, the one recurring idea that keeps coming up through their notes and writings one after another is this single notion. And on this, there is unanimous agreement:

The key to success and the key to failure is that you become what you think about.

Marcus Aurelius, the great Roman emperor, said, 'A man's life is what his thoughts make of it.' British Prime Minister Benjamin Disraeli said:

> Everything comes if a man will only wait ... I've brought myself, by long meditation, to the conviction that a human being with a settled purpose must accomplish it, and nothing can resist a will that will stake even existence on its fulfilment.

The American poet Ralph Waldo Emerson said, 'A man is what he thinks about all day long.' Pioneering American psychologist William James summarized it like this:

The greatest discovery of my generation is that human beings can alter their lives by altering their attitudes of mind. We need only in cold blood act as if the thing in question were real, and it will become infallibly real by growing into such a connection with our life that will become real. It will become so knit with habit and emotion that our interests in it will be those which characterize belief.

But he did offer a few words of caution:

If you only care enough for a result, you will almost certainly obtain it ... if you wish to be rich, you will be rich ... if you wish to be learned, you will be learned ... if you wish to be good, you will be good ... only you must then, really wish these things, and wish for them exclusively, and not wish at the same time a hundred other incompatible things just as strongly.

Dr Norman Vincent Peale, the pioneering thinker and author of *The Power of Positive Thinking* (1952), said:

This is one of the greatest laws in the universe. Fervently do I wish I had discovered it as a very young man. It dawned upon me much later in life, and I found it to be the greatest discovery outside my relationship to God.

The great law, briefly and simply stated, is this: 'If you think in negative terms, you will achieve negative results. If you think in positive terms, you will achieve positive results.'

'That simple fact', he went on to say, 'is the basis of an astonishing law of prosperity and success: believe and succeed.'

You can choose how you think

I don't know how you're feeling right now, or how you generally view your life, your circumstances or whatever you might refer to as luck. But what I do know is this: you could well be missing the big picture because so many of us are. And the big picture is that you and I and every other human being have a distinct advantage over every other living creature on planet Earth because we have 100 per cent control – yes, 100 per cent control – over how we choose to think. And it's not just control over how we think, but how we *choose* to think. We can deliberately change this at any point during any given day.

You have a choice. It's not just a concept rooted in the philosophy that comes through in the quotes above, but one firmly rooted in science and applied every day by doctors and psychologists to change negative behaviours into positive, enabling and empowering behaviours.

Think about how smokers are cured, for example. One of the basic rules for quitting a habit such as smoking is to change the thought pattern that surrounds it. Doctors refer to the moments when smokers instinctively reach for a cigarette as 'triggers', such as the moment you sit down for a morning cup of coffee, the moment you complete a certain task at work, or the last thing you do before you lock the house at night and go to bed.

Regular smokers will slide unknowingly into a deeper addiction over time where they get cravings – little feelings of unease or anxiety – that are calmed only by lighting a cigarette. Ultimately, cigarettes become a coping mechanism, ironically boosting emotional wellbeing while seriously harming physical wellbeing.

For many, stopping smoking is simply about changing the behaviour associated with those triggers. The science behind it is called Cognitive Behavioural Therapy (CBT), which treats the habit of smoking cigarettes as a learned behaviour, which in simple terms (though it's often a hard task in execution) is about simply replacing the action associated with a trigger. The ultimate intended outcome is to return the power of choice to smokers who have become enslaved by near-robotic behaviour as a result of their addiction.

But the biggest thing for me about CBT is what it reveals about how you make subconscious choices (lighting a cigarette), without even realizing you are doing it, and how once you acknowledge and accept this mindset, you're able to do something about it.

Choice. You have it. So do I. And it's very, very powerful.

At the beginning of this chapter, in the collection of powerful quotes by some of humanity's greatest thinkers there was one recurring theme. The way you choose to look at your life is key to you being able to create the outcome and life you want to lead.

That's easy enough to say when everything is going well; you feel powerful and successful and can easily propel yourself forward. But life is about ups and downs and at some point we will all face some sort of challenge or failure. It's at those critical junctures, your defining moments or defining choice points, that your ability to harness your winning mentality will set you apart.

If you want to be inspired, take some time to research on Google the ways some of the most successful people in the world, the very people who inspire you, once hit rock bottom.

A very famous failure

J. K. Rowling is one of the most successful writers of all time, by any measurement. Her books about the world's favourite boy wizard, Harry Potter, are distributed in 200 countries, translated into 68 languages and have sold over 400 million copies, earning her a net worth of £650 million.

This great success began only in her early thirties and, prior to that, things hadn't been quite so easy. I'll let Rowling share her story in her own words, delivered during her now famous Harvard University commencement address in 2008:

> Ultimately, we all have to decide for ourselves what constitutes failure, but the world is quite eager to give you a set of criteria if you let it. So I think it fair to say that by any conventional measure, a mere seven years after my graduation day, I had failed on an epic scale. An

exceptionally short-lived marriage had imploded, and I was jobless, a lone parent, and as poor as it is possible to be in modern Britain, without being homeless. The fears that my parents had had for me, and that I had for myself, had both come to pass, and by every usual standard, I was the biggest failure I knew.

Now, I am not going to stand here and tell you that failure is fun. That period of my life was a dark one, and I had no idea that there was going to be what the press has since represented as a kind of fairy-tale resolution. I had no idea then how far the tunnel extended, and for a long time, any light at the end of it was a hope rather than a reality.

So why do I talk about the benefits of failure? Simply because failure meant a stripping away of the inessential. I stopped pretending to myself that I was anything other than what I was, and began to direct all my energy into finishing the only work that mattered to me. Had I really succeeded at anything else, I might never have found the determination to succeed in the one arena I believed I truly belonged. I was set free, because my greatest fear had been realized, and I was still alive, and I still had a daughter whom I adored, and I had an old typewriter and a big idea. And so rock bottom became the solid foundation on which I rebuilt my life.

You might never fail on the scale I did, but some failure in life is inevitable. It is impossible to live without failing at something, unless you live so cautiously that you might as well not have lived at all – in which case, you fail by default.

Failure gave me an inner security that I had never attained by passing examinations. Failure taught me things about myself that I could have learned no other way. I discovered that I had a strong will, and more discipline than I had suspected; I also found out that I had friends whose value was truly above the price of rubies.

What J. K. Rowling speaks about is resilience and an inner strength that sometimes you discover only through experiencing challenging times. Rising above, reeling from the knocks but not losing the faith that you can do more, be better and still make something out of your life.

She couldn't have ever envisaged the colossal success she would accomplish, but she did know she had more in her and that her future was still unwritten.

Is your future still waiting to be written or turned into reality?

There is one more part of her speech I want to draw your attention to, something else she said a little later on as she was recounting another story of her life:

One of the many things I learned at the end of that Classics library corridor down which I ventured at the age of 18, in search of something I could not then define, was this, written by the Greek author Plutarch: 'What we achieve inwardly will change outer reality.'

All it takes is your attitude

If you look at some of the other famous failures of our time, what is it that differentiates them? What is it that created the mental strength, the personal resilience to take the knocks, pick themselves up, dust themselves off and go again?

Yes, these individuals may have a clear definition of what success looks like, feels like and acts like.

Yes, they might have created laser-beam focus and set their goals.

Yes, their personal standards of excellence might have been way up there at 100 feet.

Yes, their why might have been compelling and the fear of failure a driving force, but ...

... the one additional ingredient they have in their armoury is their ability to hone, polish, develop and refine their winning mentality and positive attitude.

> Your attitude will always determine your altitude in life.

If programming your winning mentality and shaping your positive attitude are so critical to your success, the question is how do you do it and why haven't more people mastered this essential life skill?

Defining positive attitude

First, you need to be able to define positive attitude.

How would you define it? Is it seeing the glass as half full, not half empty, looking for the opportunity in the difficulty not the difficulty in the opportunity, or just having a can-do attitude?

I'd agree with all of these but I'd caution they don't run deep enough. Cursory expressions such as these may be completely true, but they're the tip of the iceberg and must be supported by substantially more depth, feeling, understanding and emotion.

Accelerator exercise 12.1: Define a positive attitude

So, I want you to STOP and in your mind, or preferably with a pen and paper or on your gadget, answer this question: What is a positive attitude? How would you define it?

My short definition is that it's the way you dedicate yourself to the way that you think. A more detailed definition might include:

- how you **choose** to dedicate yourself to the way you think
- how you **choose** to dedicate yourself to being positive
- how you **choose** to dedicate yourself to reacting in a positive way.

Remember Dr Norman Vincent Peale's great law: 'If you think in negative terms, you will get negative results. If you think in positive terms, you will achieve positive results.'

Or, as George Bernard Shaw stated so eloquently:

> People are always blaming their circumstances for what they are. I don't believe in circumstances. The people who get on in this world are the people who get up and look for the circumstances they want, and if they can't find them, make them.

What are we doing wrong?

If you have total control over the fundamentals for developing your winning mentality and a positive attitude, why aren't more people doing it and achieving the levels of success of high achievers? To demonstrate why not, let's review a scenario that compares the human mind to a farmer planting seeds.

Suppose the farmer has a plot of good fertile land. The land gives the farmer a choice. She can plant whatever she chooses. The land doesn't care what is planted. It's up to the farmer to make the decision. But the land, just like your mind, will return what you plant.

Now let's assume the farmer has two seeds in her hand: one of corn, the other of nightshade, a deadly poison. She digs two little holes in the earth, plants both seeds, covers up the holes, waters and takes care of the land, nurturing them both.

What do you think will happen? Invariably the land will return what is planted: 'As ye sow, so shall ye reap.' Remember, the land doesn't care. It will return poison in just as wonderful abundance as it will corn. So the two plants are cultivated, one helpful and constructive, one destructive and deadly.

The human mind is far more fertile, far more incredible and mysterious than the land, but it works in a similar way. It does not care what we plant, whether success or failure – a concrete, worthwhile goal or confusion, misunderstanding, fear and anxiety. It's all the same to the human mind, which is happy to manifest either in abundance.

So why don't we use our minds more?

Your mind comes as standard equipment at birth. It's free, and we don't tend to value the things that we get for free anything like as much as we should. Everything worthwhile is given to you for free: your mind, your soul, your body, your hopes, your dreams, your ambitions, your intelligence, your love of family and children, friends and country. All these priceless possessions are free.

The human mind is not used to its full potential because we take it for granted. Familiarity breeds contempt. It's one of our most disappointing basic human instincts. The insight from this chapter is your opportunity to redress that balance and leverage one of the greatest assets you own and have at your disposal.

Your mind. Your 'necktop computer'. Your winning mentality. Your positive attitude.

Attitude challenges are everywhere

Now, there are external challenges to watch out for. Why wouldn't there be? Attitude challenges are everywhere.

Switch on the news and what's the focus of most of the headlines? Negativity. The same applies when you pick up a newspaper. Crime rate, murder, the state of the economy, an A-listed celebrity who has had an affair (as if we care), politicians who have behaved inappropriately … the list goes on. We are bombarded with negative stories and tales of gloom and doom. Estimates suggest that more than 90 per cent of the messaging we see and hear on a daily basis is negative.

It's all over the Internet, all over the front pages of news papers – everywhere.

I have a colleague who lives in South Africa, a country that by any measure is going through growing pains and challenges. He suggests there are two sets of thoughts you can have on a daily basis and he reminds himself of them every day, in order to maintain and protect his winning mentality.

On the one hand, South Africa is beset by political strife, a struggling economy, a currency that is constantly fluctuating, social challenges around poverty, exceptionally high levels of crime, declining educational standards and overall corruption apparent in almost every nook and cranny.

On the other hand, it is a growing democracy that has successfully avoided its worst potential future of recent years – civil war and international pariah status – which continues to look for solutions to its problems and will probably find them, and which in the meantime has a warm sunny climate, beautiful landscapes, quirky, friendly, funny people and a vast number of entrepreneurial opportunities.

Both sets of thoughts are true. But if you focus on one, you'll struggle to overcome your paranoia, fear and dread enough to get out of bed each morning, while, if you focus on the other, it's a world of great abundance where every day has the potential to be a great one.

The point is that you have to own your mind filter, not blindly ignoring the bad because we're certainly not striving for naivety, but accepting the bad as only part of the story – and not the one that has to be the most relevant at any given moment.

Using the mind filter

One of my favourite stories drives the point home:

Once upon a time, a shoe company sent two salespeople to Africa to determine the market potential for their products. One salesperson was sent to the east coast of Africa, while the other was sent to the west. Both salespeople completed a basic survey of the target market and called the office to describe what they had found.

The salesperson sent to the east coast of Africa called the office and said: 'Nobody wears shoes. There's no market for us here. I'm coming home on the next available flight and I suggest we explore other markets.'

The salesperson sent to the west coast of Africa called the office with genuine excitement in their voice and said: 'Nobody wears shoes. There's a massive market for us here. I'm setting up an office and a warehouse. Please send me 20 container loads of shoes as soon as you can.'

Life is about choices

Are you a Blue Monday or a National Happiness Day person?

Blue Monday

The Monday at the beginning of the third week in January has the depressing nickname 'Blue Monday'. It's supposedly the most depressing day of the year based on the following formula:

$$1 / 8W + (D - D) - 3 / 8 \times T + M \times NA$$

The key components of the formula include:

W	=	Weather
D	=	Debt
D	=	Money due in January pay
T	=	Time since Christmas
M	=	General motivational levels
NA	=	The need to take action

What this is essentially saying is that we're in the doldrums for a variety of reasons:

- The weather: it's at its darkest in January, and sunlight is a big determinant of happiness. In

269

fact, in many northern countries, such as those in Scandinavia, the suicide rate trends sharply upward around this date.

- Debt: imagine you're sitting at the kitchen table on the third Monday in January with three documents: a bank statement, a credit card statement and a payslip, and you can see you spent too much in December.

- Motivation: you said you'd visit the gym three times per week, it's the third week in January and you've been once. You've now got a mountain to climb to get started because you feel you've failed at a resolution already.

By the time we get to the first Monday in February, we experience what is known as National Absenteeism Day. For the past few years this day has been the highest absenteeism day in the entire working calendar, probably because of lack of motivation more than sickness.

National Happiness Day

Fast-forward a couple of months and we have the opposite. The Friday at the end of the second week in June, known as National Happiness Day, is explained through another mathematical formula:

$$O + (N \times S) + C_{PM}/T + H_E$$

O	=	Being outdoors and outdoor activity
N	=	Nature
S	=	Social interaction
C_{PM}	=	Childhood summers and positive memories
T	=	Temperature
H_E	=	Holidays and looking forward to time off

External stimuli, the outdoors, nature, the warmer temperature – all have a big impact. Summer is a fun time, when you can shed some clothing, spend time outdoors and when social activities are much more the norm.

Which camp are you in?

We all know people who still feel that it is Blue Monday even on National Happiness Day. Some people carry negativity around with them 365 days a year. You know the type of person I'm talking about. This person sees the glass as half empty, looks for the difficulty in the opportunity, and will come up with every reason under the sun for why you can't do something.

But the reverse is also true. We all know individuals who seem to feel that it's National Happiness Day even when it's Blue Monday. These positive, self-actualized people believe they have choices and choose to exercise them frequently, especially on Blue Monday when the odds are against them.

Spend time with the first type of person and you feel you'll have to plug yourself into the wall socket to get charge back into your system. They drain your positivity battery quickly, if you choose to let them. Spend time with the second group, and any bad day or attitude challenges you might be experiencing can soon be framed, contextualized and dealt with.

We all know individuals who fall into one of these camps. But the big question is which camp are you in?

Your two choices

Choice 1: The EV (the emotional vacuum)

Negative people are worse than negative experiences. Why? Because an experience can be over in ten minutes, but a negative person can hang around for a lifetime.

271

I call these types of people EVs, short for emotional vacuums. They see the world bleakly and spread their bleak view because for them it's real. One big reason for this is that misery loves company, and if you're an EV, you're likely to be attracted to, and to attract, other EVs. Imagine being in *that* room, listening to *that* conversation. Talk about stripping yourself of all your happy thoughts.

Choice 2: The positivity magnet

Positivity loves company too. It's contagious. It will be far easier for you to make positive choices if you surround yourself with the right company.

I have a colleague who is a wonderful person with a great attitude and, as a result, she always seems to be the resident agony aunt for the people around her who turn to her to unload their woes. She's so strong, considered and resilient that they are drawn to her and they draw their strength from her. But I have to caution her from time to time to be careful that she doesn't constantly just give her great energy away without getting a regular recharge for herself.

Making your choices conscious and deliberate

How do you know whether you're making great choices? What kind of mindset do you need to adopt to ensure you're giving yourself every opportunity to be the best version of you? The simple answer is: be **conscious and deliberate**, as the architect of your own destiny, about how you program, develop, maintain and, yes, protect your positive attitude.

There are those people who choose to play the victim in life because it allows them to renounce responsibility for their own experience. I already know you don't fall into this camp as you wouldn't have made it this far through the book if you did. But what I would like you to do is use this chapter to think deeply about whether you are being conscious and deliberate in choosing a great attitude. For many, it may be a default choice, but if we're not working on it consciously and deliberately, you can very easily wobble now and then and allow your positivity to falter.

Remember these three key points:

- Attitude is your **choice**, not your circumstance
- Attitude is the way you **respond** to the situation, not the situation itself
- You have total **control** over the way you choose and the way you respond, so choose wisely.

Your attitude compass

Below are six attitude enablers that make up your 'attitude compass'. Together they will give power to your winning mentality.

Attitude enabler 1: You become what you think about all day long

I've referenced Earl Nightingale, the founder of the self-help concept, previously in this book, but this is one of his foundational ideas. You become what you think about all day long.

Some of the most important conversations you have are the ones inside your head – with yourself. It's critical to pay attention and truly listen to your inner voice and the quality of the internal conversations taking place. The mind is such a powerful force and, no matter what programs you've previously run or what thoughts you've given greatest attention to in the past, the great news is that you can override even years of poor programming with the right focus.

If your waking hours are consumed with positive, enabling thoughts, ideas and strategies on how you're going to turn your compelling vision of the future into reality, what's going to happen? You will become those thoughts and your vision *will* become your reality.

Attitude enabler 2: Failures are just stepping stones to your ultimate success

There is no such thing as a failure. Failures are just stepping stones to your ultimate success. Remember J. K. Rowling. Another part of her story that I haven't yet shared is that her first Harry Potter book had been rejected multiple times by multiple publishers before it was published.

J. K. Rowling wasn't alone. Stephen King, another of the most successful authors of all time, was told that he would never amount to anything as a writer. For both authors, those rejections and criticisms fell on deaf ears as they pushed ahead, determined to succeed.

The annals of history are filled with two types of people: those who failed and stopped and those who failed and tried again. It's all about attitude. Do you see failure as an end result or merely as a stepping stone on the way to success?

A key part of programming your winning mentality is to reframe each failure as just another step on your glorious path. You change your mindset; you change the game. Success is simply the ability to go from one failure to the next, learning and growing as you go and never losing enthusiasm as you keep the end goal in the front of your mind.

Attitude enabler 3: Dynamic language is everything!

The things you say and words you use have equal power to shape your thoughts. Be aware of your choice of words, what they mean and the impact they can have on yourself and others.

There is a great scene in *Star Wars Episode V: The Empire Strikes Back* where Luke Skywalker is being coached in the Jedi skills by Yoda. Luke says he is going to 'try' to lift a rock with his mind, only to be rebuked by Yoda for letting himself off the hook before he even starts.

'Do or do not. There is no "try",' Yoda says. It's a great metaphor for life. Either you commit and get it done, or you don't commit and do not. Half measures are of no worth in achieving your goals. When you use words like 'I will try', or 'Maybe I can', or 'perhaps', 'could', 'might', 'should', what happens? Nothing happens.

As the life coach guru Tony Robbins says, 'You never get your shoulds in life, you end up "should-ing" all over yourself.' You get action when you change 'I should' to 'I must.' When it's a 'must', then you will do whatever it takes to make it happen.

Choose dynamic language and lean into it. Use positive, action words and thoughts to drive your actions because they will empower you, not disempower you. And if you catch yourself falling into the trap of the shoulds and maybes, take a moment to re-anchor back to the 'why' of what you're doing. If the 'why' is strong enough, the language will reflect your commitment to making it happen. When it's a 'must', you'll figure out the 'what' and the 'how'.

Attitude enabler 4: Who you spend time with is who you become

You can't always choose your family but you can choose your friends. Choose wisely. Pick people who want to celebrate your success and whose friendship and support make you want to celebrate theirs as you build your buildings higher and higher. Beware those who would rather knock the foundations out from under your feet even as they look you in the eye and smile.

Attitude enabler 5: Nothing's as bad as you're making it out to be

The framing technique or reality checker, aka 'get a grip', is that nothing's as bad as you're making it out to be.

There are people in the world who face real adversity, real challenges, whose life is so difficult every day that you wonder how they manage to cope. And then in the very next thought, you slip into a really bad mood, depressed, angry or fed up because something small and comparatively insignificant hasn't gone quite the way you wanted.

To develop a great winning mentality every day, you've got to overcome the natural human tendency to blow small things out of proportion. Work on having a rational amount of perspective about things.

Most of us have our ups and downs. Good fortune and bad fortune can easily be confused if you don't take a much broader view of your life. The following Chinese fable illustrates this very point.

A Chinese fable

A farmer and his son had a beloved stallion that helped the family earn a living. One day the horse ran away and their neighbours exclaimed, 'Your horse ran away, what terrible luck!'

The farmer replied, 'Maybe so, maybe not. We'll see.'

A few days later the horse returned home, leading a few wild mares back to the farm as well. The neighbours shouted out, 'Your horse has returned, and brought several horses home with him. What great luck!'

The farmer replied, 'Maybe so, maybe not. We'll see.'

Later that week, the farmer's son was trying to break in one of the mares and she threw him to the ground, breaking his leg. The villagers cried, 'Your son broke his leg, what terrible luck!'

The farmer replied, 'Maybe so, maybe not. We'll see.'

A few weeks later, soldiers from the national army marched through town, recruiting all the able-bodied boys for the army. They did not take the farmer's son, still recovering from his injury. Friends shouted, 'Your boy is spared, what tremendous luck!'

To which the farmer replied, 'Maybe so, maybe not. We'll see.'

The moral of this story is of course that no event, in and of itself, can truly be judged as good or bad, lucky or unlucky, fortunate or unfortunate. As time passes, what you may see as a disaster may turn out to be actually great fortune.

Perspective: it's critical to your winning mentality.

Attitude enabler 6: Override derailing thoughts with incantations

You've probably heard the term 'affirmation', the action or process of affirming something. Think back to your schooldays when you learned your times tables. You didn't just affirm and repeat your times tables to learn them; you incanted them.

An incantation or enchantment is a set of words, spoken or unspoken, which are considered by their user to evoke meaning and purpose. The difference between an affirmation and an incantation is that when you 'affirm' something you're just repeating it over and over, but when you 'incant' an idea it becomes hotwired to your physiology, your entire sensory experience, your whole being.

If I were asked, at 45 years of age, to recite my times tables or even the Lord's Prayer from my schooldays, I could do both. That's the power of an incantation. And you can use it right now to override any limiting or derailing beliefs that might be holding you back.

'I'M ALWAYS LATE'

If you are running a negative program through your intalk like 'I'm always late', the way to overcome it is to run a positive, empowering incantation in its place. The mind is a powerful force and the reality is what you say will be the way. Even if you have been running a negative deroiling programme for years, you can still override it.

I'm sure you've heard people run a program that goes something like this: 'I'm always late for meetings.' And if you run that negative incantation for long enough, you will always be late for meetings as your conscious mind does everything to play out the self-fulfilling prophecy you've created.

In this situation you need to try running a second program – a positive enabling incantation: 'I'm always five minutes early for meetings.' Incant that program for long enough and – guess what? – you will start turning up five minutes early.

The executive who hated public speaking

I recently coached a senior executive who hated public speaking. His whole body was consumed by trepidation every time he thought about speaking at the company conference or in front of shareholders and it really affected his performance.

There were a couple of different ways to resolve this. The first was to change the approach, for example by asking him questions while he sat on a chair on stage, interview style, to avoid him having to stand up in front of everyone. The second approach was to reprogram his inner voice, which was feeding him negative intalk.

Before he was due to speak a voice inside his head would say things like, 'What if you forget what you're going to say? What if you look like an idiot?' This voice would chip away at his confidence and his breathing would go shallow as he suffered a physical reaction to his fear. When the time came to deliver a presentation, he would be in no state to deliver it.

I knew he had to override that internal voice with an incantation. The incantation's power would be in its simplicity and etched into his memory as a fully fledged belief. With my help, the executive created an incantation for himself that went: 'I'm about to go on stage and deliver the best nerve-busting presentation of my life.'

Repetition is an incredibly powerful force. For two months prior to the annual company conference, he recited his new empowering incantation a hundred times a day – sometimes in his mind, sometimes out loud, even while out running or in the shower. He would recite it in a variety of ways – slowly, then quickly, and even adding a beat to it as if he were rapping – until it had become etched into his conscious and subconscious mind and the default 'state' he would revert to whenever he thought about public speaking.

He also repeated it 50 times while waiting to kick off his presentation. Just imagine how pumped up and in the performance zone he was as he walked on to the stage. He delivered the best nerve-busting presentation of his life. He was awesome!

Remember … the only difference between an in**CAN**tation and an in**CAN'T**ation is where you put the emphasis on one letter. What negative programs are you currently running that are sabotaging your efforts to reach your full potential? Perhaps it's time to create an empowering, enabling incantation to unlock your potential, eliminate any limiting beliefs and start living the life you were meant to lead.

Choosing a winning mindset

A winning mentality is not only critical to your success; it's entirely yours to choose. If you're not yet practising a winning mentality every day by conscious, deliberate choice, start now. It's not an overstatement to suggest that it can literally change *everything*.

The ideas, strategies and tools in *Rise* have been carefully developed to give you the framework you need to start living the life you were meant to lead, but there is one additional critical enabler: a winning mentality. When these work in unison, they become an unstoppable force, giving you control and enabling you to set the pace, the cadence and the direction of your life, aligned to your definition of success.

Australian Nick Vujicic is living proof of this. Nick was born with tetra-amelia syndrome, a rare disorder characterized by the absence of arms and legs, giving him a severely challenging start in life. But he sums up his life like this: 'It's not what happens to you … it's what you do with what happens to you that makes the difference!'

He is one of the most inspirational human beings you will ever get to meet or listen to. Watching him share his thoughts and insights on his life is so humbling and such an extraordinary experience, that it puts your own life into perspective. Nick has a winning mentality that has propelled him from adversity, the likes of which you and I can scarcely imagine, to success, the likes of which you and I might aspire to.

Skills and tools alone are not enough to win in this game of life. What makes the difference is the mindset that enables you to make the most of them.

Take action: achieve more

We become what we think about. What are you thinking about?

This chapter explored the power of your thoughts, the choices you make and the ways in which you can create a winning attitude and mindset to set you up for success.

We have total control over how we choose to think – not just over how we think, but how we *choose* to think. We can deliberately change it at any point during any given day, during any situation. We have a choice. It is your choice, not your circumstance.

I shared one winning Accelerator exercise (12.1) to help you define a positive attitude and winning mindset. My short definition is the way you dedicate yourself to the way that you think. My more detailed definition is:

- how you *choose* to dedicate yourself to the way you think
- how you *choose* to dedicate yourself to being positive
- how you *choose* to dedicate yourself to reacting in a positive way.

Reflecting on the six attitude enablers will help you choose a great attitude every day.

Your defining moments come when life's ups and downs throw out a challenge to you. How you harness your winning mentality at those precise moments will be what sets you apart.

Being your own performance coach

'If it's to be ... it's up to me!'

Congratulations on making it to this penultimate chapter. This is the big one because, from this point on, it's about turning everything we've covered into momentum-building action. It's about accelerating your success, both personally and professionally, and turning your dreams, aspirations and goals into reality. I want you to align the things you say with the actions you take so you join the ranks of the truly successful: those who walk their own talk.

This chapter is called 'Being your own performance coach' because the whole concept of *Rise* is about you owning *your* life, *your* actions and *your* results. Three possible scenarios could play out and your Learning Director has a critical role to play, keeping you accountable as your own performance coach.

- **Scenario 1: The hot-bath effect** How many times have you attended a seminar or workshop or watched a webinar and felt enthused and energized, ready to take on the world ... only to do nothing with the insights, ideas and strategies once you returned to the autopilot of your normal daily routine? Don't fall into this trap.

- **Scenario 2: Spray-and-pray implementation** You could implement some ideas from this book in an ad hoc fashion, a spray-and-pray approach, and you may see some short-term gains. However, they will never be enduring or sustainable. The holistic nature of *Rise* is a structured framework of interlocking ideas that feed off one another for sustainable change. You will not leverage the full potential of the ideas and tools until you think and apply them with rigour, consistency and discipline.

- **Scenario 3: A disciplined, systematic, structured approach** Of course, this is my recommended scenario, and why the book is structured in the way it is. It is designed for applied learning, the integration of the ideas into your daily, weekly and monthly disciplines, which ultimately become your success habits, leading to your unlocked potential.

In Chapter 3: Why success is not an accident, I shared the five secrets of success, covering the first three in detail:

1 Defining what success means to you
2 Creating your success formula
3 Success modelling to fast-track your timeline.

I'll now talk about Secrets 4 and 5 in detail:

4 Developing your success disciplines
5 Honing your success habits.

Secret 4: Developing your success disciplines

> 'Once you have commitment, you need the discipline and hard work to get you there.'
>
> *Haile Gebrselassie*

More than 140 years ago there was a fascinating scientific discovery called the Ebbinghaus Effect, named after the German psychologist Hermann Ebbinghaus. His research indicated that your ability to recall information declines significantly over a short space of time. If you look at Figure 13.1 you'll notice that, after ten minutes, information recall drops off by 60 per cent and, after three months, to less than 10 per cent. This is a phenomenon known as the Ebbinghaus Curve of Forgetting.

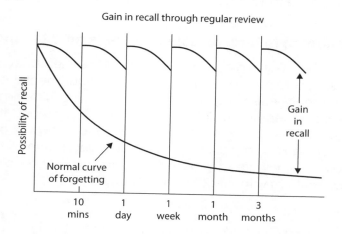

Gain in recall through regular review

FIGURE 13.1 The Ebbinghaus Curve of Forgetting

In order to bring this to life, let me give you a simple example. If you train in the gym, you don't work out for an hour, then walk back to the changing room, stand in front of the mirror and say, 'Wow don't I look fantastic!' No, you work out day after day, week after week, month after month, combining discipline and consistency, in order to develop muscle strength and tone.

If you take a two-week summer vacation and miss your training, the week you come back and start training again, it's painful, because the muscles regress quickly. The drop-off is severe, just like the Ebbinghaus Effect.

Repetition really is the master of skill. You can't become great at something by doing it once or by continually stopping and restarting.

You've heard the expression 'If you're going to do it, do it well'. Doing anything well requires dedication, discipline and commitment. Behind every overnight success is a story of hours of sacrifice, practice and repetition. Mohammed Ali captured it brilliantly when he said: 'The fight is won or lost far away from witnesses – behind the lines, in the gym, and out there on the road, long before I dance under those lights.'

Physical or mental muscle ... there is no difference

Just as you visit a gym to build physical muscle, you've got to visit the 'gym of the mind' to develop your mental muscle memory. Attending a workshop or seminar, listening to a podcast, reading or listening to *Rise* just once and then forgetting about it, won't cut it. You have to 'show up' on a regular basis creating, honing and polishing thoughts and ideas until they are so grooved and wired you'll be able to draw on them without conscious thought.

The problem with procrastination

'When all is said and done, more is *said* than *done*!'

Even with all your positive intentions, there is one major pitfall of human behaviour that enhances the Ebbinghaus Effect – procrastination.

We all procrastinate from time to time. Sometimes it's the mundane things, but often it's the bigger things that we know logically will have an important effect on our lives. Somehow we still manage to sabotage our own success by failing to take action.

Of course, people come up with all sorts of creative reasons why 'now isn't the right time'. We are too busy, too broke, too stressed; it's too risky, too uncertain; we are too inexperienced, too old, too young, too disruptive. Occasionally, those reasons are valid. But, more often, they are simply excuses to avoid doing the real work and experiencing the emotional discomfort that comes from making meaningful change in your life.

Have you ever been too late to book the concert tickets you wanted, or sat up all night finishing an assignment due the next day, because you only started that evening? Have you had a great idea for a new business, only to discover 12 months later that someone has 'stolen your idea and done it first'? This is precisely what I'm talking about, and the biggest problem with procrastination is that it is insidious. The longer you go without taking action, the less likely it is that you ever will. And if you're not careful it becomes a self-fulfilling prophecy and, before you know it, you become known for being the world's best procrastinator.

The world is full of people with good intentions, people who talk a good game about what they're going to do – but never do it. Then there are those brave souls, committed and courageous warriors of action who quietly go about their life making stuff happen. Their energy is not consumed in talking a good game, it is channelled and focused into *playing* a good game. For them, the saying above is flipped on its head: 'When all is said and done, more is *done* than *said*!'

When you think about potentially delaying, making an excuse or putting off an action until 'the perfect conditions present themselves', just remember one thing:

Procrastination is the saboteur of ambition and prevents the realization of your biggest ideals and goals.

So what can you do right now to combat the Ebbinghaus Effect and delete procrastination from your vocabulary, making sure it's not subconsciously embedded in your behaviour? I have the following six solutions.

Solution 1: Have an attitude of action

As demonstrated in the examples throughout this book, one of the traits that differentiates successful individuals from all the rest is their attitude of action. They will have a clear goal of what they want to achieve, they will have placed a 'stake in the ground' in determining timescales, and, yes, they will have a plan of how they are going to get there. But it doesn't have to be the perfect plan, and most of the time it's not.

Successful people don't waste time reviewing, tweaking and perfecting their plan or analysing it from all angles. They don't suffer from paralysis by analysis. They have the attitude of action. For the individual with a mindset and attitude of action, it is more 'Ready – Fire – Aim' than the traditional approach of 'Ready – Aim – Fire'.

One of my clients has this view: 'When our thinking is at 80 per cent, we go, because we always know the final 20 per cent will need adjusting along the way.'

Successful people maintain a positive focus in life, no matter what is going on around them. They stay focused on their past successes rather than their past failures, on the next action steps which get them closer to their goals rather than the distractions that could derail them. When it's apparent that a goal cannot be reached, they don't automatically adjust the goal; they first adjust the action steps required to reach it.

If you're faced with challenges, find a route to get around them. If there are hurdles, jump over them. If people are repeatedly saying no to your request, view a 'no' as a delayed 'yes'. Work out how you can influence them to change their point of view to embrace your vision and what you're trying to achieve.

Simply getting on with changing and turning a situation to your advantage is a very powerful trait to possess. Combine that with passion and persistence and you have three powerful forces working for you.

Solution 2: Recognize and prepare for your 'ability blip'

The ability blip (Figure 13.2) is an important concept for you to be aware of. It's the downturn in performance you'll experience while you adopt a new skill, approach or way of thinking intended to produce improved results. Recognize and look out for it from now on, and be prepared to hold your nerve and work through it. The rewards are worth it on the other side of your ability blip.

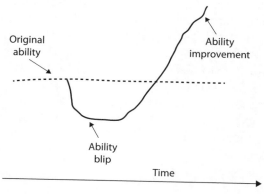

Original ability

Ability improvement

Ability blip

Time

FIGURE 13.2 The ability blip

If you're a golfer, you will know that if you change your grip to improve your performance, even if you're already a decent golfer, your game will almost certainly go through a period of deterioration while you get used to the new way of holding your club. That's precisely what happened to Tiger Woods at the height of his success. A recurring shoulder problem meant he had to learn how to swing his club differently and it cut short a brilliant winning streak while he got used to it. Once he did, of course, he was back – and better than ever.

Unfortunately, many teachers, trainers and coaches do not call out the ability blip, which creates one of the biggest frustrations when it comes to doing something new or differently – and why most people give up too early.

Working through an ability blip

Let me share a story about a time when I experienced my own ability blip and the way I worked through it.

I am regularly hired by organizations to deliver key-note addresses and sessions on a variety of topics, including many contained in this book. While I am now totally comfortable on stage and even feel excitement at the prospect, this wasn't always the case.

The first time I spoke publicly was at a business breakfast session for around 20 or 25 people. I stood up after being introduced, intending to wow everyone, but within two minutes I began to sweat, my voice began to wobble, and I completely forgot what I was going to say. It must have been excruciating for the audience. There was no way I could ask them to pay as I was so embarrassed by my poor performance.

But once I recovered from the experience, I realized I had a choice, just as you do when you hit your own ability blip:

- I could never do it again, closing down a new avenue before I'd even started
- I could lock in my core, get disciplined about practice, find out what I was missing or lacking, and set myself goals for improvement to get me back in the arena quickly.

I took the second option. I scoured bookshops and the Internet, finding everything I could about public speaking, researching how the best of the best do it. I practised for hours in front of the mirror so I could be sure my body language echoed my words. I was determined to become comfortable, natural and engaging. And as the years have passed, this is exactly what has happened.

It always amazes me, when I'm coaching or running a session, when someone says, 'Royston, I tried that idea and it didn't work.'

And I say, 'How many times did you try it?'

And they reply, 'Oh at least half a dozen.'

And I say, 'How many times did you really try it?'

And they'll look at me with a wry smile and respond with, 'OK, maybe three or four.'

So I'll ask the same question again.

'How many times did you really try it?'

Usually the response will be, 'Well, I tried it once and it didn't work.'

When you experience ability blips and your current core level of competence, expertise or excellence drops, hold your nerve and stay the course. Be persistent in the application of the new way of thinking, behaving or new skill. Allow momentum to carry you through, catapulting you to new levels of competence, expertise or excellence. And once you reach the other side of your ability blip, you will achieve levels of performance you never imagined possible.

Solution 3: Practice makes perfect – or does it?

I said earlier that repetition is the master of skill. There are enormous benefits to be gained through repetition. But a word of caution: the saying 'Practice makes perfect' is not always true.

I learned this lesson to my peril one summer when Jane, my wife, bought me a golf lesson. That particular summer, golf was my game. I'd visit the driving range three or four times a week, pay for a bucket of 150 balls and spend an hour or so practising. That's 150 balls, four times a week, over an eight-week period. That's a lot of balls – 4,800 to be precise. During these practice sessions, especially when using my driver, the balls would veer off to the left.

Unfortunately, the lesson Jane bought me was in week eight of my summer obsession with golf, and during this lesson the golf pro said to me, 'Royston, let me just watch you hit a couple of balls.'

Guess what? The balls veered off to the left, exactly like the 4,800 balls I had hit that summer. The golf pro said, 'Royston, all I want you to do is change one movement. I want you to take your left hand and I want you to turn it a couple of degrees on the club in a clockwise direction.'

So I did. I hit another six balls and every single ball went straight up the fairway. It was one of those 'Aha!' moments. I'd spent all summer practising, honing, refining my skills but I was actually practising, honing, refining and making permanent a bad habit.

Practice doesn't make perfect; practice makes permanent. And there's another word that should be added in:

The **RIGHT** practice makes **PERMANENT**!

Rise has given you the mindset, the skillset and the toolset to start living the life you were meant to lead. It's now over to you as your own performance coach to do the *right* practice to make them permanent.

Solution 4: Focus on one thing

I want to introduce you to a word you may not be familiar with: entelechy. It means turning theory into practice. I must thank Neil Rackham, the author of *SPIN Selling* (1988), for first putting this word into my vocabulary. Entelechy is achieved through three key ideas:

1 **Do one thing at a time.**

   Focus is the process of zoning in on something and giving it the energy it really needs to get it right. If you decide to focus on three things at once, what do you think will happen? You won't do any of them very well. Try doing one thing, get it absolutely right, and then move on to the next. Each time you master one, not only do you get closer to your overall goal, the practice you put in makes it easier and easier to get it right.

2 **Do it over and over.**

This goes straight to the heart of the ability blip, where you do something and you're so bad at it you feel like giving up. The difference between people who achieve mastery in anything is simply that they don't quit just because they're not good at it. They know the journey always starts at novice status but, by continuing to improve, expert status will be within their grasp.

3 **Aim to do it many times rather than doing it well.**

This sounds counter-intuitive, but if you've got the previous two ideas locked in your head, you'll see the sense in this too. We improve by becoming comfortable with things and getting used to them so that they become second nature. You can achieve that only by doing something again and again. If you're playing golf and insist on getting your grip absolutely right before even hitting a ball, you're in for a very long haul. If you just try first, you'll have a much better idea of what you need to improve.

Solution 5: Use your Rise Performance Tracker

There are many actionable, momentum-building parts to *Rise*: 14 chapters, Accelerator exercises, tools to use and actions to complete. Your *Rise* Performance Tracker (Figure 13.3) will give you the framework for being your own performance coach, ensuring that you keep the Ebbinghaus Effect at bay by constantly refreshing your mind with regular, scheduled actions and activities, such as your monthly Me Unlimited board meetings.

The *Rise* Performance Tracker
'Turning positive intention into tangible ACTION!'

Toolkit	The Chairperson	The Sales & Marketing Director	The Finance Director	The Planning & Administration Director	The Wellbeing Director	The Learning Director	The Communications Director
	Me Unlimited	Personal brand tracker	Financial model … determining your number	Transformational visioning and goal-setting tracker – complete		Success modelling questions	
	Defining what success means to you					Recommended reading list	

Recommended frequency of use

Frequency	The Chairperson	The Sales & Marketing Director	The Finance Director	The Planning & Administration Director	The Wellbeing Director	The Learning Director	The Communications Director
Daily							
Weekly		Personal brand… Focused Five					
Monthly	Me Unlimited	Personal brand tracker		Transformational visioning and goal setting tracker			
Quarterly							
Half-yearly	Defining what success means to you					Success modelling questions	
Yearly			Financial model… determining your number			Recommended reading list	

Review your copy of Rise regularly

Figure 13.3 The *Rise* Performance Tracker

If you still haven't downloaded your *Rise* toolkit, here's the link: https://www.roystonguest.com/RISE-toolkit/. I've also included a video in which I explain exactly how to get maximum benefit from it.

Solution 6: Share Rise *with an accountability buddy*

'Tell me and I forget, teach me and I may remember, involve me and I learn.'

Benjamin Franklin

Within 90 days of reading *Rise*, find an individual who you think will benefit from applying *Rise* in their own life: a friend, your partner or a trusted colleague at work. Give them a copy to read. Remember, who you spend time with is who you become.

When you've both finished reading *Rise*, get together and be an 'accountability buddy' for each other. It's a fact that the highest level of learning is achieved when we verbalize the lessons we are learning. The process of talking out loud embeds them in your mind and deepens your understanding of the subject better than any other method.

By having an accountability buddy, not only will you get more intimate with the material and achieve better results but you will also hold each other accountable for action.

> By implementing the six solutions above, you'll have built your bridge to transition you from success disciplines to success habits.

Secret 5: Honing your success habits

'We are what we repeatedly do. Excellence, then, is not an act but a habit.'

Aristotle

How long does it take to form a new habit?

You may be familiar with the saying 'It takes 21 days to change a habit', but you may not be so familiar with where it originated. In 1960 Dr Maxwell Maltz, a plastic surgeon, published his theory on how long it took to change a habit. Observing his patients post-surgery Dr Maltz noticed how each patient, irrespective of their operation (an amputated arm or face reconfiguration) would take about 21 days to adjust to their new circumstance. What Dr Maltz, who published his theory in a book which went on to sell 30 million copies, actually said was that it took 'a minimum of about 21 days to change a habit'. Over time this has been shortened to the more clear-cut 'It takes 21 days ...'. A crucial difference!

The reality is quite different again, according to Phillippa Lally, a health psychology researcher at University College London, who published a study on the topic in the *European Journal of Social Psychology*. During an extensive study period, she discovered that it takes on average 66 days for a new behaviour to become automatic – and it can take up to 254 days. That may sound like a journey in itself, but think about what you're trying to achieve: long and lasting changes in your habits, habits that you might have had for years. It should come as no great surprise that it might just take a little longer than 21 days!

Let's confront reality head on, so you know what you're signing up to and can set your expectations appropriately, creating lasting behavioural change as you prepare yourself to achieve real success on your journey to personal mastery.

Your journey to personal mastery

If you make the decision to master anything, you're going to have to commit to putting in the time and effort to improve. Achieving personal mastery is one of the most rewarding things you can do, but it is also a never-ending journey, with the returns often far into the future.

Of course, talent plays a role in ultimate success, but talent isn't everything by a long shot. The world is packed with talented people who never achieve success because they lack focus. At the same time the world is packed with people far less naturally talented, who achieve great success because they have focused on improvement and worked hard to achieve personal mastery in a specific area. This is *not* mastery over 100 things but mastery in a specific area. As I discussed in Chapter 3: Why success is not an accident, great achievement never happens by chance. It happens by design, on purpose, in a focused long-term pursuit of a goal.

Malcolm Gladwell, author of *Outliers: The Story of Success* (2008), says the journey to mastery is one of 10,000 hours, which is the amount of practice needed to be truly masterly at anything. In his book he cites the success of The Beatles and Microsoft founder Bill Gates as proof that the 10,000 hours rule is a golden rule. Whether you believe that or not, there can be no doubt that focused practice over time is the way to mastery.

One example of this is *Britain's Got Talent* winner Tokio Myers, a pianist who today sells out concert stadiums around the world. He is a great example because he was perhaps the last person you would have earmarked for success as a pianist. He grew up in what he describes as a really rough London council estate where the odds of his joining a gang were considerably higher than his learning music.

But one day his dad brought him home a keyboard. Tokio became fixated on playing his keyboard, seeing it as a way to a better future. He would play whenever he could, sneaking into his music school and playing the piano when he didn't have lessons and becoming a devotee of his music teacher.

He was 33 when he won *Britain's Got Talent*, in 2017. His success didn't happen overnight. He had worked hard to master his technique, and he had worked hard to find a good piano to play on. Today, he's considered one of the best in the world, thanks to the thousands of hours he invested in personal mastery.

No crowds lining the extra mile

As you've heard already, masters of their craft, whatever their specialist field, are part of a select group of people who really live this saying because the extra mile is where they spend most of their time. Their journey is a never-ending pursuit of personal mastery, and their disciplines over time lead to habit.

They recognize that mastery takes time and they are dedicated to its pursuit. Choosing mastery is about choosing to focus on constant improvement, hunting out those daily marginal gains and finding that extra fuel in your tank. Even when you think you've arrived, you kick on to the next level and squeeze that extra potential from within.

To be a master in your chosen field, it is never OK to be OK; it's all about excellence. This means *being your own performance coach.*

Are you ready for your journey to personal mastery?

Take action: achieve more

It's about taking ownership of your life, your actions and your results

This chapter brought together the remaining two of my five secrets of success: developing your success disciplines and honing your success habits. It focuses on turning everything we've covered so far into momentum-building action. You don't just talk the talk; you walk the talk.

While there were no specific Accelerator exercises, this chapter is about being your own performance coach, which could be viewed as one big Accelerator exercise. Your Learning Director has a critical role to play, keeping you accountable as your performance coach – especially in the face of procrastination, the biggest reason we fail to get started and fail to follow through.

Remember the saying, 'If it's to be, it's up to me!'

While I challenge you to do this for yourself, you've got support – not only through this book and the Accelerator exercises I've shared but through the *Rise* toolbox to help keep you motivated. To get maximum benefits from *Rise* I encourage you to use it. Download it here: https://www. roystonguest.com/RISE-toolkit/. It's yours.

The extra mile is where only the elite few spend their time. Will you choose to join them?

Turning your future into reality

'It's never too late to be who you might have been.'

George Eliot

It's never too late to make your dreams come true, and there's no time like now to begin. But dreams don't become reality through magic: it takes focus, sweat, determination and hard work. The exciting news is that you have the framework; the mindset, the skillset and the toolset are now in your hands to help you bridge the gap between where you are now and the picture of your future self, living the life you were meant to lead.

Action and discipline are key

If your past hasn't turned out the way you wanted it to, that doesn't mean your future can't be better than you ever imagined (Figure 14.1). Don't let the shadows of your past darken your future. Your destiny is in your hands to shape however you choose.

'YOUR FUTURE IS CREATED BY WHAT YOU DO TODAY NOT TOMORROW'

Figure 14.1

Throughout this book, I've shared the power of momentum. These are the very small, regular marginal gains that, compounded over time, result in an overwhelming force of action. You don't have to start big in order to chase big dreams. You just have to start, and be consistent, every day from now on. Every journey of 1,000 miles starts with the first step.

If you did one extra push-up per day, saved one extra pound or dollar per day, read one extra page of a book per day, or reached out to one new connection per day, over time you'd be fitter, have more money, have new ideas and know new people who could help you implement those ideas.

But remember to watch out for marginal erosion, the opposite effect of marginal gains. If you're not making gains, however small, you'll find yourself substantially behind all the other people who are. Those individuals who cared for their health, looked after their finances, and expanded their knowledge and their network will be the winners in this journey called life.

If the gateway to marginal gains is action, the gateway to marginal erosion is procrastination. And your job now is to take massive action and apply all you have discovered on your *Rise* journey.

Your pathway to action

What steps are you going to take right now to turn your vision into your reality?

It is my hope that your copy of *Rise* is dog-eared and worn, with scribbled notes on every page, passages underlined and whole strings of exclamation points in the margins to indicate the parts that resonated with you strongly. My goal for *Rise* is that it becomes your active blueprint to dip into on a regular basis, helping you maintain your focus and momentum, with the Accelerator exercises and the *Rise* Performance Tracker pulling everything together into one complete framework.

Reread this book often – when there is a specific area you want to refresh or when you feel your motivation waning.

Remember, be the authentic you; play to your strengths, accept your weaknesses and find ways to compensate for them. We all have them. Hal Elrod, author of *The Miracle Morning* (2012), captured it brilliantly when he said: 'Give up being perfect for being authentic.'

Accept your past without regrets, handle your present with confidence and face your future without fear. Invest in your dreams now, put in the hard yards and you will shine bright.

This is your cue to *Rise* like never before. I know you've got it in you to build a life of enduring greatness and live the life you were meant to lead.

Royston, your success coach
Take action: achieve more

NOW *is your point of power!*

In Chapter 14: Turning your vision into reality, I called out that ACTION and DISCIPLINE are now key. Your future is created by what you do today, not tomorrow.

So you're at a choice point. You can choose what comes easy, knowing it won't last. Or choose what lasts, knowing it won't come easy. There's no crowds lining the extra mile!

My desire for you is to choose the latter, and to help you with your pathway to action here are some further ideas:

Mindset

Your copy of *Rise* is your living blueprint to dip into on a regular basis, helping you to maintain your focus and momentum. Carry it with you and use it as your reminder to take action and maintain your momentum.

Toolset

Throughout the book I referenced a number of resources and tools available to help you personalize some of the insights and Accelerator exercises. Don't miss out on your FREE Rise toolkit. Simply download at https://www.roystonguest.com/RISE-toolkit/or by scanning the QR code below:

Masterclass and Bootcamp

Skillset

Join me and my team for a one- or two-day high-energy Masterclass or Bootcamp and walk away with key ideas, strategies and tools to personalize your own success formula to unlock and realize your potential.

Visit https://www.roystonguest.com/events/rise-masterclass for more information.

Conference speaking

For over a decade I have been sharing my tried-and-tested ideas for increased business and personal success through key notes and high-impact speaking sessions. My sessions are revered as game-changing, transformational experiences, and without false modesty I can say that my energy and enthusiasm are contagious.

If you have a conference or event in the near future and want me to speak, visit https://www.roystonguest.com/work-with-royston/speaking/ for more information.

Corporate programme

For businesses who are truly focused on growing, developing and retaining their people, access a people development programme that really means business. living**your**future™ is an award-winning personal transformation programme building on all the content covered in *Rise*, plus more!

Visit https://www.roystonguest.com/work-with-royston/living-future-corporate/ for more information.

Feeling galvanized?

I'd love to hear your story, your questions or your feedback. Email me at royston@roystonguest.com.

Connect with me at ...

Facebook.com/RoystonGuestOfficial
LinkedIn.com/in/roystonguest
Twitter @Royston_Guest
Instagram.com/roystonguest

Blog and resources

Visit https://www.roystonguest.com/blog/ to access my weekly blog, videos, webinars and other free resources.

Recommended reading

Fraser, Henry, *The Little Big Things* (London: Seven Dials, 2017)

Gladwell, Malcolm, *Outliers: The Story of Success* (London: Penguin, 2009)

Guest, Royston, *Built to Grow* (London: Wiley, 2016)

Kerr, James, *Legacy* (London: Constable, 2013)

Peale, Norman Vincent, *The Power of Positive Thinking* (London: Vermilion, 2004).

Peters, Steve, *The Chimp Paradox: The Mind Management Programme to Help You Achieve Success, Confidence and Happiness* (London: Vermilion, 2012).

Pink, Daniel, *Drive* (New York: Riverhead Books, 2009)

Rackham, Neil, *SPIN Selling* (London: Routledge, 2008)

Woodward, Clive, *Winning* (London: Hodder & Stoughton, 2004)

Also by Royston Guest ...
Built to Grow

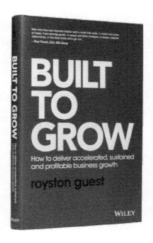

It's a reality that most businesses and individuals never reach their full potential, always yearning for the 'thing' that will catapult them into significance, but never really finding it.

Whether you're an entrepreneur starting out, or a director, executive or business leader climbing the corporate ladder, the building blocks of *Built to Grow* are universally applicable.

Developed in the real-world laboratory of thousands of businesses in 27 countries spanning over two decades, *Built to Grow* is a proven, time-tested formula to unlock the real potential in your business.

Avoid the common pitfalls of a trial-and-error approach to business growth. *Built to Grow* is full of practical strategies, tools and ideas, backed up with real-world case studies to illustrate what can be achieved – leaving you equipped to transform your business' performance and drive tangible results.

Available on Amazon in hardcover and eBook format, and as an audio book an Amazon Audible.

Index

Text credits

The author and publisher would like to give their thanks for permission to publish the following text:

Chapter 12 Extract from J. K. Rowling's Commencement Address at Harvard University, 2008 – *Very Good Lives: Copyright © J.K. Rowling 2008.*